ANGUILLA

BUSINESS AND INVESTMENT OPPORTUNITIES YEARBOOK

VOLUME 1

STRATEGIC, PRACTICAL INFORMATION AND OPPORTUNITIES

International Business Publications, USA
Washington DC, USA

ANGUILLA

BUSINESS AND INVESTMENT OPPORTUNITIES YEARBOOK

VOLUME 1 STRATEGIC, PRACTICAL INFORMATION AND OPPORTUNITIES

UPDATED ANNUALLY

Cover Design: **International Business Publications, USA**

We express our sincere appreciation to all government agencies and international organizations which provided information and other materials for this yearbook

2016 Edition Updated Reprint International Business Publications, USA
ISBN 1-4387-7611-X

This yearbook provides basic information for starting or/and conducting business in the country. The extraordinary volume of materials covering the topic, prevents us from placing all these materials in this yearbook. For more detailed information on issues related to any specific investment and business activity in the country, please contact Global Investment Center, USA
Please acquire the list of our business intelligence and marketing reports and other business publications. We constantly update and expand our business intelligence and marketing materials. Please contact the center for the updated list of reports on over 200 countries.

in the USA: **Global Investment Center, USA.**
P.O.Box 15343, Washington, DC 20003
Phone: (202) 546-2103, Fax: (202) 546-3275, E-mail: rusric@erols.com

For additional analytical, marketing and other information please contact Global Investment Center, USA

Printed in the USA

ANGUILLA

BUSINESS AND INVESTMENT OPPORTUNITIES YEARBOOK

VOLUME 1

STRATEGIC, PRACTICAL INFORMATION AND OPPORTUNITIES

TABLE OF CONTENTS

STRATEGIC AND DEVELOPMENT PROFILES

Status	British Overseas Territory
Capital and largest city	The Valley
Official languages	English
Ethnic groups ([1])	• 90.1% West African • 4.6% multiracial • 3.7% European • 1.5% other
Demonym	Anguillian
Government	Parliamentary dependency under a constitutional monarchy
• Monarch	Elizabeth II
• Governor	Christina Scott
• Deputy Governor	Stanley Reid
• Chief Minister	Victor Banks
• Responsible Minister[b] (UK)	James Duddridge MP
Legislature	House of Assembly
	Establishment
• Overseas territory	1980
	Area
• Total	91 km^2 (220th) 35 sq mi
• Water (%)	negligible
	Population
• 2006 estimate	13,600[2] (215th)
• 2011 census	13,452
• Density	132/km^2 (n/a) 342/sq mi
GDP (PPP)	2004 estimate
• Total	$108.9 million
• Per capita	$8,800
Currency	East Caribbean dollar (XCD)
Time zone	(UTC-4)
Drives on the	left
Calling code	+1-264
ISO 3166 code	AI
Internet TLD	.ai

a. "National Song of Anguilla". Official Website of the Government of Anguilla. Archived from the original on 23 July 2011. Retrieved 10 July 2011.

b. For the Overseas Territories.
UK Postcode: AI-2640

Anguilla is a British overseas territory in the Caribbean. It is one of the most northerly of the Leeward Islands in the Lesser Antilles, lying east of Puerto Rico and the Virgin Islands and directly north of Saint Martin. The territory consists of the main island of

Anguilla itself, approximately 16 miles (26 km) long by 3 miles (5 km) wide at its widest point, together with a number of much smaller islands and cays with no permanent population. The island's capital is The Valley. The total land area of the territory is 35 square miles (90 km^2), with a population of approximately 13,500 (2006 estimate).

Anguilla has become a popular tax haven, having no capital gains, estate, profit or other forms of direct taxation on either individuals or corporations. In April 2011, faced with a mounting deficit, it introduced a 3% "Interim Stabilisation Levy", Anguilla's first form of income tax

GEOGRAPHY

Location: Caribbean, island in the Caribbean Sea, east of Puerto Rico

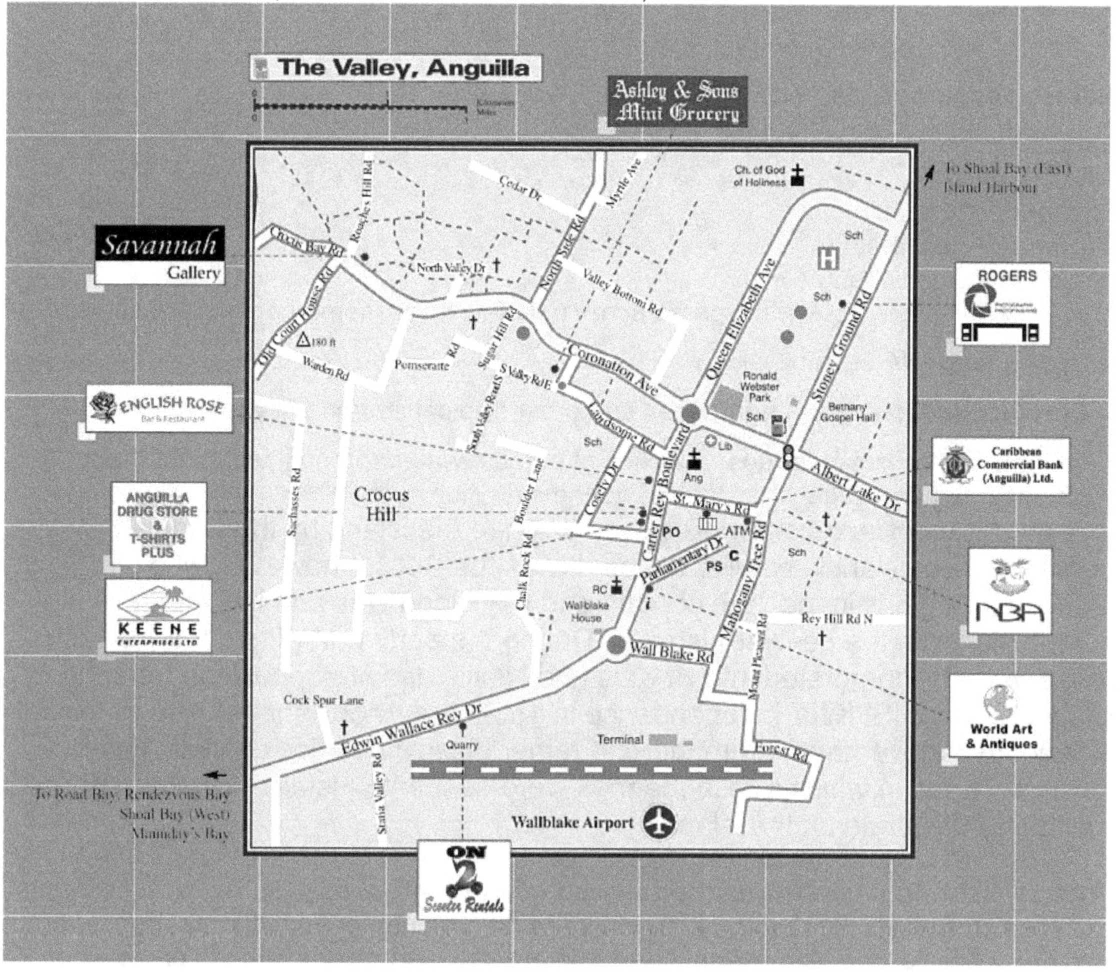

Geographic coordinates: 18 15 N, 63 10 W

Map references: Central America and the Caribbean

Area:

total: 91 sq km

land: 91 sq km
water: 0 sq km

Area - comparative: about half the size of Washington, DC

Land boundaries: 0 km

Coastline: 61 km

Maritime claims:
exclusive fishing zone: 200 nm
territorial sea: 3 nm

Climate: tropical; moderated by northeast trade winds

Terrain: flat and low-lying island of coral and limestone

Elevation extremes:
lowest point: Caribbean Sea 0 m
highest point: Crocus Hill 65 m

Natural resources: salt, fish, lobster

Land use:
arable land: 0%
permanent crops: 0%
permanent pastures: 0%
forests and woodland: 0%
other: 100% (mostly rock with sparse scrub oak, few trees, some commercial salt ponds)

Irrigated land: NA sq km

Natural hazards: frequent hurricanes and other tropical storms (July to October)

Environment - current issues: supplies of potable water sometimes cannot meet increasing demand largely because of poor distribution system

The name *Anguilla*, meaning 'eel', was given to the island by the Spanish because of the island's eel-like shape. It was the British, however, who first settled on Anguilla in the 17th century and the island was administered in conjunction with the Leeward Islands. During the early part of the 19th century, Anguilla was incorporated into St Kitts and Nevis, despite opposition from the islanders. Upon St Kitts' independence in 1967, the Anguillans refused to accept independent government from there; a rather bizarre and occasionally comical 'crisis' followed in which British marines were sent in to install a Commissioner to maintain British rule on the islands.

Anguilla is the most northerly of the Leeward Islands, 146 miles (235 km) east of Puerto Rico and 6 miles (10 km) to the north of St. Martin. The name 'Anguilla' means 'eel' and well describes its long, thin shape. Its people are of mixed origins, though primarily of African descent. The island is very flat with its highest point at a little over 200 feet (70 metres). Rainfall levels are low and the resulting vegetation is mostly small trees and bush.

Anguilla's position and basic geology has contributed much to its appeal; it is quiet, secluded and peaceful. It is widely regarded as having the best beaches in the Caribbean. With its exclusive resorts and fine dining Anguilla appeals to the discerning visitor.It has also, in more recent times, continued to grow as a centre for offshore banking. Anguilla's other attractions include diving & snorkelling, cruising & fishing, its sights and places of interest and opportunities to shop. Anguilla has a distinct culture, a product of its peculiar history, reflected greatly in the events celebrated throughout the year.

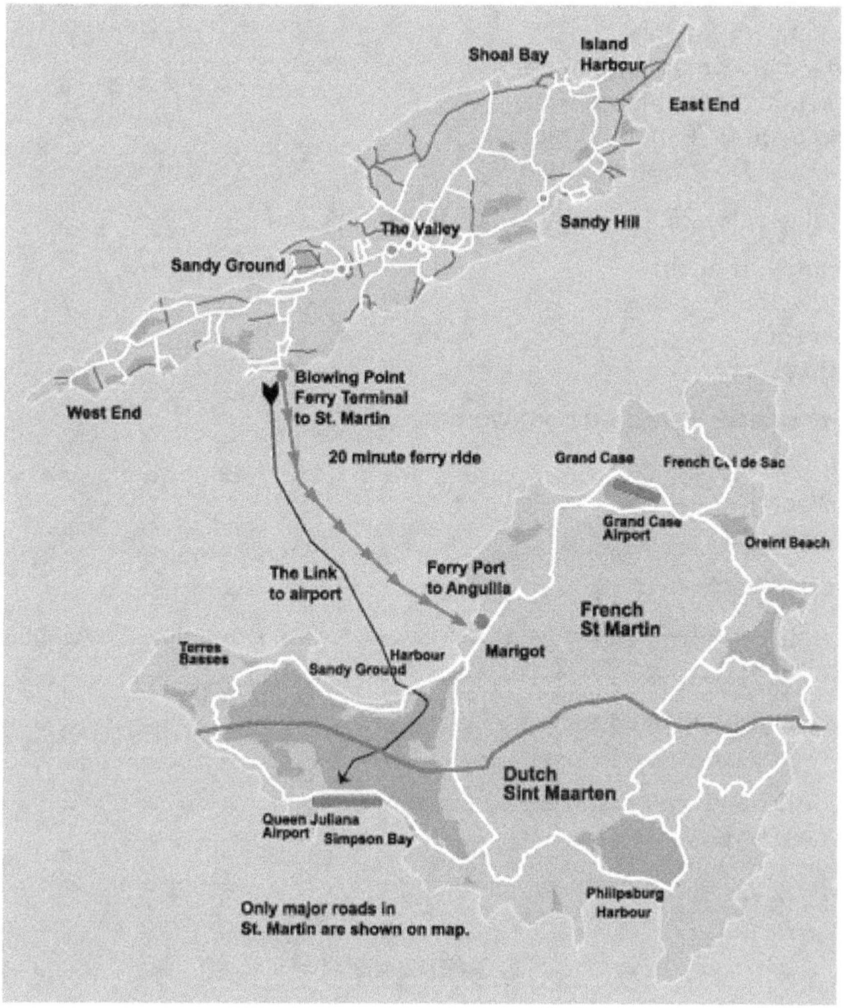

In all, Anguilla is ideal for those who want a peaceful destination offering exclusivity, privacy and comfort.

PEOPLE

Population: 11,797

Age structure:
0-14 years: 26% (male 1,565; female 1,519)

15-64 years: 67% (male 4,040; female 3,839)
65 years and over: 7% (male 369; female 465)

Population growth rate: 2.93%

Birth rate: 15.34 births/1,000 population

Death rate: 5.76 deaths/1,000 population

Net migration rate: 19.75 migrant(s)/1,000 population

Sex ratio:
at birth: 1.03 male(s)/female
under 15 years: 1.03 male(s)/female
15-64 years: 1.05 male(s)/female
65 years and over: 0.79 male(s)/female
total population: 1.03 male(s)/female

Infant mortality rate: 25.44 deaths/1,000 live births

Life expectancy at birth:
total population: 76.11 years
male: 73.22 years
female: 79.09 years

Total fertility rate: 1.8 children born/woman

Nationality:
noun: Anguillan(s)
adjective: Anguillan

Ethnic groups: black

Religions: Anglican 40%, Methodist 33%, Seventh-Day Adventist 7%, Baptist 5%, Roman Catholic 3%, other 12%

Languages: English (official)

Literacy:
definition: age 12 and over can read and write
total population: 95%
male: 95%
female: 95% (1984 est.)

GOVERNMENT

Country name:
conventional long form: none
conventional short form: Anguilla

Data code: AV

Dependency status: overseas territory of the UK

Government type: NA

Capital: The Valley

Administrative divisions: none (overseas territory of the UK)

Independence: none (overseas territory of the UK)

National holiday: Anguilla Day, 30 May

Constitution: Anguilla Constitutional Order 1 April 1982; amended 1990

Legal system: based on English common law

Suffrage: 18 years of age; universal

Executive branch:

chief of state: Queen ELIZABETH II (since 6 February 1952); represented by Governor Alistair HARRISON (since 21 April 2009)

head of government: Chief Minister Victor Banks

Victor Franklin Banks (born 8 November 1947) is an Anguillan politician. A member of the Anguilla United Front (AUF), he has served as Chief Minister since 23 April 2015.

cabinet: Executive Council appointed by the governor from among the elected members of the House of Assembly

elections: the monarchy is hereditary; governor appointed by the monarch; following legislative elections, the leader of the majority party or the leader of the majority coalition usually appointed chief minister by the governor

Legislative branch:

unicameral House of Assembly (11 seats; 7 members elected by direct popular vote, 2 ex officio members, and 2 appointed; members serve five-year terms)

election results: percent of vote by party - NA; seats by party - AUM 4, AUF 2, APP 1

Judicial branch:

High Court (judge provided by Eastern Caribbean Supreme Court)

Political parties and leaders: Anguilla Democratic Party or ADP [Victor BANKS]; Anguilla National Alliance or ANA [Osbourne FLEMING]; Anguilla United Party or AUP [Hubert HUGHES]

International organization participation: Caricom (associate), CDB, Interpol (subbureau), OECS (associate), ECLAC (associate)

Diplomatic representation in the US: none (overseas territory of the UK)

Diplomatic representation from the US: none (overseas territory of the UK)

Flag description: blue, with the flag of the UK in the upper hoist-side quadrant and the Anguillan coat of arms centered in the outer half of the flag; the coat of arms depicts three orange dolphins in an interlocking circular design on a white background with blue wavy water below

ECONOMY

Anguilla has few natural resources, and the economy depends heavily on luxury tourism, offshore banking, lobster fishing, and remittances from emigrants. Increased activity in the tourism industry has spurred the growth of the construction sector contributing to economic growth. Anguillan officials have put substantial effort into developing the offshore financial sector, which is small but growing. In the medium term, prospects for the economy will depend largely on the tourism sector and, therefore, on revived income growth in the industrialized nations as well as on favorable weather conditions.

GDP (purchasing power parity):

$175.4 million
country comparison to the world: 221
$191.7 million (2008 est.)
$108.9 million (2004 est.)

GDP (official exchange rate):

$175.4 million (est.)

GDP - real growth rate:

-8.5% (est.)
country comparison to the world: 219

GDP - per capita (PPP):

$12,200 (2008 est.)
country comparison to the world: 104

GDP - composition, by end use:

household consumption: 74.5%
government consumption: 20.1%
investment in fixed capital: 22.1%
exports of goods and services: 43.7%
imports of goods and services: -60.4%
(2013 est.)

GDP - composition, by sector of origin:

agriculture: 2.5%
industry: 23.6%
services: 73.8% (2013 est.)

Agriculture - products:

small quantities of tobacco, vegetables; cattle raising

Industries:

tourism, boat building, offshore financial services

Industrial production growth rate:

2% (2013 est.)
country comparison to the world: 127

Labor force:

6,049 (2001)
country comparison to the world: 220

Labor force - by occupation:

agriculture/fishing/forestry/mining: 4%
manufacturing: 3%
construction: 18%
transportation and utilities: 10%
commerce: 36%
services: 29% (2000 est.)

Unemployment rate:

8% (2002)
country comparison to the world: 89

Population below poverty line:

23% (2002)

Household income or consumption by percentage share:

lowest 10%: NA%
highest 10%: NA%

Budget:

revenues: $69.52 million
expenditures: $78.37 million (2012 est.)

Taxes and other revenues:

39.6% of GDP (2012 est.)
country comparison to the world: 45

Budget surplus (+) or deficit (-):

-5% of GDP (2012 est.)
country comparison to the world: 166

Public debt:

20% of GDP (2013 est.)
country comparison to the world: 135
21.7% of GDP (2012 est.)

Fiscal year:

1 April - 31 March

Inflation rate (consumer prices):

3.1% (2013 est.)
country comparison to the world: 117
4.4% (2012 est.)

Central bank discount rate:

6.5% (31 December 2010 est.)
country comparison to the world: 55
6.5% (31 December 2009 est.)

Commercial bank prime lending rate:

9.4% (31 December 2013 est.)
country comparison to the world: 93
9.38% (31 December 2012 est.)

Stock of narrow money:

$16.89 million (31 December 2013 est.)
country comparison to the world: 189
NA% (31 December 2012 est.)

Stock of broad money:

$384.4 million (31 December 2013 est.)
country comparison to the world: 183
$373.2 million (31 December 2012 est.)

Stock of domestic credit:

$498.1 million (31 December 2013 est.)
country comparison to the world: 167
$483.3 million (31 December 2012 est.)

Current account balance:

-$54.3 million (2013 est.)
country comparison to the world: 70
-$44.8 million (2012 est.)

Exports:

$12.2 million (2013 est.)
country comparison to the world: 211
$7.3 million (2012 est.)

Exports - commodities:

lobster, fish, livestock, salt, concrete blocks, rum

Imports:

$140.1 million (2013 est.)
country comparison to the world: 207
$129.3 million (2012 est.)

Imports - commodities:

fuels, foodstuffs, manufactures, chemicals, trucks, textiles

Debt - external:

$8.8 million (1998)
country comparison to the world: 198

Exchange rates:

East Caribbean dollars (XCD) per US dollar -
2.7 (2013 est.)
2.7 (2012 est.)
2.7 (2010 est.), 2.7 (2009)

COMMUNICATION

Telephones - main lines in use:

6,000 (2012)
country comparison to the world: 207

Telephones - mobile cellular:

26,000
country comparison to the world: 209

Telephone system:

general assessment: modern internal telephone system
domestic: fixed-line teledensity is roughly 40 per 100 persons; mobile-cellular teledensity is roughly 170 per 100 persons
international: country code - 1-264; landing point for the East Caribbean Fiber System submarine cable with links to 13 other islands in the eastern Caribbean extending from the British Virgin Islands to Trinidad; microwave radio relay to island of Saint Martin/Sint Maarten

Broadcast media:

1 private TV station; multi-channel cable TV subscription services are available; about 10 radio stations, one of which is government-owned (2007)

Internet country code:

.ai

Internet hosts:

269
country comparison to the world: 192

Internet users:

3,700
country comparison to the world: 208

TRANSPORTATION

Airports:

2
country comparison to the world: 197

Airports - with paved runways:

total: 1
1,524 to 2,437 m: 1

Airports - with unpaved runways:

total: 1
under 914 m:
1

Roadways:

total: 175 km

country comparison to the world: 210
paved: 82 km
unpaved: 93 km

Ports and terminals:

major seaport(s): Blowing Point, Road Bay

MILITARY

Manpower available for military service:

males age 16-49: 3,641 (2010 est.)

Manpower fit for military service:

males age 16-49: 3,009
females age 16-49: 3,397

Manpower reaching militarily significant age annually:

male: 111
female: 113

Military - note:

defense is the responsibility of the UK

TRANSNATIONAL ISSUES

Disputes - international:

none

Illicit drugs:

transshipment point for South American narcotics destined for the US and Europe

ECONOMIC, POLITICAL AND BUSINESS CLIMATE

ADVANTAGES

- UK Overseas Territory
- Well-regulated financial services industry
- Common law legal system based on English law
- Well developed professional infrastructure
- Same day company incorporation service
- World standard telecommunications system
- Easy air access to North America and Europe
- Neutral tax jurisdiction
- No foreign exchange restrictions
- Multi-year work permits available for professionals within the financial services industry

STATUS, ECONOMIC, LEGAL SYSTEM & INFRASTRUCTURE STATUS

Anguilla is one of Britain's Overseas Territories in the Caribbean and as such it enjoys a high degree of political stability. All political parties are strongly committed to the growth of Anguilla as a quality financial services centre.

Although the country is essentially self governing, its legislature is the democratically elected House of Assembly. The Constitution gives the British appointed Governor certain fundamental reserve powers. All legislation must be assented to by the Governor as H.M. The Queen's representative.

Economic
The significant growth in Government revenues earned from the financial services sector over the last few years is a testament to the success of the policies to date. Anguilla is well positioned as a major player in the international arena.

Legal
Anguilla is a common law jurisdiction. Its judicial system is administered by the Eastern Caribbean Supreme Court the appeal process culminates with the Privy Council. The Court system is serviced by a number of firms of fully qualified and experienced lawyers.

Infrastructure
The professional infrastructure is well developed, with major accounting firms represented on the island. The telecommunications system is of a world standard providing direct access worldwide.
Legislation:

- The Proceeds of Criminal Conduct Act 2000
- The Money Laundering Reporting Authority Act 2000
- The Company Management Act 2000
- The Trust Companies and Offshore Banking Act 2000
- International Business Companies Act 2000

- The Companies Act 2000
- The Limited Liability Company Act 2000
- The Limited Partnership Act 2000

TAXATION & EXCHANGE CONTROL

Taxation

Unlike many financial services centres, Anguilla is truly a neutral tax jurisdiction. There are no income, capital gains, estate, profit or other forms of direct taxation on either individuals or corporations, whether resident in Anguilla or not. This makes Anguilla a very attractive location for financial services professionals to base themselves. The Government recognises the desirability of expanding Anguilla's professional infrastructure and has very recently established a new programme allowing for multi-year work permits of up to four years duration and relaxed residency rules.

Exchange Control

There are no exchange controls in Anguilla. Although the official currency is the Eastern Caribbean Dollar the United States Dollar is commonly used.

Corporate Structures

Anguilla has three types of companies:

- The Ordinary Company
- The International Business Company
- The Limited Liability Company

Companies must be incorporated through a local agent all of whom, are licensed under the new Company Management Ordinance and regulated by the Inspector of Company Managers. The Government and private sector are working closely together to establish best practice guidelines for company managers. These will be designed to ensure that through the application of due diligence procedures and the adoption of high standards of practice, Anguilla attracts the best business and that its reputation is maintained.

The relevant IBC, LLC, Limited Partnership and Trust Ordinances all provide a statutory exemption from all forms of corporate, income withholding or other like taxes in respect of international Anguilla Companies business.
Companies are usually formed instantly using the ACORN system.

ANGUILLIAN COMPANIES

The Ordinary Company

The ordinary company, which can be used both within Anguilla and as an offshore vehicle, is governed by the new Companies Ordinance. The Ordinance contains many attractive features:

- Companies may be incorporated by one incorporator and have one director.
- Companies may be limited by shares, by guarantee or by both shares and guarantee.
- The Ordinance abolishes the doctrine of *ultra vires.*
- Companies may acquire, purchase or own their own shares.
- Filing formalities have been streamlined.
- Companies may continue in or out of Anguilla.
- A special class of Specific Private Companies that are exempted from some record keeping and accounting requirements

The International Business Company

The International Business Company is based on the traditional model and provides for the easy incorporation and subsequent administration of a flexible and cost effective corporation.

Companies incorporated in any other jurisdiction may be continued in Anguilla as an IBC. An Anguilla IBC can, where the laws of another jurisdiction permit, redomicile to such jurisdiction.

The Limited Liability Company

Anguilla is one of the few jurisdictions to have an Act or Ordinance dealing specifically with limited liability companies. Although the LLC Ordinance has its roots in the original Wyoming legislation, Anguillian LLCs have developed the concept much further.

An Anguillian LLC can readily be structured so that it possesses less than three of the four corporate characteristics recognized by the U.S. Internal Revenue Service, namely (a) continuity of life, (b) limited liability, (c) centralized management and (d) free transferability of interests. In such case the LLC will be treated as a partnership. Properly structured, therefore, an Anguillian LLC will provide its members with limited liability, but provide the advantages of income and losses passing through to the members.

The Anguillian LLC Ordinance has many features not found in the original Wyoming legislation, including a provision that its term can be perpetual or as otherwise provided for in the LLC agreement.

Trusts

The new Trusts Act is the culmination of an exhaustive study of the trusts legislation of many other jurisdictions. The decision was taken to repeal the existing trusts legislation and replace it with a completely new Ordinance, rather than attempt to amend it.

The Trusts Ordinance, which has its roots in English trust law, provides a framework so flexible that the only limitation to its use is the imagination of the trust practitioner. Specifically, the Ordinance permits commercial or charitable purpose trusts, unit trusts, spendthrift trusts, asset protection trusts and what are termed variant trusts. The provision for variant trusts permits a settlor to create a trust (in whatever form and by whatever name) of a type recognized by the law or rules of his religion or nationality or which is customarily used by his community.

The Ordinance provides for a protector of the trust (who may be the trustee). The protector may be provided with the power to remove the trustee and to appoint new or additional trustees.

The Rule Against Perpetuities has been abolished and accumulation of income throughout the full term of a trust is possible.
The Fraudulent Dispositions Ordinance provides that a fraudulent disposition is voidable by a creditor provided that the settlor was insolvent at the time of the disposition or became so as a result thereof and provided that the creditor commences his action within three years of the date that the assets were settled into trust. The burden of proving that the settlor was or became insolvent as a result of the transfer is on the creditor.

In relation to asset (or creditor) protection trusts, therefore, Anguilla has deliberately taken a more conservative approach than some jurisdictions.
Where a trust is created under the laws of Anguilla, the Court shall not vary it, set it aside or recognize the validity of any claim against the trust property pursuant to the law of another jurisdiction or the Order of another Court in respect of:

- marriage or its termination;
- succession rights;
- the claims of creditors in an insolvency;
- the imposition of any foreign tax or duty.

Other characteristics of an Anguilla trust include choice of governing law and flight provisions.

Partnerships & Limited Partnerships

The Partnership Ordinance 1994 sets out:

- The definition of partnership
- The rules for determining the existence of a partnership
- The power of partners to bind the firm
- The nature of partnership property
- The interests and duties of partners
- The types of dissolution
- The rights of third parties against apparent members of the firm
- The rights and duties of partners on dissolution
- The distribution rules on final settlement of accounts
- Confidentiality

The Limited Partnership Ordinance 1994 sets out:

- The essential elements of a limited partnership
- Registration and record keeping
- Returns of Contributions
- Transactions by partners with the limited partnership
- Dissolution
- Proceedings
- Tax Exemptions

The Limited Partnership Ordinance provides an attractive investment vehicle, particularly for the raising of venture capital, permitting the limited partners to be insulated from liability.

FINANCE & BANKING

The Government of Anguilla has positioned the Territory as a well regulated financial services centre attracting only quality business. There are no "brass plate" banks and none will be accepted. Generally, only banks which are subsidiaries or branches of banks with an established track record which are subject to the effective consolidated supervision of their home authority will be licensed as offshore banks in Anguilla.

Banking

Banking Services:

- Barclays Bank plc
- Caribbean Commercial Bank (Anguilla) Limited
- National Bank of Anguilla Ltd
- Scotiabank Anguilla Ltd

REGULATED & SECURE

Today, no financial services jurisdiction can hope to succeed unless it is well regulated. Anguilla is no exception.

The financial services sector in Anguilla is the responsibility of the Governor, although day to day regulation is delegated to the Department of Financial Services. In carrying out its functions and in considering applications by organisations wishing to establish businesses within the sector, the Department aims to adopt a firm but flexible regulatory approach.

It is of paramount concern to the Government that Anguilla's reputation is not tainted by the use of the jurisdiction for money laundering or other illegal purposes. For this reason, all licensed institutions are expected to carry out proper due diligence and "know your customer" checks so that they are satisfied as to the identity of their clients and the legitimate origin of their clients' funds.

Although commercial confidentiality is ensured by legislation, the authorities in Anguilla will co-operate fully with law enforcement agencies and regulators in other jurisdictions in the case of illegality. In common with other reputable jurisdictions, the Department of

Financial Services is, subject to safeguards to protect legitimate business, able to share regulatory information with overseas regulatory authorities.
Anguilla already has a well established professional infrastructure. The Government recognizes that, as a relatively new jurisdiction, an expansion of the sector would benefit the economy.

Applications from suitable professionals and organisations within the industry are, therefore, welcome. Any organisation wishing to establish within the sector will be required to demonstrate that it is prepared to establish a real business on-island and a multi-year work permit program has been introduced to facilitate this. Alternatively, in the case of a licensed institution, an administered or managed basis for the issue of a license will be considered. This would entail the full management and administration of the licensee's business by an equivalent licensed institution on island.

IMPORTANT INFORMATION FOR DOING BUSINESS

OVERSEAS TERRITORY

Anguilla is a British Overseas Territory. Britain is responsible for all the island's matters of foreign affairs and for the defense of the island. The local Legislative Council is responsible for internal matters. The Queen appoints a Governor and Deputy Governor to oversee the island.

LEGISLATIVE COUNCIL

The Chief Minister heads the Legislative Council. He is selected from the political party that wins the majority of the Council seats at a General Election. The elections are held every five years. There are presently seven constituencies in Anguilla, each represented by one elected member.

POPULATION
The population of Anguilla is approximately 11,000. The working population is about 4,000 of the 11,000. The rate of unemployment is possibly the lowest in the world.

LANGUAGE USED
The official language in Anguilla is English.

TELECOMMUNICATIONS
Anguilla has a modern telephone system, which is fully digital, and an Internet Service, both operated by Cable & Wireless (W.I.) Ltd. The area code is 264.

LEGAL SYSTEM : COMMON LAW SYSTEM
The legal system of Anguilla is based on the Anguilla Constitution order 1982, statutes and British common law system. English precedents and those of other British Commonwealth Countries are persuasive in court.

EASTERN CARIBBEAN SUPREME COURT
The island judiciary falls under the umbrella of the Eastern Caribbean Supreme Court.

The islands covered by the Eastern Caribbean Supreme Court are: Anguilla, Antigua, Barbuda, British Virgin Islands, Dominica, St. Lucia, St. Kitts, Nevis and Montserrat. The island is served by a Puisne Judge who presently resides on Anguilla. The judge serves the Islands of Montserrat and Anguilla. The High Court of Anguilla sits in its civil and criminal jurisdiction at least three times per year: January/February; June/July and October/November.

CIVIL AND CRIMINAL JURISDICTION IN ANGUILLA
The High Court deals with the most serious offenses and all civil matters involving property valued at EC $15,000 (US $5,800) and above. The Magistrate Court deals with minor offenses (misdemeanors). There is a resident magistrate on Anguilla. The Magistrate Court sits all year round.

FIVE REASONS WHY YOU SHOULD DO BUSINESS IN ANGUILLA
1. No Income Tax
2. No Corporate Tax
3. No Inheritance Tax
4. No Foreign Exchange Control Regulations
5. Secrecy under Confidential Relationship Act 1981

TAX SHELTER
Anguilla is a tax shelter, similar in many ways to other British tax shelters. The British Virgin Islands, Bermuda, The Bahamas, Barbados, Antigua, St. Kitts, Nevis and the Cayman Islands also offer similar facilities and services.

TAX TREATY
The United Kingdom Income Tax Convention with St. Kitts-Nevis-Anguilla to Denmark, Norway, Sweden, Switzerland, New Zealand and the United States is applicable to Anguilla. However, since Anguilla no longer has income tax, the treaties are one sided and not much weight is given to them.

TAXES
There is no personal income tax or company tax on the island. The government taxes are derived from stamp duty on the transfer of property, duty on the importation of goods to the island, hotel accommodation taxes, and stamp duty on the Alien Land Holding License.

STAMP DUTY ON ALIEN LAND HOLDING LICENSE
At present, the tax on transfer of real property is 5%. On the Alien Land Holding License it is 12.5%, making a total of 17.5% tax for an alien purchasing property on the island. Duty on motor vehicles is approximately 25%. This is possibly the lowest in the British West Indies.

REPATRIATION OF PROFITS
Companies are allowed to repatriate all profits, dividends and management charges.

CURRENCY The official currency is the Eastern Caribbean Dollar. The EC Dollar, as it is commonly called, is tied to the U.S. Dollar. The exchange rate is US $1.00 to EC

$2.6882. American dollars are accepted in all hotels and stores. All four Banks are 'A' Class Banks and offer very good services.

FREE TRANSFER OF FUNDS

There is no currency or exchange control in Anguilla. No approval need be obtained for the transfer of dividends, interest, royalties, other profits and repatriation of capital.

CONFIDENTIALITY

The Confidential Relationship Ordinance 1981 prohibits the disclosure of information relating to a person's financial business on the island of Anguilla. The Ordinance does not cover acts, which are criminal offenses in Anguilla. Anguilla is a participant of the Mutual Legal Treaty Assistant with Britain and the United States and by virtue of this treaty, Anguilla is obliged to assist in the investigation of criminal offenses, except for matters related to tax. The Common Law implied term of confidentiality between the client and his lawyer, or banker, applies to Anguilla, as it does to the United Kingdom.

STARTING A BUSINESS In general, one has the same options in Anguilla as in any of the British Commonwealth Countries, depending on the financial status of the individual or group. One may start as a sole trader, partnership, unlimited company, public limited company, specific private company, limited liability company, limited duration company and/or hybrid company. International clients, whose purpose is either for tax planning or doing business off-shore, may wish to choose an Inter-national Business Company (IBC).

THE INTERNATIONAL BUSINESS COMPANY

This form of company combines the best features of the now-familiar models used in a number of offshore jurisdictions, and is suitable for companies that will not be doing business on the island. Ease of formation and limited re-porting requirements make this option appropriate where an international company is needed. The International Business Companies Ordinance 1994 has many modern features. For example: A company may have only one director, who may be a nominee or any recognized person under Anguillian law, including a company, trust or partnership. A company may purchase or redeem its shares. Treasury and bearer shares are permitted. Share register inspection is restricted to registered share-holders. There are no financial audit or statement requirements. Domicile can easily be transferred to and from Anguilla. Meetings may be held anywhere, by telephone or other electronic means. An International Business Company may be used in con-junction with other entities, such as a trust, or various forms of partnership, as circumstances may require.

THE PRIVATE COMPANY

This entity is exempt from any of the filing and reporting requirements of an ordinary or public company, and may also be designed to function in conjunction with a trust created under the Trusts Ordinance 1994. Other attractive features of this form of company are: The acceptance of electronic signatures as evidence, not-withstanding the usual Evidence Act provisions; Exclusion of the ultra vires doctrine; Nominees may be used in place of principals; Meetings may be held anywhere, by telephone or other electronic means; No Anguillian shareholder or director requirement; Provision for domiciliation of companies incorporated under the law of other jurisdictions.

THE HYBRID COMPANY

A company formed under this provision may be limited by guarantee or by both shares and guarantee. As such, it will have some of the features of both a partnership and a company. It is a particularly attractive vehicle in civil law jurisdictions, which may not recognize the traditional common law trust concept. Civil law jurisdictions may view a transfer to a trust as no more than a transfer to an individual (with consequent gift or transfer tax implications) or a void abinitio, thus defeating the very purpose of the transfer. The hybrid company can effectively separate shareholder members from guarantor members and limit the rights of shareholders and guarantors so as to comply with the laws of the member's domicile in the most tax efficient way.

ASSOCIATION FOR NON-PROFIT

This provides a structure for private clubs and associations engaged in charitable works.

A PUBLIC COMPANY

Such a company has all the attributes and requirements of a company offering shares to the public.

THE LIMITED LIABILITY COMPANY

The Limited Liability Company Ordinance 1994 provides a comprehensive framework for the operation of a limited liability company, also known as a limited duration company. This form of non-incorporated association has some features of a company, including capacity to sue and be sued, separate legal identity, ability to own and transfer property, and limited liability of participants. It also has some of the features of a partnership, and if correctly structured, United States tax laws treat them as "pass through" entities, so that only the members and not the entity are subject to tax. This entity, based on a concept first enacted in Wyoming in 1977 and the subject of subsequent favorable IRS revenue rulings, has now been legally created in many states in the United States of America. The Anguillian legislation is modeled on the best of the Limited Liability Company Acts to emerge.

PARTNERSHIP LEGISLATION

It is sometimes useful to combine a company or trust with a partnership or limited partnership. A limited partnership in particular can be an efficient vehicle for venture capitalists who wish to limit their exposure to management and partnership liability. The Partnership Ordinance 1994 and the Limited Partnership Ordinance of 1994, which is part of the same legislative revision exercise, provide a thorough frame work for such structures. Please check with your Company Formation Agent or Attorney-at-Law for the annual corporate and other fees before starting a business.

TRUSTS

The Trusts Ordinance 1994 is the most comprehensive legislation to address developing areas in the law of trusts including asset protection trusts. To this end, it provides the utmost flexibility to the financial planner. Accordingly, the Ordinance, among other innovations, includes:

SPECIFIC PROVISIONS PROTECTING THE TRUST

The law specifically provides that where a trust is created under the laws of Anguilla, the

Court shall not vary it or set it aside or recognize the validity of any claim against the trust property pursuant to the law of another jurisdiction or the order of a Court of another jurisdiction in respect of: 1. The personal and proprietary consequences of marriage or the termination of marriage; 2. Succession rights (whether testate or intestate) including the fixed shares of spouses or relatives; 3. The claims of creditors in an insolvency; 4. The imposition of any foreign tax or duty. The Trusts Ordinance expressly provides that the Reciprocal Enforcement of Judgments Ordinance cannot be used to circumvent the above provisions.

STRENGTHENED PROTECTION AGAINST CREDITORS

The confidentiality of the trust is further protected by the Fraudulent Dispositions Ordinance 1994. Designed to work primarily with the Trusts Ordinance 1994, it strengthens the degree of protection provided to the Anguilla asset protection trust against creditors claims. The enactment strengthens the ability of the trustee to avoid creditor's claims by shifting the burden of proof of fraudulent transfer from the debtor to the creditor. Actions to set aside an alleged fraudulent transfer must be commenced in the Anguilla High Court within three years of the date that the assets were settled in the trust.

INCENTIVES TO INVESTOR

The Government has granted duty free concessions on the importation of various materials and, in some cases, on vehicles. Such concessions could save the investor as much as 10% to 25% of his building material cost. The granting of concessions is discretionary. Therefore, it is in the interest of the investor to discuss his project with Government before embarking on his project.

FREEDOM TO IMPORT RAW MATERIALS

There is no restriction on the importation of raw materials. However such materials are subject to stamp duty ranging from 5 to 25% on the cost of goods imported into the island unless exempt from stamp duty by the Government of Anguilla.

LABOUR LAWS

There are at present six statutes governing labour relations in Anguilla. These are: (1) The Labour (Minimum Wage) Act Cap 334 (2) The Labour Ordinance (3) Trade Dispute (Arbitration and Injury) Act Cap 352 (4) Workmen's Compensation Act (5) The Trade Union Act Cap 353 (6) Fair Labour Standards Ordinance Labour relations in Anguilla are very good. There has been no major trade dispute on the island for over 10 years. The main disputes on the island are from non-payment of wages by defunct overseas investors. The minimum wage in Anguilla is approximately EC $400/ US $150 monthly for unskilled personnel. All employers are required to pay 10% social security on behalf of each employee up to a maximum of EC $1,200. Five percent (5%) is taken directly from the employee's salary.

RESIDENCE AND WORK PERMITS

All non-belongers of Anguilla are subject to immigration control on arrival in Anguilla. On arrival one may be permitted to remain on the island for a period of thirty days. Extension of the period may be granted after application to the Chief Immigration Officer. Application for Residence Status has to be made to the Government of Anguilla. The granting of residence status is discretionary and is entirely a matter for the Government.

However, the Government may consider genuine investors who are developing large projects that would bring into the island large sums of foreign exchange and will also take into account the job creation aspects of the project. A non-belonger of Anguilla shall not engage in gainful occupation without a valid work permit. The Policy of the Government of Anguilla is to grant work permits only in cases where the required skills are not available in Anguilla. Application for a Work Permit must be submitted to the labour officer. It is advisable that the employer or prospective employer pays a visit to the labour officer to discuss the skills required before making the application. Documents to be submitted with the application are:

(1) Three passport-sized photographs (2) Police record of good conduct (no more than 6 months old) (3) Evidence of qualifications (4) Medical Report Prospective employers should register with the social security office as an employer before submitting application to labour officer on behalf of employee. Fees payable per annum on issue of work Permits: (1) Ministers of Religion – EC $200.00/US $74.63 (2) Domestic servants (employed in homes) – EC $300.00/ US $111.94 (3) Nurses and Teachers EC $1,000.00/US $373.13 (4) Domestic and unskilled manual workers EC $500.00/US $186.57 (5) Semi-skilled or skilled manual workers, tradesmen, secretarial and clerical workers EC $1,000.00/US $373.13 (6) Professional persons, technical managerial and administrative persons EC $2,000.00 /US $746.27 (7) Self -Employed persons (including professionals) EC$3,500.00/ US $1,305.97

POLITICAL AND ECONOMIC STABILITY

Anguilla was formerly part of the Associated State of United Kingdom with St. Kitts-Nevis-Anguilla. The Associated State of St. Kitts – Nevis - Anguilla was controlled by a central administration based in St. Kitts under the leadership of Robert L. Bradshaw. In 1967, through much dissatisfaction concerning the lack of economic development on the island, Anguilla declared its independence from the Associated State of St. Kitts-Nevis-Anguilla. In 1971, Anguilla returned to colonial status under Britain. The island is now referred to as a British Dependent Territory. Prior to 1967, Anguilla's major source of income came from salt, boat building, livestock, cultivation and financial help from Anguillians abroad. Today, Anguilla has the fastest growing tourist industry in the Caribbean region, and has diversified its sources of income, with yacht building, lobster fishing, sale of stamps and off-shore financial services.

BANKING

The Bankers Books (Evidence Act) Cap 8 and the Banking Act 1967 are the two statutes covering banking on the Island of Anguilla.

BANKERS BOOK ACT

The purpose of the Bankers Book (Evidence Act) is to prevent random searches of banking records. To obtain an order from the Court under this Act one must state the specific account(s) the allegations are made against. The Court will not allow a fishing expedition of the bank records.

REGISTRATION OF BANKS

All persons wishing to establish a bank on the Island of Anguilla must first seek the approval of the Ministry of Finance. The applicants must satisfy the Ministry that they have sufficient funds to capitalize the bank, that they or their staff have banking experience and that they are of good character. Once approved, and the fees paid, the Ministry instructs the Registrar of Companies to proceed with incorporation of the Bank. To proceed, the Registrar must first approve of the name of the company. Once approved, the filing of articles of association is straightforward. Your attorney/company formation agent handles these matters on your behalf. In practice, only banks which are already regulated in their own country are likely to be registered in Anguilla.

CAPITAL AVAILABILITY

The banks on the island are conservative in their lending policies. However, with the rapid growth in the economy of the island, this pattern may change in the near future.

'A' CLASS BANK

In Anguilla there are two classes of banks; A Class and B Class. The 'A' Class license is granted for carrying on banking business with persons resident or temporarily visiting the island. They are allowed to accept deposits of money which may be withdrawn on demand.

'B' CLASS BANK

The 'B' Class Bank is normally referred to as an off-shore bank. The off-shore bank is not allowed to do business with the general public on the island, although it may have a physical presence on the island and employ workers on the island. 'B' Class is usually formed for tax avoidance purposes, which is not an offense in most British territories.

OFF-SHORE BANK FEES

License fee for bank with office and staff on island: US $4,000 approximately. License fee for bank without office on island: US $8,000 approximately. N.B. These fees are payable annually. Registration and legal fees range from US $9,000 to US $11,000, depending on services requested. Please consult your local Attorney or the Inspector of off-shore banks and trust companies.

INSURANCE COMPANIES

Types of Insurance Under the Insurance Act 1968 as amended by Insurance Act (amendment) Ordinance 1985 supported by Insurance Regulations 1970, insurance is divided into three classes: (1) Marine Insurance (2) Life Insurance (3) Non-Marine Insurance (all other forms of insurance business)

REGISTRATION

Application for Registration must be made to the Registrar of Insurance who also is the Registrar of Companies. The registrar will request the following information prior to registration: (1) A copy of the articles of association (2) Statement as to the type(s) of insurance to be carried on by the company. (If life insurance is one of the types then the Registrar will request a certificate by a recognized company stating that company is in good standing.) (3) Appointment of local agent

FEES

For further information please consult the Registrar of Insurance (Tel: (264) 497 2451) or your local Attorney.

HOW TO GET TO ANGUILLA

Anguilla is approximately 160 miles east of Puerto Rico, 900 miles south-east of Miami and six minutes flying time from neighbouring St. Maarten. American Airlines has daily flights to Puerto Rico. There are connecting flights on a regular basis by Liat, Air Anguilla, Tyden Air and Winair. Tyden Air and Air Anguilla offer charter flights with services which include taking care of your baggage. If you are tired after a long journey by air and need a change, the local ferry boats are efficient and fast, taking only 15 minutes to cross from French St. Martin to Anguilla.

TRANQUILLITY

The island boasts some of the best beaches in the Caribbean and the warmest people one could find anywhere in the world. After business is over, it is hard to resist the temptation to relax at one of the beautiful beaches. Anguilla is the ideal place for combining business and pleasure. But please re-member business first. Do not forget to obtain a driving license before driving in Anguilla. (Most rental agencies supply temporary licenses). In today's global climate, the reasons for doing business in Anguilla are many. The protection of one's assets, the lack of both personal and corporate income tax, and the safety found in such a tranquil setting are amoung but a few. Add on top of that a legal system which is based firmly on English common law, and a financial service industry designed by strong, protective legislation, and one can see that Anguilla affords the perfect mix for securing one's future.

PRACTICAL INFORMATION FOR OFFSHORE ACTIVITY

Anguilla Chamber of Commerce & Industry
P.O. Box 321 The Valley Anguilla, B. W. I
Tel: 1-264-497 2839 E-Mail : acoci@anguillanet.com

APPLICATION PROCEDURE FOR OFFSHORE BANKS/TRUSTS

Offshore financial legislation in Anguilla is being thoroughly up-dated and reviewed on an on-going basis. In parallel with this process, regulatory provisions and application procedures are evolving. Brief general guidance is given below as to how applicants for licences should approach the application procedure.

CURRENT LEGISLATION:

The main regulatory statutes governing financial services are the Offshore Banks and Trust Companies Ordinance 1991 and the Company Managers Ordinance 1994. The latter governs company managers and company formation agents. Insurance is still regulated under the provisions of the Anguilla Insurance Act 1968.

NEW LEGISLATION

INSURANCE:

The Insurance Act will be replaced in the near future by more up-to-date legislation covering both domestic and offshore insurance activities. The precise form of this new legislation is still being debated, but it is probable that the new provisions will closely resemble legislation currently in force in other British dependencies in the region.

TRUST COMPANIES:

Capitalistic and fee requirements for trust companies are currently under review. The intention is to align basic prudential and fee provisions with the requirements in other British Caribbean dependencies. It has been decided that the minimum capitalisation level for companies seeking a general trust licence will be US$250,000.00; that for restricted trusts will be fixed shortly.

BASIC REGULATORY REQUIREMENTS

PARAMETERS:

Good financial services regulation requires the following basic parameters of all applicants for licences, whether the activities regulated are banking, insurance or company management:

- transparency of beneficial ownership
- 'fit and proper' character of shareholders, directors and managers- relevant professional experience of directors and managers
- adequate capitalisation, reserves and working capital resources
- adequate internal procedures and controls
- regular reporting by external auditors
- efficient lines of communication with the office of the regulator, which may also involve external auditors
- compliance with regulatory stipulations specific to the industry; eg for banks, there is a formal requirement for 'effective consolidated supervision' as well as other banking provisions (in accordance with 'Basle Committee' principles).

Guidelines providing details of such parameters and requirements are issued from time to time by the regulator.

ROLE OF THE SUPERINTENDENT OF OFFSHORE FINANCE

Regulation of offshore financial services is under the direct responsibility of the Governor and his appointed officials. The Superintendent of Offshore Finance (whose office is situated in the Anguilla Offshore Finance Centre, next to the Registry of Companies) handles all technical issues. To the extent that current domestic legislation may require it, the regulator of on-shore activities may also become involved in the application procedure; this would be the case for example with insurance companies which will need to be registered by the Registrar of Insurance. Domestic banking is regulated by the Eastern Caribbean Central Bank, which is headquartered in St Kitts with a representative office in Anguilla.

Initiation of Application (estimated time required 1-2 weeks)
The Superintendent's first task is to get to know and understand the business of an

applicant. The first stage of an application is therefore the provision of a summary business plan, normally in the form of a letter outlining basic business objectives, organisation and resources.

This will allow the regulator to have a general idea of whether the business is suitable or not for further consideration.

The next stage should ideally be a meeting with the regulator, preferably in Anguilla, although meetings can also be arranged elsewhere (the Superintendent is involved in frequent presentations and regulatory conferences abroad).

Formal Application (estimated time to completion 4-6 weeks)
Once the fundamental issues have been discussed in depth and an informal understanding reached with the Superintendent about the basic requirements (ie those mentioned on pages 1 and 2 above), the applicant can proceed with a formal, fully detailed application which will include:

- detailed business plan and 3-5 year projections
- personal questionnaires on shareholders, directors and managers
- professional and personal references on shareholders, directors and managers
- any other requirements that the regulator may make, which can usually be specified at the initial phase;
- relevant supporting documentation - this should, if possible, include financial statements and promotional material of any related companies.

The formal application procedure, including forms and questionnaires, is specified in the relevant law, copies of which are available from the Superintendent.

Application fees (if any) should not be paid until the definitive and final application has been completed and submitted to the Superintendent. The payment of the application fee in no way determines the success or otherwise of an application.

Once complete, it is intended that a response on most applications will be provided within a 4-6 week period (but this remains subject to the timing and acceptability of responses required from third parties).

The Government of Anguilla wishes to encourage applications by experienced professionals in the offshore industry. The Superintendents's office intends to deal with applications efficiently. The office will also attempt to assist, where possible, with the queries of applicants related to business licences, work and residency permits, accommodation, etc.

REGISTRY GUIDELINES

Whereas it is provided by section 16 of the Companies Registry Ordinance, 1998 that the Registrar may issue Registry Guidelines in respect of any matters for which he is authorised to issue guidelines and whereas the Registrar must publish such Guidelines in the Gazette;

Now therefore, I, Alan Jones, Registrar of Companies, in exercise of the power conferred upon me by the said Ordinance, do hereby publish Registry Guidelines issued by me on 16 November 1998:

1. Interpretation and commencement

1.1 These Guidelines are issued by the Registrar of Companies under section 16 of the Ordinance. They apply to documents filed under any of the Registry Ordinances, which are defined in the Ordinance as meaning

(a) the Companies Amendment Ordinance, 1998;

(b) the International Business Companies Amendment Ordinances, 1998;

(c) the Limited Liability Company Amendment Ordinance, 1998;

(d) the Limited Partnership Amendment Ordinance, 1998; and

(e) the Trusts Ordinance, 1994.

1.2 The expressions defined in section 2 of the Ordinance shall, insofar as they occur in these Guidelines and unless the context otherwise requires, have the same meanings as those expressions have in the Ordinance.

1.3 In these Guidelines -

(a) "authorised person" means a person authorised to filed documents in electronic form under section 5(3) or section 5(5) of the Ordinance;

(b) "designated e-mail address" means the e-mail address designated by an authorised person in an application made in accordance with paragraph 5 or such new e-mail address as may have been notified to the Registrar under paragraph 8.2;

(c) "Ordinance" means the Companies Registry Ordinance, 1998;

(d) "Registrar" means the Registrar of Companies and includes any person acting under his authority; and

(e) "Registry System" means the hardware and software (including operating system) for the time being used by the Registrar to receive documents filed in electronic form.

1.4 These Guidelines shall come into force at 1:00pm on 16th November 1998.

2. Paper documents

2.1 Any document that is required or permitted to be filed under a Registry Ordinance may be filed as a paper document.

2.2 To ensure that documents can be scanned by the Registry and readily filed within its filing system, all paper documents filed must meet the specifications set out in paragraph 2.3.

2.3 A paper document filed with the Registry -

(a) must be in the form prescribed or, where no form has been prescribed, in a form agreed with the Registrar;

(b) must not display or reproduce any corporate or firm logo;

(c) must be printed or hand written in black ink on plain, letter size, white paper between 80gsm and 100gsm weight with a matt finish;

(d) must, on each page, have a blank margin all round of not less than 10mm;

(e) must contain characters that are clear, legible and of uniform density; and

(f) if the document contains more than one page, must be securely fastened at the top left hand corner.

2.4 The Registrar may accept for filing a clear photographic or photostatic copy of a paper document, but will not accept a carbon copy or a copy produced on thermal paper or by spirit duplication.

2.5 The Registrar may accept for filing a facsimile transmission of a paper document transmitted either from a dedicated facsimile machine or using a computer running fax production and communication software if the following conditions are met -

(a) the person transmitting the facsimile must be an authorised person;

(b) the facsimile must be sent to such facsimile number as the Registrar may specify for the filing of documents by facsimile transmission;

(c) the facsimile must be accompanied by a cover sheet setting out

(i) the name and address of the person sending the facsimile transmission,

(ii) a telephone number which the Registrar's staff can use to speak to the person sending the facsimile transmission, and

(iii) a facsimile number to which notification may be sent under paragraph 2.6;

(d) the document is transmitted using the highest resolution of which the transmitting fax machine or computer is capable; and

(e) the document bears the signature of any person required to sign it or a printed or mechanical reproduction of the signature.

2.6 Following the receipt for filing of a facsimile transmission of a document, the Registrar will either

(a) accept the facsimile transmission in place of the original document, in which case he will notify the sender of the acceptance of the facsimile transmission:

(i) by e-mail to the sender's designated e-mail address; or

(ii) by facsimile transmission to the facsimile number of the sender as set out on the cover sheet; or

(b) in his discretion, reject the facsimile transmission and require that the document be re-transmitted or that the original document be filed as an original document, in which case he will notify the sender accordingly by either of the methods specified in paragraph 2.6(a).

3. Signing of paper documents

Where a document is required to be signed, subject to the provisions of any other law or regulation to the contrary, the Registrar will accept for filing a paper document bearing a printed or mechanical reproduction of a person's signature.

4. Documents approved for filing in electronic form

4.1 Authorised persons may file approved documents in electronic form in accordance with these Guidelines.

4.2 The documents approved for filing in electronic form are set out in Schedule 1.

5. Application to file documents in electronic form

5.1 An application by a licensee for authorisation for himself or an overseas agent to file documents in electronic form must be made in the form specified in Schedule 2 and must -

(a) confirm that the computer hardware and software (including operating system) that will be used to access the Registry System meet the minimum requirements set out in Schedule 3;

(b) confirm that arrangements have been made to ensure the confidentiality and security of data transmitted to and from the Registry System and to prevent unauthorised access to the Registry System through the accessing computer system;

(c) specify an e-mail address to which the Registrar should send notices or documents whether computer or manually generated;

(d) in the case of an application made for the authorisation of an overseas agent, specify the procedures in place to ensure that adequate due diligence is carried out by the overseas agent, where appropriate, before the filing of documents and for the verification by the licensee of the due diligence carried out by the overseas agent.

6. Hardware and software requirements

A person will not be authorised to file documents in electronic form unless he establishes, to the satisfaction of the Registrar, that the computer hardware and software (including the operating system) that he will use to access the Registry System meets the minimum specification set out in Schedule 3

7. Authentication of documents filed in electronic form

A document filed in electronic form will not be accepted for filing unless -

(a) the identity of the sender is authenticated by the verification software for the time being utilised by the Registry System;

(b) the contents and completeness of the document is verified by the Registry System;

(c) the document filed in electronic form fully complies with section 5(7) of the Ordinance; and

(d) the person filing the document in electronic form is a person authorised to file documents in electronic form under section 5 of the Ordinance.

8. Designated e-mail addresses

8.1 All notices sent by the Registrar or the Registry System to an authorised person shall be deemed to have been received by that person if sent to his designated e-mail address.

8.2 An authorised person may change his designated e-mail address by giving written notice to the Registrar.

8.3 A change in designated e-mail address is effective from the time that the written notice given under paragraph 8.2 is received by the Registrar.

9. Payment of fees

9.1 The Registrar will maintain an account with such bank as he may from time to time determine and notify to authorised persons, to be known as the "ACORN Advance Payment Account".

9.2 An authorised person may, from time to time, pay moneys into the ACORN Advance Payment Account, which sums will be credited to his account in the records of the Registrar.

9.3 The cost, fee or charge incurred by an authorised person in respect of the filing of any document or the use of any service provided by the Registrar through the Registry System will be satisfied by a transfer of moneys from the ACORN Advance Payment Account to the Registrar and deducted from his account in the records of the Registrar.

9.4 An authorised person will not be permitted to file a document in electronic form or to use a service provided by the Registrar through the Registry System unless he has deposited sufficient moneys in the ACORN Advance Payment Account to pay any costs, fees or charges payable in respect of the filing or service.

10. Authentification of documents issued by the Registrar in electronic form

Documents issued in electronic form by the Registrar will be sent using the verification software for the time being utilised by the Registry System and will be capable of being authenticated by and verified by the verification software supplied by the Registrar to the authorised person.

11. Exchange rates

11.1 This paragraph applies where it is necessary for a currency to be converted to any other currency for the purposes of assessing the fee payable to the Registrar or otherwise.

11.2 The Registrar will, using such independent source or sources as he may from time to time specify, set exchange rates between such pairs of currencies as he considers appropriate as at 16.00 hours Anguilla time each working day.

11.3 The exchange rates set by the Registrar under paragraph 11.2 will be -

(a) made available to authorised users on request; and

(b) will be utilised by the Registrar to convert currencies in respect of all documents filed between 16.00 hours Anguilla time on that day and immediately before 16.00 hours on the following working day.

11.4 If it is necessary to convert a currency for which an exchange rate has not been set under paragraph 11.2, the Registrar will, using the same or a different independent source, set an exchange rate for the conversion as at a time as close as possible to the time that the document was filed.

REGISTRAR OF COMPANIES

SCHEDULE 1

Documents approved for filing in electronic form.

Name Search (All types of company including Limited Partnerships)

Name Availability Acceptability Search
Multiple Name search - (Alphabetic or Phonetic)
Keyword Search
Single Name Search (Foreign Scripts)
Browse Company Name Registers

Name Reservation (All types of companies including Limited Partnerships)
Initial Reservation
Formal Reservation

International Business Companies filings
Articles of Incorporation
Articles of Amendment
Notification of Change in Reg Office / Agent
Articles of Continuance
Certificate of Departure
Articles of Dissolution
Recision of Articles of Dissolution
Application for Restoration to the Register
Optional Registration of Directors / Shareholders
Notice of change in Directors / Shareholders
Cancellation of optional Registration
Payment of Annual Fee
Articles of Consolidation
Merger Subsidiary
Articles of Merger

All Filings under the Companies Ordinance

All Filings under the Limited Liability Companies Ordinance

SCHEDULE 3

Minimum Computer Hardware and software specifications

Operating Environment

- Windows 95 / 98 or NT 4.0
- Microsoft Internet Explorer 4
- Microsoft Word 97
- VeriSign Inc, Digital ID Class 2 Certificate. Certificates, issued through the registry.

Minimum Hardware Requirements

- IBM compatible PC, X86-166Mhz with at least a Pentium processor (or clone) and 32MB of RAM
- An internal or external modem with a line speed of 28.8kbpse.
- An Internet connection from your local ISP.

CONSUMPTION-ORIENTED TAX SYSTEM

REWARDS PRODUCTIVITY AND THRIFT

Anguilla is a small society in the Caribbean with a successful tourism economy. **The growth-oriented tax system is based on consumption, not income, and rewards productive behavior.** Anguilla has a government, so it has taxes, but it doesn't have a sales tax, VAT, GST, income tax, profits tax, capital gains tax, or inheritance tax.

Those who use the services, pay the taxes on them. When you buy something that is imported into Anguilla, and most things are imported, the price includes import duties. **Duties are a type of consumption tax, like a sales tax**. Anguilla collects about 25% duty at the border on most items (actually 5% on food and computers to 30% on beer and cigarettes). Import duties go into the general island revenues which are used to pay for things like medical services and education, which are quite good by the standards of the developing world.

In many countries, there is also a **universal "Value Added Tax"** that applies to every sale of goods or services in the economy. VAT turns each electrician and gardener into either an unpaid government bookkeeper/tax collector, or into a tax cheat in the underground economy. Currently, there is a 7% GST in Canada and 10%-40% VAT in Europe, and it is imposed in addition to heavy income taxes. Anguilla does not currently have a VAT.

The system for raising revenues in Anguilla is relatively **eco-friendly** in that the consumption of non-renewable resources is taxed fairly heavily. Those who use the roads pay a heavy annual vehicle licencing fee, and an annual driving license fee. Those who consume gasoline pay the import duty on gasoline, and those who buy cars pay a a heavy import tax for them.

Taxes in Anguilla are on consumption, not productivity. When you buy land, you pay a 5% stamp tax, 17.5% if you are not a "belonger" (local citizen). Those who use the airport pay a $10 departure tax and those who use the less expensive ferry service pay a lesser tax, only $2. There is an 8% tax on hotel rooms, but a night at Lloyds Guest House for $65 per night only collects $5 tax, while staying in an $800 suite at Cap Juluca adds $64 to the bill. **(All figures on are in US dollars.)**

Instead of deducting **half of family income** from paychecks for income taxes, surcharges, and social security taxes, Anguilla collects only a 5% social security tax (plus 5% from the employer, and the maximum is $186/month combined).

There are no taxes on savings and investment. This encourages people to save and invest. Many Anguillians, even those with very modest incomes, really know how to save.

Instead of punishing those who build a successful business by taxing away half their **capital gains** when they sell, Anguilla **rewards hard work, boosts savings, and**

encourages growth of the economy. The result? The country has gone from poverty to regional prosperity in one generation.

And there is **no inheritance tax** in Anguilla. Family land is the most important thing in Anguilla and inheritance tax that had to be paid in cash would eliminate passing down land to your children.

Anguilla employs both the US dollar and the EC dollar in local commerce, without exchange controls. By having the most rational currency regulations in the OECS (Organization of Eastern Caribbean States), Anguilla has more foreign currency deposits than any other OECS state. Banks use the normal "know your customer" rules to avoid money laundering.

Compared to many countries, the USA is considered tax efficient and it uses that to attract foreigners. Many creative and productive Europeans, Asians and Latin Americans make personal choices to create their businesses in Silicon Valley or Miami instead of Paris or Berlin ("Go West, Young Frenchman", *Business Week*, March 9, 1998: "A torrent of talent is leaving France"). Even more foreigners use the excellent financial services of the United States and the Internet makes this easier still. From Anguilla you can open an account at Jack White, discount brokers in San Diego, and have full financial services over the Internet, all provided by a US firm. Or if you open an account at Dollarbank while visiting the USA, you can do all your banking over the Internet. If it is okay for the USA to use it's low tax rates to attract most of the brain power of the world, why does it call what Anguilla does "harmful tax competition".

You can think of Anguilla as a laboratory experiment in alternative tax policies. **Tax policy in Anguilla isn't perfect, but it works.** Anguilla, along with Hong Kong, New Zealand, and Chile, have shown that small places can prosper despite serious handicaps. In the 30 years since Anguilla separated from St.Kitts/Nevis, Anguilla's people have built a successful, productive economy, and now attract guest workers from neighboring islands. And these other islands have tax systems of the European/US model that sap the growth of new small business and protect the large, entrenched firm with its lobbyists and tax specialists.

BUSINESS CONTACTS FOR OFFSHORE ACTIVITY

ACCOUNTING FIRMS

Audain & Associates
Hansa Bank Building
P.O. Box 671
The Valley
Anguilla, B.W.I.
Tel: +1 264 497 5621
Fax: +1 264 497 5220
E-mail: mraudain@anguillanet.com
Website: N/A
Contact: Marva Audain-Thompson

Counsel Limited
Physical Address:
The Hansa Bank Building - 1st Floor
Landsome Road
The Valley
Anguilla, B.W.I.

Mailing Address:
P.O. Box 727
The Valley

TV1 02P
Anguilla, B.W.I.

Tel: +1 264 498 3800
Fax: +1 264 498 3805
E-Mail: counsel@counsel.ai
Website: www.counsellimited.com
Contact: Donald R Curtis

KPMG Peat Marwick
P.O. Box 136
The Valley
Anguilla, B.W.I.
Tel: +1 264 497 5500
Fax: +1 264 497 3755
E-Mail: kpmg@anguillanet.com
Website: www.kpmg.com.ai
Contact: Claudel Romney

BANKS

Firstcaribbean International Bank (Barbados) Limited
P.O. Box 140
The Valley
Anguilla, B.W.I.
Tel: +1 264 497 2301
Fax: +1 264 497 2980
E-mail: N/A
Website: N/A
Contact: Mr Bernard Leonce

National Bank of Anguilla
P.O. Box 44
The Valley
Anguilla, B.W.I.
Tel: +1 264 497 2101
Fax: +1 264 497 3310
E-mail: nbabankl@anguillanet.com
Website: N/A
Contact: Icilma Vanterpool

Caribbean Commercial Bank (Anguilla) Ltd.
P.O. Box 23
The Valley
Anguilla, B.W.I.
Tel: +1 264 497 2571
Fax: +1 264 497 3570
E-mail: ccbaxa@anguillanet.com
Website: N/A
Contact: Landia Richardson

Scotiabank Anguilla Ltd.
Fairplay commercial Complex
P.O. Box 250
The Valley
Anguilla, B.W.I.
Tel: +1 264 497 3333
Fax: +1 264 497 3344
E-mail: scotia@anguillanet.com
Website: N/A
Contact: Walter MacCalman

LAW FIRMS

Caribbean Juris Chambers
P.O. Box 328

Caribbean Associated Attorneys
P.O. Box 1010

The Valley
Anguilla, B.W.I.
Tel: +1 264 497 3470
Fax: +1 264 497 3177
E-mail: caribjur@anguillanet.com
Website: www.benjamine.ai
Contact: John Benjamin / Bernadine Romney / Carol Nelson

J.A.G. Gumbs & Co
The Anguilla Professional Complex
P.O. Box 1398
The Valley
Anguilla, B.W.I.
Tel: +1 264 497 1212
Fax: +1 264 497 1214
E-Mail: jaggumbs_co@anguillanet.com
Website: N/A
Contact: Mrs Josephine A G Gumbs-Connor

Hodge's Chambers
Hodge's Chambers
PO Box 840
The Valley
Anguilla, B.W.I.
Tel: +1 264 497 3793
Fax: +1 264 497 2863
E-mail: N/A
Website: N/A
Contact: V. R. Hodge

Lake & Kentish
PO Box 259
The Valley
Anguilla, B.W.I.
Tel: +1 264 497 2582
Fax: +1 264 497 5496
E-mail: laken@anguillanet.com
Website: N/A
Contact: Bernice V Lake QC / Joyce Kentish / Lorna Rogers

Richardson Sinel & Associates
NBA Corporate Building
P O Box 1474
The Valley
Anguilla, BWI

The Valley
Anguilla, B.W.I.
Tel: +1 264 497 5405
Fax: +1 264 497 3975
E-mail: caa@caribbean-attorneys.com
Website: www.caribbean-attorneys.com
Contact: Courtney Abel

Harney Westwood & Riegels
Harlaw Chambers
P.O. Box 1026
The Valley
Anguilla, B.W.I.
Tel: +1 264 498 5000
Fax: +1 264 498 5001
E-Mail: hwr@anguillanet.com
Website: www.harneys.com
Contact: Alex Richardson

Keithley Lake & Associates
The Law Building
P.O. Box 14
The Valley
Anguilla, B.W.I.
Tel: +1 264 497 2069
Fax: +1 264 497 3012
E-mail: information@anguilla-attorney.com
Website: www.anguilla-attorney.com
Contact: Keithley Lake, Kenneth Porter or Yvette Wallace

Myrna R. Walwyn & Associates
The Valley
Anguilla, B.W.I.
Tel: +1 264 497 2484
Fax: +1 264 497 3706
E-mail: N/A
Website: N/A
Contact: Myrna R. Walwyn

Samuel McCleery
Hansa Bank Building
P.O. Box 1027
The Valley
Anguilla, B.W.I.

Tel: +1 264 498 5544
Fax: +1 264 498 5545
Email: arichardson@sineltrust.com
Website: N/A
Contact: J Alex Richardson

Tel: +1 264 497 2527
Fax: +1 264 497 5638
E-Mail: ultra@anguillanet.com
Website: www.smccleery.com
Contact: Samuel McCleery

T W R Astaphan
P.O. Box 350
The Valley
Anguilla, B.W.I.
Tel: +1 264 497 5555
Fax: +1 264 497 5310
E-mail: N/A
Website: N/A
Contact: Thomas WR Astaphan

Webster Dyrud Mitchell
P.O. Box 58
The Valley
Anguilla, B.W.I.
Tel: +1 264 497 2060
Fax: +1 264 497 3096
E-mail: information@websterdyrud.com
Website: www.websterdyrud.com
Contact: Palmavon J Webster

Wigley's Chambers
P.O. Box 821
The Valley
Anguilla, B.W.I.
Tel: +1 264 497 8129
Fax: +1 264 497 8289
E-Mail: information@offshore-lawyer.com
Website: www.offshore-lawyer.com
Contact: John Wigley

COMPANY MANAGERS

Anglo-Overseas Trust Company Limited
Intertrust Office
The Valley
Anguilla
British West Indies
E-mail: intertrust@anguillanet.com
Website: N/A
Contact: Anthony Shiffers

Angwal Corporate Services Limited
Myrna R. Walwyn & Associates Chambers
P.O. Box 397
The Valley
Anguilla
Tel: (264) 497-2484/3868
Fax: (264) 497-3706
E-mail: angwal@anguillanet.com
Website: N/A

Antilles International Management Services Limited
The Valley
Anguilla
E-mail: ault@kensingtontrust.com
Website: N/A
Contact: Douglas Calder

Astaphan & Kelsick
Herbert's Commercial Center
The Valley
Anguilla
British West Indies
E-mail: astaphankelsick@anguillanet.com
Website: N/A
Contact: Thomas Astaphan

AXA Offshore Management Limited

Banx Professional Services Ltd

The Law Building
P.O. Box 687
The Valley
Anguilla, B.W.I.
Tel: +1 264 497 3142
Fax: +1 264 497 5753
E-mail: axa-offshore@anguillanet.com
Website: www.axaoffshore.com
Contact: Esther Fleming

Benjamine Company Svcs. Ltd.
Hannah-Waver House
P.O. Box 801
The Valley
Anguilla, B.W.I.
Tel: +1 264 497 5270
Fax: +1 264 497 5271
E-mail: caribjur@anguillanet.com
Website: www.benjamine.ai
Contact: Bernadine Romney / John Benjamin / Carol Nelson

CMF International Ltd
c/o C.E.G. Limited
P.O. Box 294
Heywood House
Anguilla, B.W.I.
Tel: +1 264 497 6468
Fax: +1 264 497 6080
E-mail: info@ceg.ai
Website: www.ceg.ai
Contact: Graham Crabtree

Counsel Limited
Physical Address:
The Hansa Bank Building - 1st Floor

Caribbean Commercial Centre
P.O. Box 20
The Valley
Anguilla, B.W.I.
Tel: +1 264 497 5388
Fax: +1 264 497 3286
E-mail: banksv@anguillanet.com
Website: N/A
Contact: Olivia Gumbs Hodge

C.E.G. Limited
Heywood House
P.O. Box 294
The Valley
Anguilla, B.W.I.
Tel: +1 264 497 6468
Fax: +1 264 497 6080
E-mail: info@ceg.ai
Website: www.ceg.ai
Contact: Graham Crabtree

Codan Trust Company (Anguilla) Limited
Principal Office
Clarendon House
2 Church Street
P.O. Box HM 666
Hamilton HM CX
Bermuda
Tel: +1 284 852 1010
Fax: +1 284 852 1011

Anguilla Office
c/o Intertrust Offices
P.O. Box 147
The Valley
Anguilla, BWI
Tel: 264 497 2189
Fax: 264 497 5007

E-Mail: GThomas@cdp.bm
Website: www.cdp.bm/bvi/bvi.cfm
Contact: Gareth Thomas

Euro-American Trust and Management Services Limited
Principal Office

Landsome Road
The Valley
Anguilla, B.W.I.

Mailing Address:
P.O. Box 727
The Valley
TV1 02P
Anguilla, B.W.I.

Tel: +1 264 498 3800
Fax: +1 264 498 3805
E-Mail: counsel@counsel.ai
Website: www.counsellimited.com
Contact: Malcolm Hope-Ross

First Anguilla Trust Company Ltd
Mitchell House
P.O. Box 174
The Valley
Anguilla, B.W.I.
Tel: +1 264 498 8800
Fax: +1 264 498 8880
E-mail: information@firstanguilla.com
Website: www.firstanguilla.com
Contact: John O. Dyrud

Hansa Bank & Trust Company Limited
NBA Corporate Building
First Floor
St. Mary's Road
The Valley
Anguilla, B.W.I.
TV1 02P
Tel: +1 264 497 3800
J.Fax: +1 702 447 8567
E-Mail: hansa@attglobal.net
Website: www.hansa.net
Contact: Lynwood S. Bell

Icaza, Gonzalez-Ruiz & Aleman
Principal Office
Aquilino de la Guardia Street, No. 8
IGRA Building
5th Floor
PO Box 87-1371 - 7

R.G. Hodge Plaza, 3rd Floor
P.O. Box 3483
Wickhams Cay 1
Road Town
Tortola
British Virgin Islands

Anguilla Office
P.O. Box 1388
The Valley
Anguilla, B.W.I.
Tel: +507 269 2272
Fax: +507 269 2714

E-Mail: eamsbvi@surfbvi.com
Website: N/A
Contact: Pauline Robinson

First Management Company Ltd.
#40 Caribbean Commercial Centre
P.O. Box 68
The Valley
Anguilla, B.W.I.
Tel: +1 264 497 5578
Fax: +1 264 497 5589
E-mail: firstmanagement@anguillanet.com
Website: N/A
Contact: Icilma Woodley

HWR Services (Anguilla) Limited
Harlaw Chambers
P.O. Box 1026
The Valley
Anguilla, B.W.I.
Tel: +1 264 498 5000
Fax: +1 264 498 5001
E-Mail: hwr@anguillanet.com
Website: www.harneys.com
Contact: Alex Richardson / Heather Wallace

ICS Trust (Anguilla) Limited
The Hallmark Building, Old Airport Road
PO Box 227
The Valley
Anguilla, B.W.I.
Tel: +852 2854 4544

Panama
Republic of Panama

Anguilla Office
P.O. Box 1388
The Valley
Anguilla, B.W.I.

Tel: +507 263 5555
Fax: +507 259 4891
E-Mail: igranet@icazalaw.com
Website: www.icazalaw.com
Contact: Dr. Roberto R. Alemán H. and/or Dr. Domingo A. Díaz S.

Fax: +852 2543 5555
E-Mail: ew@icstrust.com
Website: www.icstrust.com
Contact: Eliza S. Y. Wu

Intertrust (Anguilla) Limited
P.O. Box 1388
The Valley
Anguilla, B.W.I.
Tel: +1 264 497 2189
Fax: +1 264 497 5007
E-mail: Anguilla@intertrustgroup.com
Website: www.intertrust-group.com
Contact: Joseph Brice

J.A.G. Gumbs & Co
The Anguilla Professional Complex
P.O. Box 1398
The Valley
Anguilla, B.W.I.
Tel: +1 264 497 1212
Fax: +1 264 497 1214
E-Mail: jaggumbs_co@anguillanet.com
Website: N/A
Contact: Mrs Josephine A G Gumbs-Connor

Samuel McCleery
Hansa Bank Building
P.O. Box 1027
The Valley
Anguilla, B.W.I.
Tel: +1 264 497 2527
Fax: +1 264 497 5638
E-Mail: ultra@anguillanet.com
Website: www.smccleery.com
Contact: Samuel McCleery

KPMG Corporate Services LLC
P.O. Box 136
The Valley
Anguilla, B.W.I.
Tel: +1 264 497 5500
Fax: +1 264 497 3755
E-mail: kpmg@anguillanet.com
Website: www.kpmg.com.ai
Contact: Claudel Romney

Lake & Kentish
P.O. Box 259
The Valley
Anguilla, B.W.I.
Tel: +1 264 497 2582
Fax: +1 264 497 5496
E-mail: laken@anguillanet.com
Website: N/A
Contact: Bernice V Lake QC / Joyce Kentish / Lorna Rogers

Lutea (Anguilla) Limited
c/o Intertrust Offices
The Valley
Anguilla
E-mail: jfleetwood@lutea.com
Website: N/A
Contact: John Fleetwood

M & R Corporate Services
P.O. Box 671
The Valley
Anguilla, B.W.I.
Tel: +1 264 497 5620
Fax: +1 264 497 5220
E-mail: mraudain@anguillanet.com
Website: N/A
Contact: Marva Audain-Thompson

Offshore Incorporations (Anguilla) Limited
Principal Office
9/F Ruttonjee House
11 Duddell Street
Central
Hong Kong
Anguilla Office
Harlaw Chambers
The Valley
Anguilla, B.W.I.

Tel: +852 2521 2517
Fax: +852 2810 4525
E-Mail: administration@offshore-inc.com
Contact: Wendy O'Donnell

On-Island (Anguilla) Corporate Svcs. Ltd.
P.O. Box 1010
The Valley
Anguilla, B.W.I.
Tel: +1 264 497 5405
Fax: +1 264 497 3975
E-mail: abelc@anguillanet.com
Website: www.on-island.com
Contact: Courtney Abel

Overseas Management Company (Anguilla) Limited
Victoria House
The Valley
Anguilla
E-mail: eileen@omcpty.com
Contact: Eileen Marquez

Professional Corporate Services (Anguilla) Ltd.
The Hallmark Building, Old Airport Road
PO Box 227
The Valley
Anguilla, B.W.I.
Tel: +1 264 497 3573
Fax: +1 264 497 3577
E-mail: procorp@profgroup.com
Website: www.profgroup.com
Contact: Scott Hauser

ProServices (Anguilla) Limited
Victoria House
The Valley
Anguilla
E-mail: haleue@amicorp.vg
Website: N/A
Contact: Humphry Leue

Rathbone (Anguilla) Ltd.
P.O. Box 136
#7 Herberts Commercial Centre
The Valley
Anguilla, B.W.I.
Tel: +1 264 497 5500
Fax: +1 264 497 3755
E-mail: rathbone@surfbvi.com
Website: N/A

Sinel Trust Anguilla Limited
Sinel Chambers
PO Box 1269
The Valley
Anguilla, BWI
Tel: +1 264 497 3311
Fax: +1 264 497 5659
E-mail: jbrice@sineltrust.com
Website: www.sineltrust-anguilla.com

Contact: Mr. Peter W Poole or Ms. Annetta Williams

Sterling Trust (Anguilla) Ltd
Principal Office
Sterling ACS, Ltd.
British American Building
Ground Floor
Malborough & Navy Lyon Road
Nassau
Bahamas
Tel: +1 242 325 7574
Fax: +1 242 325 8030
Anguilla Office
National Bank Corporate Building
Airport Road
The Valley
Anguilla, B.W.I.

Tel: +1 264 497 5578
Fax: +1 264 497 5589
E-Mail: hwoltz@sterlinggroup.bs
Contact: Howell Woltz

Sucre & Sucre Anguilla Limited
Principal Office
48th East Street, Bella Vista
Sucre Building
P.O. Box 6277, Zone 5
Panama
Republic of Panama

Anguilla Office
P.O. Box 58
Victoria House
The Valley
Anguilla, B.W.I.

Tel: +507 264 1355
Fax: +507 264 1168
E-mail: sucre@sucre.net
Website: N/A
Contact: Mr. Carlos Sucre, Mr. RamÓn Anzola, Ms. Yavel Francis or Ms. Thays de Salas

Contact: Joseph Brice

Stott & Company Limited
P.O. Box 2
The Valley
Anguilla, B.W.I.
Tel: +1 264 497 2744
Fax: +1 264 497 3350
E-mail: information@stottco.com
Website: www.stottco.com
Contact: Denise Stott-Brown

OVERSEAS AGENTS

ALCO Trust B.V.
Sophialaan 33
1075 BL-Amsterdam
The Netherlands
Email: manager@alcotrust.nl
Contact: Albert Verstijnen
Local Agent: C.E.G. Limited

ARPAD Corporate Services, Inc
Karikas
42 Rue
Raoul Servant
69007
Lyon
France
Email: arpad-corporate-services@attglobal.net
Contact: Michel Rakoczi
Local Agent: Wigley & Associates Inc.

ATU General Trust (BVI) Limited
076 Sir Francis Drake Highway
P.O.Box 3463
Road Town
Tortola
British Virgin Islands
Email: atu@atubvi.com
Contact: Michael Parton
Local Agent: Euro-American Trust and Management Services Limited

Thomas Azzara
54 Sandyport Drive
Nassau
Bahamas
Email: taxman@mail.batelnet.bs
Contact: Thomas Azzara
Local Agent: Wigley & Associates Inc.

Colombo Fiduciaria SA
Via San Salvatore 10
6902 Paradiso
The Swiss Confederation
Email: diego@colombo-group.com
Contact: Diego Colombo
Local Agent: Professional Corporate Services (Anguilla) Ltd.

Corporate Agents Group
Werfstraat 6
P.O. Box 3914
Willemstad
Curacao
Netherlands Antilles
Tel: +1 305 358 7872
Fax: +1 305 358 7873
E-Mail: wal001@aol.com
Website: www.corporate-agents.com
Contact: James Walfenzao
Local Agent: HWR Services (Anguilla) Limited

Morris K Ebeling
44 W. Broadway, Suite 601
Salt Lake City
Utah 84101
Tel. No: +1 801 983 5000
Fax No.: +1 801 983 5005
Email: morty@goluxul.com
Contact: Morris Ebeling
Local Agent: Professional Corporate Services (Anguilla) Ltd.

Equinox Trustees Limited
Thorp House
Rouge Bouillon
St Helier
Jersey
Email: clive.tomes@clivetomes.com
Contact: Clive Tomes
Local Agent: Sinel Trust Anguilla Limited

Euro-American Trust and Management Services Limited (BVI)
Euro American Building
Box 3161
Road Town, Tortola
British Virgin Island
Email: eamsbvi@surfbvi.com
Contact: Kay Reddy
Local Agent: Euro-American Trust and Management Services Limited (Anguilla)

Euro-American Trust and Management Services Limited (Guernsey)
St. Peter Port
The Grange
Guernsey
Channel Islands, 971 2QJ
Email: howep@ffg.co.gg
Contact: Kay Reddy
Local Agent: Euro-American Trust and Management Services Limited (Anguilla)

Euro-American Trust and Management Services Limited (Panama)
PO Box 4281
Panama City
Republic of Panama
Email: eamspty@sinfo.netv
Contact: Martha Salazar
Local Agent: Euro-American Trust and Management Services Limited (Anguilla)

Fiduvalor Services Limited
Flat 500
78 Marylebone High Street
Marylebone
London W1U 5AP
United Kingdom
Tel: +44 709 216 4250
Fax: +44 709 216 4253
E-Mail: fiduvalor@valorgroup.biz
Website: www.valorgroup.biz
Contact: René Wetzel, TEP
Local Agent: Professional Corporate Services (Anguilla) Ltd.

FINAB International Corporate Management Services, Ltd
Genesis Building 3/F
Georgetown
Grand Cayman
Cayman Islands
BWI
Email: finab@candw.ky
Contact: Valdemar B Lopes
Local Agent: Professional Corporate Services (Anguilla) Ltd.

First Class Company Services Limited
72 New Bond Street
London W1S 1RR
UK
Email: jdixon@4business.com
Contact: John Dixon
Local Agent: Professional Corporate Services (Anguilla) Ltd.

Goodman & Richter, LLP
501 West Broadway
Suite 1720
San Diego
California, 92101
Email: srichter@goodman-richter.com
Contact: Steven Richter
Local Agent: Benjamine Company Services Limited

Gordon Down and Partners
23 Allenbank Road
Heath
Cardiff
Wales
UK
CF14 3PN
Email: l.cohen1@ntlworld.com
Contact: Laurence Cohen
Local Agent: Benjamine Company Services Limited

Hebert Schenk, P.C.
1440 E Missouri
Suite 125
Phoenix
AZ 85014
Email: prr@hs-law.com
Contact: Philip Rupprecht
Local Agent: Anguilla Offshore Management Limited

HWR Services Limited (BVI)
Craigmuir Chambers
Road Town
Tortola
British Virgin Islands
Email: acorn@hwr.org
Contact: Richard Peters
Local Agent: HWR Services (Anguilla) Limited

ICS Trust (Anguilla) Limited
The Hallmark Building, Old Airport Road
PO Box 227
The Valley
Anguilla, B.W.I.
Tel: +852 2854 4544
Fax: +852 2543 5555
E-Mail: ew@icstrust.com
Website: www.icstrust.com
Contact: Eliza S. Y. Wu
Local Agent: Professional Corporate Services (Anguilla) Ltd.

Interface Management International (UK) Ltd
Green Dragon House, 64-70 High Street
Croydon, United Kingdom
CRO 9XN
Email: dolores@interface-management.com
Contact: Dolores McCarthy
Local Agent: HWR Services (Anguilla) Limited

International Business Company Formation, Inc.
101 Main Street, Suite One
Tappan
New York 10983
USA
Email: poneill@ibcf.com
Contact: Patrick O'Neill
Local Agent: HWR Services (Anguilla) Limited

Intertrust (Hong Kong) Limited
2001 Central Plaza
18 Harbour Road
Wanchai
Hong Kong
Email: HongKong@intertrustgroup.com
Contact: Katherine Chiu
Local Agent: Intertrust (Anguilla) Ltd.

Intertrust (Isle of Man) Limited
Clinch's House
Lord Street
Douglas
Isle of Man, IM99 IRZ
Email: richardorton@intertrustlimited.com
Contact: Melanie Sarapuk
Local Agent: Intertrust (Anguilla) Ltd.

Intertrust Management S.A. - Geneva Branch
Rue de la Pélisserie 16
P.O. Box 3292
CH - 1211 Geneva 3
Switzerland
Tel: +41 22 317 8000
Fax: +41 22 317 8011
E-mail: Geneva@intertrustgroup.com
Website: www.intertrustgroup.com
Contact: Walter Stressemann
Local Agent: Intertrust (Anguilla) Ltd.

Intrust Ltd.
66 Wigmore Street

Jordans Limited
21 St Thomas Street

London
WIH OHQ
England
Tel: +44 20 7467 4000
Fax: +44 20 7467 4081
E-mail: info@intrust.com
Contact: Peter Stone
Local Agent: Professional Corporate Services (Anguilla) Ltd.

Everett, Krebs
256 Bronte Road
Oakville
Ontario, L6L 3C6
Canada
Tel: +1 905 825 8535
Fax: +1 905 469 9967
E-mail: lawgod@offshore-tax.com
Website: www.offshore-tax.com
Contact: Randall J. Krebs
Local Agent: Wigley & Associates Inc

Newport Pacific Financial Group SA/Le Groupe Financiér Newport Pacific SA
Suite 1860, Manulife Place
10180 - 101 Street
Edmonton
Alberta
Canada T5J 3S4
Tel: +1 780 424 5700
Fax: +1 780 428 5100
E-mail: mritter@newpac.com
Website: www.newpac.com
Contact: Michael P. Ritter
Local Agent: HWR Services (Anguilla) Limited

Offshore Incorporations Limited
9/F Ruttonjee House
11 Duddell Street
Central, Hong Kong
Email: administration@offshore-inc.co
Contact: Wendy O'Donnell
Local Agent: HWR Services (Anguilla) Limited

Bristol BS1 6JS
England
Tel: +44 117 923 0600
Fax: +44 117 923 0063
Email: international@jordans.co.uk
Website: www.jordans-international.com
Contact: Anna Goddard
Local Agent: Finsco Limited

Mr. Duncan MacDonald
c/o Stephen Bullock & Co.
Barristers & Acting Solicitors
PO Box 625
244. Main Street
GIBRALTAR
Tel: +350 41380
Fax: +350 76363
E-mail: solicitor@fastmail.fm
Website: N/A
Contact: Duncan MacDonald
Local Agent: Finsco Limited

OCRA World Wide
Grosvenor Court
Tower Street
Ramsey
Isle of Man, IM8 1JA
British Isles
Tel: +44 1624 811000
Fax: +44 1624 811001
E-mail: ocra@ocra.com
Website: www.ocra.com
Contact: Christopher Oldfield
Local Agent: Professional Corporate Services (Anguilla) Ltd.

Overseas Management Company (Asia) Limited
2706 NatWest Tower
Times Square
1 Matheson Street
Causeway Bay
Hong Kong
Email: omcasia@omchk.com.hk
Contact: Irma Herrera
Local Agent: Overseas Management Company Anguilla Limited

Overseas Management Company (Jersey) Limited
P.O. Box 740
31 Broad Street
St Helier
Jersey
JE4 8ZP
Tel: +44 1534 737776
Fax: +44 1534 759909
E-mail: omcj@omcjersey.com
Website: www.omcgroup.com
Contact: Mrs Brigette Homer or Miss Carol Beaugie
Local Agent: N/A

Overseas Management Company Inc (Panama)
Via Espana # 122
Bank of Boston Building
Panama
Republic of Panama
Email: corp.ops@omcpty.com
Contact: Eileen Marquez
Local Agent: Overseas Management Company Anguilla Limited

Overseas Services International Corp (Miami)
1001 Brickell Bay Drive, Ste. 1716
Miami
Florida
33131
Email: andromaji@omcpty.com
Contact: Andromaji Tzanetatos
Local Agent: Overseas Management Company Anguilla Limited

Jason Ellis Perry
918 Town Colony Drive
Middletown
Connecticut
06547
USA
Email: jadmperry@aol.com
Contact: Jason Perry
Local Agent: C.E.G Limited

ProServices Limited
Ellen L. Skelton Building, 4th Floor
Fisher's Estate
Road Town
Tortola
B.V.I
Email: haleue@amicorp.vg
Contact: Humphry Leue
Local Agent: ProServices (Anguilla) Limited

Sovereign Trust International
1601-1603 Kinwick Centre
32 Hollywood Road
Central
Hong Kong
Tel: +852 2542 1177
Fax: +852 2545 0550
E-mail: hk@sovereigngroup.com
Website: www.sovereigngroup.com
Contact: Stuart Stobie or Michael Tsang
Local Agent: Professional Corporate Services (Anguilla) Ltd.

SUCRE, ARIAS, CASTRO & REYES
48th East Street
Bella Vista
Sucre Building
Panama
Republic of Panama
Email: sucre@sucre.net
Website: www.sucre.net
Contact: Mr Carlos Sucre, Mr Ramon Anzola, and Ms Thays De Salas

SUCRE, BRICEÑO & CO.
Samuel Lewis Avenue and 58th Street
Obarrio
ADR Tower, 8th Floor
Panama City
Republic of Panama
Email: tds@sucrelaw.com
Website: www.sucrelaw.com
Contact: Fernando Sucre and Thays de Salas

Local Agent: Sucre & Sucre Anguilla Ltd

Sterling ACS, Ltd.
PO Box CR 56766, #1202
British American Building
Ground Floor
Malborough & Navy Lyon Road
Nassau, Bahamas
Email: hwoltz@sterlinggroup.bs
Contact: Howell Woltz
Local Agent: Sterling Trust (Anguilla), Ltd

Synergia Management International Ltd
6 Petersham Mews
Kensington
London SW7 5NR
England
Tel: +44 207 584 0335
Fax: +44 870 128 6677
E-mail: tim@synergia.co.uk
Website: www.synergia.co.uk
Contact: Timothy Facer
Local Agent: Professional Corporate Services (Anguilla) Ltd.

Scott Wilson
701 Rossland Road, Suite 258
Whitby
Canada L1N 9K3
Tel: +1 905 430 5359
Email: offshore2001@rogers.com
Contact: Scott Wilson
Local Agent: Professional Corporate Services (Anguilla) Ltd.

Zetland Corporate Services Limited
13/F. Silver Fortune Plaza
1 Wellington Street, Central
Hong Kong
Tel: +852 2525 7800
Fax: +852 2140 6833
E-Mail: intray@offshore.com.hk
Website: www.offshore.com.hk
Contact: Michael H. Horne or Ms Hanna Cheung
Local Agent: On-Island (Anguilla) Corporate Svcs. Ltd.

Local Agent: Registered Agents (Anguilla) Limited

St Peters Trust Company Limited
Quay House, South Esplanade
St Peter Port
Guernsey GY 4EJ
Email: quay@quayport.demon.co.uk
Contact: Andy Stoaling
Local Agent: HWR Services (Anguilla) Limited

Angela Wang & Co
24/F, Entertainment Building
30 Queen's Road
Central
Hong Kong
Tel: +852 2869 7772
Fax: +852 2868 0708
E-mail: lawyers@angelawangco.com
Website: N/A
Contact: Kevin L Jones, Angela Wang
Local Agent: Professional Corporate Services (Anguilla) Ltd.

G. Wiseman & Associates
Rossland, BC
Canada VOG 1YO
Email: gideon@invest-wise.com
Contact: Gideon Wiseman
Local Agent: HWR Services (Anguilla) Limited

STOCK BROKERS

Global Trading Ltd
Anguilla Professional Complex
PO Box 174
The Valley
Anguilla B.W.I.
Tel: +1 264 498 2222
Fax: +1 264 498 2228
E-mail: globaltrading@anguillanet.com
Website: www.globaltradestation.com
Contact: Pauline Smith

TRUST COMPANIES

Codan Trust Company (Anguilla) Limited
c/o Intertrust Offices
P.O. Box 147
The Valley
Anguilla, BWI
Tel: 264 497 2189
Fax: 264 497 5007
E-Mail: see Contact
Website: www.cdp.bm
Contact: David Astwood or John C.R. Collis

First Anguilla Trust Company Ltd
Mitchell House
P.O. Box 174
The Valley
Anguilla, B.W.I.
Tel: +1 264 498 8800
Fax: +1 264 498 8880
E-mail: information@firstanguilla.com
Website: www.firstanguilla.com
Contact: John O. Dyrud

HWR Services (Anguilla) Ltd.
Harlaw Chambers
P.O. Box 1026
The Valley
Anguilla, B.W.I.
Tel: +1 264 498 5000
Fax: +1 264 498 5001
E-mail: hwr@anguillanet.com
Website: www.harneys.com
Contact: Alex Richardson / Heather Wallace

Intertrust (Anguilla) Limited
P.O. Box 1388
The Valley
Anguilla, B.W.I.
Tel: +1 264 497 2189
Fax: +1 264 497 5007
E-mail: Anguilla@intertrustgroup.com
Website: www.intertrust-group.com
Contact: Joseph Brice

Sinel Trust Anguilla Limited
Sinel Chambers
PO Box 1269
The Valley
Anguilla, BWI
Tel: +1 264 497 3311
Fax: +1 264 497 5659
E-mail: arichardson@sineltrust.com

Sterling Trust (Anguilla), Ltd
National Bank of Anguilla Building
St. Mary's Road
The Valley
Anguilla, B.W.I.
Tel: +1 264 497 2189
Fax: +1 264 497 5007
or U.S. number +1 714 398 8173

Website: www.sineltrust-anguilla.com
Contact: J Alex Richardson

E-mail: hwoltz@sterlinggroup.bs
Contact: Howell W. Woltz

IMPORTANT ECONOMIC DEVELOPMENTS

COMBATTING MONEY LAUNDERING: DEVELOPMENTS IN ANGUILLA[1]

Money laundering, the conversion of the profits from illegal activities into financial assets, which appear to have legitimated origins, is one of the major crimes that beset societies today and consequently is one of the major challenges of our times. In the main, people tend to associate money laundering only with drug trafficking. However, it also arises from illegal arms trafficking, organised crime, blackmail, credit card and other financial fraud.

The quantity of drug money laundered world-wide is estimated to be in the region of 300-500 billion dollars per annum, with some $60 billion reportedly laundered in the Caribbean region. Globalisation of the world economy, while acknowledged as bringing clear benefits to the world's population, also comes with acknowledged risks, causing weaknesses and vulnerabilities in both national and international financial systems. Money laundering is now considered not only a threat to the national security of individual nations but is seriously considered to be a threat to international security.

Money laundering is the process by which criminals attempts to conceal the true origin and ownership of the proceeds of criminal activities. If undertaken successfully, it allows them to maintain control over those proceeds and to provide a legitimate cover for their source of income.

Money laundering is a global phenomenon that affects all countries to varying degrees. Failure to prevent the laundering of the proceeds of crime permits criminals to benefit from their actions, thus making crime a more attractive proposition. This cannot be tolerated.

In recent years it has become increasingly recognised that if the fight against crime is to succeed criminals must be prevented, whenever possible, from legitimising the proceeds of their criminal activities by converting " dirty" funds to "clean" funds.

The ability to launder the proceeds of criminal activity through financial systems is vital to the success of criminal operations. The unchecked use of financial systems for money laundering purposes has the potential to undermine individual

[1] By John D.K. Lawrence, Director, Financial Services Department

financial institutions and, ultimately, the entire financial sector. The increased integration of the world's financial system, and the removal of barriers to the free movement of capital, have both enhanced the ease with which criminal money can be laundered and complicated the tracing process.

It is often thought that money laundering is associated solely with banks and other credit institutions and bureaux de change. Whilst the traditional banking activities of deposit-taking, money transfer systems and lending do offer a vital laundering mechanism, particularly in the initial conversion from cash, it should be recognised that products and services offered by other types of financial and non-financial sector businesses are also attractive to the launderer. The sophisticated launderer often involves many other unwitting accomplices such as trust companies; stockbrokers; accountants and lawyers; real estate agents; casinos; antique dealers and precious metals dealers.

It is important, therefore, that all businesses in Anguilla, but especially those operating within the financial services sector, understand the nature of money laundering and take measures to protect themselves, as far as possible, from becoming involved. If a business becomes involved in a money laundering scandal, the consequences can be very serious. It will risk prosecution and the loss of its good market reputation. Furthermore, the reputation of Anguilla as a financial services centre could be seriously damaged.

Anguilla, as an emerging financial services jurisdiction, must therefore play its part in ensuring that the proceeds of criminal conduct do not touch it. Furthermore, if unwittingly such proceeds do surface in Anguilla, the mechanisms are properly in place to be able to isolate these proceeds and to identify their source and take appropriate action.

International initiatives, such as the Caribbean Financial Action Task Force, of which Anguilla is an active member, now require countries with financial services sectors, both onshore and offshore, to have in place the proper legislation, regulations, procedures and practices to be able to identify and to investigate the likely proceeds of criminal conduct. These are referred to as suspicious transactions.

Anguilla has therefore recently passed the necessary legislation and regulations to meet these international standards. Failure to have done so would have made Anguilla a target for international criticism. This legislation is described in more detail below.

The Drugs Trafficking Offences Act (DTOA) and The Proceeds of Criminal Conduct Act (PCCA)

These two Acts represent what is referred to as the primary legislation. They apply to all individuals and businesses, which are subject to the jurisdiction of the court in Anguilla and not just to financial services businesses. Both pieces of legislation list a number of offences and these are the following:

(a) Assistance

The combined effect of the DTOA and the PCCA is to make it an offence for any person to provide assistance to a criminal to obtain, conceal, retain or be able to invest funds, if that person knows or suspects or, in some cases, should have known or suspected that those funds are the proceeds of criminal conduct. The term 'criminal conduct' includes any conduct wherever it occurs that would constitute an indictable offence if it had occurred in Anguilla. The specific activity of the laundering of the proceeds of drug trafficking is dealt with under the DTOA.

It should be noted that it is a defence that the person concerned or involved reported his knowledge or suspicion to the Reporting Authority established under the Money Laundering Reporting Authority Act as soon as is reasonably possible.

(b) Tipping Off

A person is guilty of the offence of tipping off if he discloses information to anyone that is likely to prejudice an investigation into money laundering:

* Whilst knowing or suspecting that an investigation into money laundering is being, or is about to be, conducted;
* Whilst knowing or suspecting that a disclosure has been made to the Authority; or
* Whilst knowing or suspecting that a disclosure has been made to the appropriate internal reporting officer at his place of employment. This applies to financial services companies

(c) Failure to Report

In the case of monies derived from drug trafficking, it is also an offence for any person who acquires knowledge or a suspicion of money laundering in the course of their trade, profession, business or employment not to report the knowledge or suspicion as soon as it is reasonably practical after the information comes to his attention.

In the case of an employee, internal reporting in accordance with the reporting procedures laid down by the employer will satisfy this requirement.

Client Confidentiality

The legislation protects those who report suspicions of money laundering from claims in respect of any alleged breach of client confidentiality or in respect of any restrictions upon disclosure imposed by statute or contract.

The Anti-Money Laundering Regulations, 2000

As already explained, the Drugs Trafficking Offences Act (DTOA) and the Proceeds of Criminal Conduct Act (PCCA) apply to all persons and businesses subject to the jurisdiction of the court in Anguilla. However, the above Regulations place additional administrative requirements on financial services providers. The Regulations cover all persons licensed or registered to carry on relevant business, as defined in the Regulations.

It should be emphasised again that all businesses risk prosecution under the DTOA or PCCA and a reputational loss, if they become involved in a money laundering transaction. In the circumstances, those who believe that they may be vulnerable to being used by criminals should consider applying the requirements of the Regulations in whole or in part, whether or not they are subject to them.

Requirements of the Regulations

The Regulations impose an obligation on regulated persons, as defined, to maintain policies and procedures to guard against their businesses and the financial systems being used for the purposes of money laundering. In essence these procedures are designed to achieve two purposes - first to enable suspicious transactions to be recognised as such and reported to the Authority and second to ensure that if a client comes under investigation in the future, the regulated person can provide its part of the audit trail. The Regulations cover:

1. Identification procedures;
2. Record keeping
3. Internal reporting procedures; and
4. The training of staff

Guidance Notes on the Prevention of Money Laundering

These Guidance Notes are designed to produce a practical handbook on both money laundering in general and on the requirements of the Regulations for the financial services providers. They cover:

* What is money laundering and the vulnerability of financial sector businesses to money laundering.
* The legislation and regulations in force
* Identification procedures "know your customer"

* Record keeping procedures
* Regulation and reporting of suspicious transactions
* Training and awareness requirements
* Examples of suspicious transactions

Money Laundering Reporting Authority Act 2000

This piece of legislation establishes an Authority to which suspicious transactions should be reported. The Authority is in process of being set up and full details will be made available shortly.

What does all this mean for the public in Anguilla ?

At the level of those involved in financial services, both as employer and employee, the primary legislation of both the PCCA and the DTOA as well as the anti-money laundering regulations and guidelines are very much applicable. Employers and their staff will have to become familiar with the regulations and the guidelines and implement the requirements of those regulations.

For other businesses, they will still be subject to the primary legislation and should be vigilant to activities and transactions that seem unusual or strange and/or cannot be properly explained.

For the ordinary citizen of Anguilla, he or she may be now subject or may become subject to the bank asking questions about monetary transactions, that never seemed to be asked before. These questions will usually be about the source of funds being transacted with the bank, especially if any amount of cash, that is to say bank notes or even traveller's cheques, is involved.

If the banker feels the need to ask where the funds have come from, please do assist him or her and do not take offence. Remember your service provider and banker has obligations to fulfill and he or she is only doing his or her job, and can only do that job properly if you, the client, are willing to cooperate.

Remember money-laundering is a crime and we all have a duty to protect the reputation of this growing island.

Financial Services Department is available to give guidance on any matter concerning issues regarding money-laundering.

ANGUILLA'S COMMERCIAL ONLINE REGISTRATION NETWORK REVIEW OF FINANCIAL REGULATION IN THE CARIBBEAN OVERSEAS TERRITORIES AND BERMUDA

The UK and the Caribbean Overseas Territories and Bermuda commissioned an independent review of financial regulation in those territories. This independent review, carried out by KPMG to assess the extent to which the Overseas Territories comply with international standards and good practice in the way they regulate their international financial sectors, is published today.

The review analysed the position of each Overseas Territory individually in terms of the extent and range of financial business conducted and the strength and effectiveness of their regulatory regimes. The KPMG report is exception-based and largely concentrates on those areas of financial regulation where action is considered necessary to comply fully with international standards.

Welcoming the publication of the review, Melanie Johnson, the Economic Secretary to the Treasury said:

"The review provides a rigorous and comprehensive evaluation of how far the Overseas Territories already match international standards and good practice, and makes recommendations for action to improve and strengthen financial services regulation in the Overseas Territories.

I look forward to seeing their plans for implementation linked to a specific timetable which each Overseas Territory has committed to publish by 15 January 2001.

It is evident that some Overseas Territories have more to do than others before they can deliver fully what is necessary. It is equally clear that not everything can be done immediately. It has been mutually agreed that the Overseas Territories, where applicable, will give priority to three particular recommendations made in the KPMG report. The three priorities for action are legislation for the establishment of independent regulatory authorities; any necessary enhancements to their laws and systems to combat money laundering; and introducing legal powers that would allow regulatory authorities to obtain key information, and share this with overseas regulators in order to assist their investigations. We will be working with each Overseas Territory to put in place suitable measures; and we expect to see the necessary steps substantively in place by 30 September 2001. Prompt and firm action in this regard will demonstrate to the global financial community the strength of the Overseas Territories' commitment to international standards."

Baroness Scotland, Parliamentary Under Secretary of State in the Foreign and Commonwealth Office responsible for the Overseas Territories, added her appreciation for the efforts made by all concerned with the delivery and publication of the review:

"The Overseas Territories White Paper - 'Partnership and Prosperity' - noted that the Overseas Territories' success in attracting financial services has been built upon, amongst other things, their reputation for sound administration, effective legal systems, and political stability. In an increasingly competitive global economy, maintaining a reputation for seeking to attract only clean and well-regulated business is vital.

I welcome the Overseas Territories' full participation in the review exercise. It has been a complex process, but one which we believe will deliver real benefits to the Overseas Territories' financial sectors. The review has underlined the Overseas Territories' commitment to adhering to international standards of financial regulation, and their willingness to co-operate internationally to help ensure a sound international financial system."

In response to the publication of the KPMG report, Hon Victor Banks, Minister of Finance in Anguilla, said:

"The Government of Anguilla welcomes the KPMG Report and recognises the hard work that has gone into its completion. The Report highlights the extent to which Anguilla already meets international standards and practices and serves as an excellent springboard for the continuing solid development of Anguilla's financial services sector. The comments in the Report on the sound regulatory aspects of Anguilla's electronic Companies Registry, ACORN, are particularly welcome. The Report should also assist the Government of Anguilla in dealing with a number of international initiatives currently underway".

This comment follows a recent meeting in London attended by Ministers, senior officials and regulators from the Overseas Territories and the UK. This meeting agreed the following conclusions:

- Each Overseas Territory would publish by 15 January 2001 a response to the recommendations addressed to it, together with a timetable for implementation.
- Following appropriate consultation and parliamentary approval within each Overseas Territory, the core recommendations relating to independent regulatory authorities, anti-money laundering regimes and exchange of information would be substantially implemented by 30 September 2001.
- The UK is willing to provide appropriate assistance to Overseas Territories in their bilateral and/or multilateral negotiations with other entities in matters relating to regulation and exchange of information.
- Finally, the UK and Overseas Territories expressed their thanks to KPMG for producing a professional report on a short timescale.

Notes for editors

1. The KPMG report comprises individual publications on each Overseas Territory. Each publication also contains the Terms of Reference for the review and Guidance Notes produced by HMG, the Caribbean Overseas Territories and Bermuda setting out the standards/practices against which the OTs would be assessed. Copies of the report can be ordered from The Stationery Office. It can also be found on the following web-site address http://www.official-documents.co.uk/document/cm48/4855/4855.htm
2. The White Paper "Partnership for Progress and Prosperity - Britain and the Overseas Territories", published in March 1999, envisaged an in-depth independent review of the Overseas Territories' financial centres by regulatory experts.
3. In December 1999, following a lengthy tendering process, KPMG was appointed to undertake this review. The review examined practices and legislation covering the banking, insurance and securities sectors, companies and trusts,

independence of regulatory authorities, as well as arrangements for co-operating with overseas and law enforcement authorities and developments in tackling money laundering.

4. The review assessed progress by the Overseas Territories in implementing accepted international standards and good practice in the areas outlined above. It determines whether further action in order to meet those standards and where necessary, makes recommendations for improvement.

ASIA PACIFIC OFFSHORE INSTITUTE (APOI) ANNUAL CONFERENCE

The Registrar of Commercial Activities Mr. Lanston Connor and the newly appointed Deputy Registrar of Commercial Activities Mr. Brent Davis returned to the island over the weekend from attending the Asia Pacific Offshore Institute (APOI) annual conference which was held in Macau during September 25 -27 2002. The conference focused mainly on issues and concerns of the members of the Asia Pacific region and how they are dealing with the initiatives of the OECD. The theme for this year's conference was ***Strategies for offshore industry in greater china - business development under the current economic and regulatory framework.***

The keynote speaker for the conference was Mr. Jeffery Owens (Head of Center for Tax Policy and Administration OECD) who delivered his presentation on the latest developments of the OECD initiatives and their impact on Asian countries. The conference also provided much information on the emerging financial services market in China, which holds great potential for Anguilla and our ACORN system and its capability to use Chinese characters. "We are very excited about the opening up of the Chinese market and we will be monitoring the activities there very closely," stated Mr. Connor.

After the completion of the conference the two senior government officials made courtesy visits to all of Anguilla's offshore agents in Hong Kong. "It is very important to establish a personal relationship with the agents in order to create a higher degree of trust and confidence in each other" explained Mr.Connor. He further stated "In the Asian culture the personal relationship is of paramount importance when doing business and it can make a difference in the level of success one achieves".

The agents were visited mainly to establish personal relationships, obtain feedback on the use and effectiveness of the ACORN system, and to address any issues and concerns they may have. The major issue was the lack of knowledge about Anguillla by their clients and potential clients.

According to Mr. Davis the main problem facing Anguilla in the financial services industry is that the island is unknown. While Anguilla has gain substantial publicity as an up market tourism destination we experience the complete opposite as a financial services center. In comparison with the establish financial centers such as the BVI, Cayman Islands and Bermuda, Anguillla has a huge marketing task ahead in order to become a major player in the financial services industry.

Mr. Connor explained that the government and the private sector must work vigorously and continuously to promote Anguillla in the Asian market as a financial services center and an up market tourism destination. "It is important that the island is known first, in order for potential clients to become comfortable and confident and establish offshore companies with us" he said. Mr. Connor further stated that it is time for another joint government and private sector promotion team to conduct a visit to Hong Kong. Promotional visits are very important for the Asian market as it shows that Anguillians value their patronage and this would translate in increase business in both tourism and financial services.

THE JERSEY AND GUERNSEY FINANCIAL COMMUNITY WELCOMES ANGUILLA'S FINANCIAL SERVICES SECTOR

The Hon Victor F Banks, The Government of Anguilla's Minister for Finance, Investment, Economic Development and Commerce, recently invited Jersey officials and financial-services practitioners to choose Anguilla as its partner in the Caribbean.

The Minister was speaking at a presentation held in Jersey recently supported by John Lawrence the Director of Financial Services and Lans Connor, Registrar of Commercial Activities from the Government of Anguilla together with Alex Richardson, President of AFSA; Harry Wiggin and Bruce Drummond of Webster Dyrud Mitchell. The Jersey community's response was positive particularly as Anguilla offers specialist company formation services via its transparent Anguilla Commercial Online Registration Network (ACORN).

"Anguilla has already forged several successful business partnerships with Jersey-based practitioners including Sinel Trust," said Minister Banks. He added: "the support of the Jersey financial community of Anguilla's Financial Services sector is a coup for Anguilla as we are very keen that they `savour the waters' of Anguilla's well-regulated and efficient, quality services."

The Minister said that the visit was the first time that such a large delegation from Anguilla has had a presence in the Channel Islands. "Ultimately it is a flag-waving exercise, however, the Anguillian brand of service and the reputation of the ACORN system is growing and it essential that we back this up by briefing and meeting in person the managers who provide our services to their clients."

Delegates who attended the presentation included senior representatives from the Jersey regulatory authority, international banks, trust-company formation companies, fund managers, law firms and leading finance corporations.

Minister Banks said that Anguilla will definitely visit the Channel Islands again to continue the dialogue that has been established by the territories.

"There is a natural synergy between the Channel Islands and Anguilla. We are island territories with experienced, quality and well-regulated, financial-services sectors; we have stable systems of Government under the protection of HMG; and have recently undergone a thorough audit by independent surveyors on behalf of the UK Government. "

Alex Richardson, President of the Anguilla Financial Services Association, and the head of a leading private sector law firm hosted a business briefing in Guernsey the following day. Senior officials from the Government of Anguilla's Financial Services department and the private sector supported Mr Richardson.

"Anguilla's presence in Guernsey was an essential activity to rekindle existing links and prove to those who had heard of us that we are a force to be reckoned with. I am very proud of the unique services that Anguilla can provide and our visit went along way in persuading potential clients why they should do business with us," said Mr Richardson.

Trust company managers, international private banks and existing overseas agents of the ACORN system, attended the briefing

IMPORTANT LAWS AND REGULATIONS AFFECTING BUSINESS

OFFSHORE BANKING BUSINESS REGULATIONS

The following is presented as guidance for determining whether business is offshore banking business and is for informational purposes only. If there is any inconsistency between this information and any provision of the laws of Anguilla, the provision in the law shall prevail.

Offshore Banking: *The establishment in or from within Anguilla of an account for, the taking of deposits from, and the making of loans to or investments for a non-resident in a foreign currency.*

Non-resident: ***A)*** *A natural person who does not satisfy any of the following conditions:*

i) A person who is a Belonger of Anguilla regardless of where domiciled and by extension his/her children and grandchildren

ii) A person who has a permanent place of abode on Anguilla to which he or she may return without restriction

iii) A person who has a legal right to be or remain, and is personally resident, in Anguilla for not less than 183 days in any 12 month period.

B) A legal person who does not satisfy any of the following conditions:

i) An entity established under the laws of Anguilla, other than a non-domestic company (as defined in the Companies Act) and the entities referred to in item C

ii) An entity established under the Limited Liability Companies Act, which, at the relevant time, engages in revenue generating activities in Anguilla.

C) The following legal persons are non-resident in every case:

i) An entity established under the International Business Company Act

ii) An entity established under the Limited Liabilities Companies Act that does not, at the relevant time, engage in revenue generating activities in Anguilla.

Foreign Currency: *A currency other than the Eastern Caribbean Dollar.*

Relevant time: *The time at which application to do business is made.*

REGULATORY FRAMEWORK FOR MUTUAL/HEDGE FUNDS IN ANGUILLA

Anguilla is a British Overseas Territory and has a stable government which is committed to promoting its mutual/hedge funds industry. The laws of Anguilla are derived from English common law and supplemented by local legislation. The Court system is well developed and the London based Privy Council is the jurisdiction's final court of appeal. Anguillian legislation ensures that funds can be structured as internationally accepted vehicles.

REGULATORY REGIME

Mutual and hedge funds are regulated under the Mutual Funds Act 2004 ("the Act"). The Act sets out two procedures for regulation based on the type of fund under consideration:

i.e. recognition for private and professional funds and registration for public funds. In addition, fund administrators and managers are licensed where they wish to operate from in or within Anguilla to provide their services to local and foreign funds. Under section 31 of the Act, the Commission has the power to exempt any person or class of persons from complying with the Act. This allows for flexibility in requiring funds to be registered or recognized and persons to be licensed as managers and administrators. This flexibility is particularly important for managers/administrators who provide their services for one name fund only.

FUND STRUCTURES

Funds in Anguilla may be formed as companies, partnerships, unit trusts or protected cell/segregated portfolio accounts. This allows investors to adopt the structure which best suits their needs which are often tax based. It appears that traditionally funds in which US taxable investors will invest directly tend to be formed as limited partnerships, funds that target European and South American investors tend to be formed as corporate funds while those that target Japanese investors tend to be formed as unit trusts. This means that Anguillian funds are able to satisfy the individual requirements of most investors globally.

PROTECTED CELL/SEGREGATED PORTFOLIO ACCOUNTS

Anguilla enacted a Protected Cell Companies Act in 2004. It allows mutual funds to be established as protected cell accounts and in essence, the legislation provides that, whilst retaining its corporate existence as a single legal entity, a corporate fund vehicle may be registered as having protected cell accounts, which are traded independently and which during the life of the company and on liquidation are protected from creditor claims arising with respect to liabilities of other protected cell accounts or the company generally.

The use of protected cell accounts as funds provides an attractive alternative to the traditional structures to address cross-class liability issues for multi-class corporate funds and provides corporate fund vehicles with the ability to operate in a way analogous to a corporate group despite utilizing just a single legal entity.

TAXATION

Anguilla is a completely zero tax jurisdiction. There are no capital gains, income, profit, corporation or withholding taxes or any legal restrictions on the investment policies and strategies of funds in Anguilla.

DEFINITION OF A MUTUAL FUND

A mutual fund is defined as a company incorporated, a partnership formed, a unit trust organized or other similar body formed or organized under the laws of Anguilla or any other country or jurisdiction which collects and pools investor funds for the purpose of collective investments and issues shares that entitle the holder to receive on demand or within a specified period after demand an amount computed by reference to the value of a proportionate interest in the whole or in a part of the net assets of the company, the partnership, the unit trust or other similar body, as the case may be. This definition includes an umbrella fund whose shares are split into a number of different class funds or sub-funds and a fund which has a single investor which is a mutual fund not registered or recognized under the Act.

CATEGORIES OF FUNDS

The Anguilla legislation provides for three types of funds. Of these three (3) types, only public funds are required to submit audited financial statements to, as well as publish and file a prospectus with, the Commission.

1. Public

A public fund is a fund which is not a private or professional fund. Usually, its prospectus indicates that it can offer its shares to the public for subscription.

2. Private

A private fund is a fund whose constitutional documents specify that it will have no more than ninety-nine investors; the constitutional documents of which specify that an invitation to subscribe for or purchase shares issued by the mutual fund is not to be made. An invitation is not made to the public if it is made to specified persons and is not calculated to result in shares becoming available to other persons or by reason of a private or business connection between the person making the invitation and the investor. The Commission also has the power to designate certain funds as not being private funds.

3. Professional

A professional fund means a fund, the shares of which are made available only to professional investors and the initial investment in which, in respect of each of the persons constituting a majority of the such investors, is not less than one hundred thousand dollars in the United States currency or its equivalent in any other currency, but this minimum initial investment limit shall not apply in respect of an investment made by the manager, administrator, promoter or underwriter of the professional funds; a mutual fund which was carrying on business or engaged in an activity as a mutual fund on the date of the coming into force of the Act; the initial investments in respect of the majority of each of the investors in the mutual fund have been not less than one hundred thousand dollars in the United States currency or its equivalent currency; and the shares of the mutual fund are, after the date of the coming into force of the Act, made available only to professional investors. The Act further defines an investor as a person whose ordinary business involves dealing in investments or who has signed a declaration that he, whether individually or jointly with his spouse, has net worth in excess of one million dollars in United States currency or its equivalent in any other currency and that he consents to being treated as a professional investor.

FUNCTIONARIES

All funds domiciled in Anguilla must have the following functionaries: a manager, administrator, investment advisor and custodian who should be in a recognized jurisdiction under Act. The Commission has issued a list of such jurisdictions which can be found on the site stated below. However, where this is not possible, the Commission requires an explanation be given as to why and permission sought to appoint the particular functionary. There is no requirement for the appointment of an auditor for professional and private funds but public funds must appoint an auditor approved by the Commission. A public fund must also maintain adequate accounting records and prepare audited financial statements for each year.

MANAGERS AND ADMINISTRATORS

Under the Act, both managers and administrators are required to be licensed. There is no requirement to use an Anguillian administrator or manager for Anguillian funds. And where the manager or administrator is only providing its services to one mutual fund, whether registered or recognized in Anguilla or another jurisdiction, as evidenced by a written undertaking, the Commission may exempt him/her from the requirement to be licensed under the Act. In addition, the Commission may use section 31 of the Act to exempt a company if it is not against the public interest.

QUALIFIED FUND ADMINISTRATOR/INTERMEDIARY (QFAI) STATUS

The Commission allows service providers with a proven track record in setting up mutual and hedge funds to apply for QFAI status. This allows the recipient of this status to launch the fund prior to review of the application by the Commission provided he/she adheres strictly to the guidance issued by it. This fast-track procedure gives Anguilla a competitive advantage over its competitors. The Commission will conduct a regulatory review within thirty (30) days of the launch of the fund, post facto, to ensure that the QFAI exercised its prerogative properly. If it fails to do so, then the registration or recognition will be revoked and the QFAI will lose its status. QFAIs are able to launch their funds within twenty-four (24) hours if they use an Anguillian corporate entity which can be formed online using the ACORN system (www.anguillafsc.com). Anguilla's competitive advantages in this area are speed and efficiency and are the hallmarks of the jurisdiction's thrust into the provision of international financial services.

NETTING LEGISLATION

Anguilla will enact shortly the Netting Act 2005 which will provide for the ability of over the counter (OTC) derivative transactions to net the mark-to-market values of all existing transactions under the master agreements upon their early termination following the default of its counterparty or other specified events. The Act is based extensively on the International Swaps and Derivatives Association (ISDA) model and is ideally suited for hedge funds thus contributing to Anguilla's attractiveness as a jurisdiction.

COMMISSION FEES

Anguilla's fees are extremely competitive with other jurisdictions. They are as follows:

Recognition – US$350 plus an application fee of US$350 Registration – US$500 plus an application fee of US$500 Licensing – US$500 (for a single licence) and US$1000 (for a double licence) plus an application fee of US$250

Where the recognition, registration or licensing is effected on or after 1st July in any year, the fees are prorated but the application fee remains the same. The annual fees are the same as the fees paid at the time the recognition, registration or licensing is effected where this is done on or before the 30th June in any year.

APPLICATION PROCEDURES

Where the service provider in question is not a QFAI, all applications must be submitted to the Commission before the corporate entity is formed at the Companies Registry. Applications forms, which can be downloaded from website www.fsc.org.ai are contained in the Mutual Funds Regulations 2004. They must be fully and properly completed and submitted, along with the requisite application fee, to the Commission at the address below. Policy guidance notes, which are also posted on the aforementioned website, provide important guidance for the completion of the forms and should be read carefully prior to completion. The Commission is very proactive and seeks to determine applications which have been fully and properly completed and which are sound in all respects, within five (5) working days.

FURTHER INFORMATION

Further information can be had from Mr. John Lawrence, Director of the Anguilla Financial Services Commission or Mr. Carlyle Rogers, the Deputy Director, at the following address:

P.O. Box 1575 The Valley Anguilla Tel. no. 1 264 497 5881 Fax no. 1 264 497 5872
John_L@anguillafsd.com Carlyle_R@anguillafsd.com www.fsc.org.ai

GUIDELINES FOR INTRODUCED BUSINESS

(Issued under Section 48 of the Financial Services Commission Act 2003)

The Anguilla Financial Services Commission ("Commission") is concerned that a number of intermediaries and/or introducers (including overseas agents) of persons licensed to conduct company management business in and/or from Anguilla are not fully complying with the due diligence requirements of the relevant anti-money laundering and combating the financing of terrorism legislation, regulations, codes and guidance notes. This concern is based on the findings of a series of recently concluded onsite examinations of company managers and information brought to the attention of the Commission by external agencies.

In light of the stated concern, the Commission hereby requires all persons (legal and natural) licensed to conduct company management business in and/or from Anguilla to establish and enforce formal procedures with their ***eligible*** intermediaries and/or introducers to ensure the following:

i) That intermediaries and introducers are complying with all applicable Anguillian legislation, regulations, codes, guidelines and/or regulatory directives.

ii) That intermediaries and introducers are able to provide the local licensee or registered agent with all due diligence and other information and/or documents requested by the Commission, within 72 hours of such a request. The information and documents must be made available to the Commission in Anguilla. The information and documents can initially be submitted via electronic means with official copies to be provided as required by the Commission.

An ***eligible intermediary or introducer*** is one that satisfies the conditions of a foreign regulated person under section 7 of the Anti-Money Laundering and Terrorist Financing Regulations, 2009, which states:

"Foreign regulated person" means a person—

(a) that is incorporated in, or if it is not a corporate body, has its principal place of business in, a jurisdiction outside Anguilla (its "home jurisdiction");

(b) that carries on business outside Anguilla that, if carried on in Anguilla, would fall within a category of business specified in Schedule 1, paragraphs (a) to (i);

(c) that, in respect of the business referred to in paragraph (b)—

(i) is subject to legal requirements in its home jurisdiction for the prevention of money laundering and terrorist financing that are consistent with the requirements of the FATF Recommendations, for the time being issued, for that business; and

(ii) is subject to effective supervision for compliance with those legal requirements by a foreign regulatory authority.

Appendix I contain a list of jurisdictions that the Commission considers complies with the conditions detailed in item (c) (i) above.

Intermediaries and/or introducers that do not satisfy the conditions detailed above for eligible introducers and intermediaries are not allowed to hold due diligence information on behalf of Anguillian licensees. Accordingly, all due diligence information for clients introduced by these intermediaries must be maintained at all times by the licensed company manager.

Compliance with this guideline will be assessed during special and routine onsite examinations of company management licensees. Onsite examinations of licensees will include a review of due diligence information held by a random sample of intermediaries and/or introducers. Failure by the intermediaries and/or introducers to comply with the due diligence requirements of the AML/CFT Act, Regulations and Code will be considered in assessing whether licensees should continue to maintain a relationship with delinquent intermediaries/introducers. Repeated noncompliance on the part of intermediaries/introducers will have an impact on a licensee's fit and proper status and its eligibility to continue to hold a company management licence.

These guidelines are issues pursuant to section 48 (1) of the Financial Services Commission Act, Revised Statutes of Anguilla, Chapter F28, and will come into effect on 31 January 2010. All Company Managers are expected to achieve compliance with these guidelines by 31 March 2010.

Financial Services Commission

JURISDICTIONS WITH LEGISLATION EQUIVALENT TO THE ANTI-MONEY LAUNDERING AND TERRORIST FINANCING REGULATIONS, 2009

The following jurisdictions are considered to be approved jurisdictions pursuant to the requirements of sections 7 (c) and 16 (2)(c) of the Anti-Money Laundering and Terrorist Financing Regulations, 2009:

FATF Member Countries:

Argentina Australia

Austria Belgium

Brazil Canada

China Denmark

European Union Finland

France Germany

Greece Gulf Co-operation Council

Hong Kong, China Iceland

Ireland Italy

Japan Kingdom of the Netherlands

Luxembourg Mexico

New Zealand Norway

Portugal Russian Federation

Singapore South Africa

Spain Sweden

Switzerland Turkey

United Kingdom United States of America

Other Countries:

Bahamas Bermuda

British Virgin Islands Cayman Islands

Gibraltar Guernsey

Isle of Man Jersey

Liechtenstein

APPROVAL PROCEDURES FOR FOREIGN PERSONS

The Anguilla Financial Services Commission will consider the following when reviewing an application for approval of a foreign regulated person, pursuant to Section 1(1)(d) of the AntiMoney Laundering Regulations, 2006:

i) The applicant's regulatory status in its home jurisdiction;

ii) The fit and proper nature of the applicant's principals;

iii) The adequacy of the applicant's operating policies and procedures for administering the business line which is the subject of the application; iv) The applicant's internal procedures for complying with the requirements of Anguilla's antimoney laundering legislation, regulations and guidelines;

v) The applicant's internal control procedures;

vi) The quality of the applicant's audit report (whether qualified);

vii) The training profile of the applicant's compliance officer; and

viii) A statement confirming that the applicant is aware of, and is prepared to comply with, the requirements of the Anguilla's antimoney laundering legislation, regulations and guidelines.

The applicant should submit the following information or documents in support of its application:

a) A letter of good standing from its home regulator; b) A completed personal questionnaire for the manager(s) or senior officer(s) responsible for the business line which is the subject of the application; c) A copy of the applicant's procedures manual, detailing its internal control procedures, for the business line which is the subject of the application;

d) A copy of the applicants most recent audit report;

e) The training profile or experience of the applicant's compliance officer;

f) The statement of confirmation referred to in item viii above; and

g) Any other information or documents the applicant consider relevant in process its application.

MUTUAL FUNDS REGULATIONS

1. WHAT IS A MUTUAL FUND?

A mutual fund as defined by the Act means a company incorporated, a partnership formed, a unit trust organized or other similar body formed under the laws of Anguilla of any other jurisdiction that collects and pools investor monies for the purpose of investing collectively. The fund must also issue shares that entitle the holder of those shares to receive on demand or within a specified period after demand an amount calculated by reference to the value of a proportionate interest in the whole or in a part of the net assets of the company, partnership, the unit trust or similar body.

The definition of a mutual fund includes an umbrella fund whose shares are split into a number of different class funds or sub-funds. The definition also includes a fund that has single investor which is a mutual fund not registered or recognized under this Act.

2. WHAT IS A UNIT TRUST?

A unit trust means an arrangement creating a trust under the laws of Anguilla or any other country or jurisdiction in which unit holders participating in the arrangement are the beneficiaries of the trust.

3. WHICH TYPE OF MUTUAL FUNDS ARE PROVIDED FOR UNDER THE ACT?

a) Public fund.

The Act defines a public fund as a fund that is not a private or professional fund. In practical terms a public fund is one that offers shares in the entity used to form it to the general public through the issuance of a prospectus. A prospectus is a document which purpose is to make an invitation to the public or any section to subscribe for or purchase shares issued by a public fund. A public fund must issue a prospectus.

b) Private fund.

The private fund is constituted of no more than 99 investors. The constitutional documents must state this. The fund must not make any invitations to the public to subscribe for or purchase shares issued by the fund.

c) Professional fund

A professional fund is a fund, the shares of which are made available only to professional investors and the initial investment in which, in respect of each of the persons constituting a majority of such investors, is not less than US$100,000 or its equivalent in another currency. This minimum initial investment shall not apply in respect of an Investment made by the manager, administrator, promoter or underwriter of the professional fund. A professional investor means a person whose ordinary business involves dealing in investments or who has signed a declaration that he, whether individually or jointly with his spouse, has a net worth in excess of US$1 million or its equivalent in any other currency and that he consents to being treated as a professional investor.

4. WHAT RIGHTS DO INVESTORS HAVE FOR MISREPRESENTATIONS MADE IN A PROSPECTUS?

If a registered public fund publishes a prospectus or any amendment to it that contains misrepresentations relating to any disclosures required under the ACT, a person who purchased any shares pursuant to the prospectus or amendment to it, is deemed to have relied on the misrepresentation and shall have specific rights. These include rescission for the purchase or damages against the fund. However, no person is liable if he/she proves that the purchaser bought the shares offered by the prospectus or amendment to it with knowledge of the misrepresentation.

5. WHO IS A PROMOTER?

A promoter means a person acting alone or in conjunction with others directly or indirectly who takes the initiative in forming or organizing a mutual fund, but does not include an underwriter who receives an underwriting commission without taking any part in the founding or organizing of the mutual fund business.

6. WHAT IS AN ADMINISTRATOR?

An administrator is a person who for valuable consideration provides a mutual fund with administrative services alone or together with accounting services and is entitled to provide mutual funds such services and facilities under the laws of a recognized country or jurisdiction. Administrators must apply to be licensed under the Act. It is an offence to conduct the business of administrator from in or within Anguilla without a licence.

7. WHAT IS A MANAGER?

A manager refers to person, who is not an employee or officer of a person licensed under this Act who for valuable consideration provides a mutual fund with management services alone or together with investment advice or administrative services or is entitled to provide mutual funds with such services and facilities as provided in the laws of a recognized country or jurisdiction. Managers, like administrators, must apply to be licensed under the Act. It is an offence to conduct the business of manager from in or within Anguilla without licence.

8. CAN ANYONE BE AN ADMINISTRATOR OR MANAGER?

No; in order to be granted a licence as an administrator or manager, the Commission must be satisfied that the applicant is a fit and proper person to be engaged in the business proposed. The applicant must also have available to him or her adequate knowledge, expertise, resources, and facilities necessary for the nature and scope of the business proposed and has appointed an auditor satisfying conditions as may be prescribed by the Commission.

9. Are all managers and administrators required to appoint an auditor?

No; a manager or administrator who provides services to one private mutual fund or one professional mutual fund and whose business is only to appoint other service providers or to receive fees or both, is exempted from the requirement to appoint an auditor.

10. Can someone be both an administrator and manager?

Yes; an applicant can hold licences at the same time.

11. What is meant by registration?

Registration refers to the process whereby a public fund is authorized to conduct business in or from within Anguilla. Only public funds are registered. No public fund can conduct business in or from within Anguilla without being registered under the Act.

12. What are the grounds for refusing to grant registration?

The Commission will refuse to grant registration if the public fund has a name which is undesirable or misleading; where the public fund or proposed public fund does not have a custodian who is independent of the manager or administrator or it determines that it is not in the public interest that registration should be granted.

13. What is meant by recognition?

Recognition refers to the process whereby a private or professional fund is authorized to conduct business in or from within Anguilla. Only private and professional funds are recognized. No private or professional fund can conduct business in or from within Anguilla without being recognized under the Act.

14. What are the grounds for refusing to grant recognition?

The Commission will refuse to grant recognition if the private or professional fund has failed to provide evidence that it is a private or professional fund and is lawfully constituted under the laws of Anguilla; and where it determines that it is not in the interests of the investors or in the public interest that recognition should be granted.

1. **Do all funds need to submit annual audited financial statements?**
2. **What are the grounds for canceling the registration or recognized of a fund or the licence of a manager or an administrator?**

No; only registered public funds have to provide these statements.

A licence may be cancelled where the holder

a. has ceased to carry on business in or from within Anguilla.

b. has contravened any provision of the Act, regulations or the Code of Practice.

c. Has been convicted of an offence under section 35 (1) of the Act or of a serious criminal offence in any country or jurisdiction.

d. Has knowingly and willfully supplied false, misleading or inaccurate information or failed to disclose information required for the purposes of any provision of the Act or regulations.

e. Is carrying on business in a manner detrimental to the interests of mutual fund investors or to the public interest; or

f. Is declared bankrupt or is being wound-up or otherwise dissolved.

17. What is the procedure for cancellation?

The Commission has to give the holder of the licence a notice in writing of the grounds on which it intends to do so; afford the holder an opportunity to make written representations to it within a period of 30 days after the receipt of the notice and take any such representations into consideration.

18. Does the Commission have the power to exempt any provision of the Act or of the regulations issued under the Act?

Where the Commission is satisfied that to do so would not be prejudicial to the public interest, it may direct that all or any of the provisions of the Act or the regulations shall not apply or apply subject to such modifications as it may specify in the direction to any person or class of persons.

19. What are the restricted "words" under the Act?

The Commission has to give its consent for persons to use the words "fund", "mutual fund" or "unit trust" either in English or another language, in the name, description, or title under which that person is carrying on business in or from within Anguilla. Further, such consent is required also where the person makes or continues to make any representation in any advertisement, billhead, circular, letter, letterhead, notice, paper or in any other manner that that person is carrying on business as a fund or mutual fund.

20. What are the basic offences and penalties under the Act?

The basic offences include oral and written misrepresentation or false statements; knowingly refusing or failing to disclose any information or fact required to be disclosed under the Act and regulations and being in charge of or having possession of or control over any information, records, books or other documents required to be maintained by a licencee or registered or recognized mutual fund and willfully neglecting to comply with any lawful directions given under the Act.

The penalties include a fine on conviction of not less than US$10,000 or more than US$25,000 or to imprisonment of a period not exceeding twelve months.

Further, any person who, without reasonable cause, contravenes a provision of the Act or the regulations for which no penalty is provided commits an offence against the Act or the regulations, as the case may be, is liable on summary conviction to a fine of no more than US$50,000 in the case of a body corporate or unincorporated, or trust; and a fine not exceeding US$5000 or imprisonment for a period not exceeding one month or to both.

21. What regulations will be issued under the Act?

The regulations will cover the application forms for the registration of public funds, recognition of private and professional funds, and the licensing of managers and administrators. It will also cover fees, arrangements which are not mutual funds, financial reporting requirements.

22. WHAT ARE THE TRANSITIONAL PROVISIONS FOR THE ACT?

Any manager or administrator who on the date of coming into force of the Act is carrying on business or engaged in any activity in relation to which he is required to be licensed under the

Act, shall within 3 months of the coming into force of this Act, comply with the provisions of the Act. Any mutual fund, which on the date of the coming into force of this Act, is carrying on its business or managing or administering its affairs in or from within Anguilla, shall within 6 months from that date comply with the provisions of the Act.

ANGUILLA FOUNDATION ACT, 2008

[Gazetted 30 June, 2008] [Commencement: Section 75]

An Act to provide for the establishment, operation and regulation of foundations and for incidental and connected purposes.

ENACTED by the Legislature of Anguilla

PART 1 PRELIMINARY

Interpretation

1. In this Act, unless the context otherwise requires—

"beneficiary" means a person designated as such pursuant to the provisions of the declaration of establishment or by-laws of a foundation or by any amendment thereto;

"by-laws" means the by-laws of the foundation adopted in accordance with the provisions of section 8;

"Commission" means the Financial Services Commission established under section 2 of the Financial Services Commission Act;

"declaration of establishment" means—

(a) in relation to a foundation established in Anguilla, a declaration of establishment or a testamentary declaration of establishment in accordance with the provisions of section 3(2) and any amendments to any such declaration; or

(b) in relation to an overseas foundation continuing in Anguilla, its articles of continuance and any amendments to such articles;

"deposited foundation" means a foundation in respect of which the relevant documents have been deposited pursuant to section 14;

"dollar" or "$" means a dollar in the currency of the United States of America;

"foundation" means a foundation established under this Act or continued into Anguilla under Part 7;

"Foundation Council", in relation to a foundation, means the person or the body of persons having the responsibility pursuant to the declaration of establishment of the foundation or section 20 of carrying out the objectives and purposes of the foundation;

"Foundation Council member", in relation to a foundation, means a person who is a member of the Foundation Council of the foundation;

"founder" means—

(a) any person who signs the declaration of establishment establishing a foundation, acting either for himself or on behalf of another; or

(b) in the case of an overseas foundation continued into Anguilla, the person who signed the declaration of establishment, articles or any document equivalent to the declaration of establishment or articles in the jurisdiction of the overseas foundation, acting either for himself or on behalf of another;

"guardian", in relation to a foundation, means the person or persons appointed as the guardian of the foundation pursuant to section 31;

"incompetent" means a person in respect of whom a custodian or curator has been appointed by any court having jurisdiction, whether in Anguilla or elsewhere, in matters concerning mental disorder;

"inspector" means an inspector appointed by an order made under section 62;

"legal entity" means a foundation, corporation, limited partnership, business, trust, limited liability company or any other juridical person;

"minor" means an individual who is less than 18 years of age;

"official seal" means an official seal prepared pursuant to section 55;

"overseas foundation" means a foundation established in a jurisdiction other than Anguilla;

"property endowment", in relation to a foundation, means the assets for the time being of the foundation;

"Register" means the Register of Foundations kept by the Registrar in compliance with section 13(1);

"registered address", in relation to a registered agent, means the address of the registered agent;

"registered agent", in relation to a foundation, means the registered agent of the foundation for the time being holding such office pursuant to sections 17 and 18;

"registered foundation" means a foundation registered under section 13;

"Registrar" means the Registrar of Foundations declared pursuant to section 54;

"regulated person" means a person holding a relevant licence;

"relevant licence" means a licence issued under—

(a) the Company Management Act; or

(b) the Trust Companies and Offshore Banking Act;

"relevant person", in relation to a foundation, means—

(a) the registered agent of the foundation;

(b) a former registered agent of the foundation;

(c) a subsidiary or holding company of the registered agent, or of a former registered agent, of the foundation;

(d) the Secretary of the foundation; or

(e) a Foundation Council member who is resident in Anguilla and is a regulated person;

"residuary assets", in relation to a foundation, means the assets of the foundation remaining after its dissolution;

"Secretary" means the person appointed to be the secretary of a foundation pursuant to section 29.

Applicable law

2. Every foundation shall be governed by the provisions of this Act as well as the declaration of establishment of that foundation and its by-laws.

Part 2

ESTABLISHMENT OF FOUNDATION

Establishment of foundation

3. (1) One or more natural or legal persons may establish a foundation in accordance with the provisions of this Act.

(2) A foundation may be established by—

(a) a declaration of establishment made in writing and signed by one or more founders during their lifetime; or

(b) a testamentary declaration of establishment made by a single founder, comprised in a will as defined in the Wills Act and complying with all formalities required by that Act and probated in the High Court.

(3) An initial property endowment, expressed in any currency of legal tender, not being of less value than $10,000, shall—

(a) be placed under the control of the intended registered agent on or before the date of registration of the foundation pursuant to section 13 or the deposit of the foundation's documents pursuant to section 14; and

(b) become the property of the foundation upon such registration or, as the case may be, such deposit.

(4) For the purposes of this section, there shall be no requirement for separate articles of a foundation but, subject to section 4 and to the terms of the declaration of establishment of the foundation, provision not required by this Act to be included in the declaration of establishment may be included in separate articles of the foundation.

(5) Where a foundation established pursuant to paragraph (2)(b) cannot be registered or its documents deposited within a reasonable period of time after the death of the testator, any interested person may apply to the High Court for the appointment of a temporary receiver of the initial property endowment referred to in subsection (3), who shall be responsible—

(a) for applying to the Registrar for the entry of the foundation on the Register, pursuant to section 13, or depositing the declaration of establishment with the Registrar pursuant to section 14, when probate of the will has been granted;

(b) for carrying out the declaration of establishment and administering the property endowment until the Foundation Council is appointed; and

(c) if necessary, for appointing the Foundation Council.

(6) The temporary receiver—

(a) shall be entitled to reimbursement for his proper charges and expenses, which shall be determined by the High Court; and

(b) may be removed by the High Court as soon as the foundation acquires legal personality.

Requirements of declaration of establishment

4. (1) A declaration of establishment shall include the particulars specified in subsection (2).

(2) The particulars referred to in subsection (1) are as follows—

(a) the name of the foundation;

(b) the initial property endowment referred to in section 3(3) accompanied by a certified confirmation, by the person designated as the registered agent of the foundation, that such initial endowment of property is readily available to the foundation and will be vested in or under its legal control immediately upon the foundation's acquisition of legal personality pursuant to section 15;

(c) the name and address of the founder or founders, but, if at any time the founder's rights are assigned, any assignee of the founder's rights shall be deemed to be a founder for the purposes of section 16;

(d) the full names and addresses of the Foundation Council members;

(e) the name and address of the registered agent;

(f) the name and address of the Secretary, if any;

(g) the name and address of the guardian, if any;

(h) the purposes of the foundation;

(i) provisions, if any, for the designation of beneficiaries;

(j) the names and addresses of any designated beneficiaries;

(k) provisions, if any, for the exercise of powers otherwise than by the Foundation Council;

(l) the method of appointing and changing Foundation Council members;

(m) provisions concerning the making of by-laws and their amendment;

(n) provisions concerning any power to amend the declaration of establishment of the foundation;

(o) provisions concerning the application of the foundation's property endowment in the event of the dissolution of the foundation;

(p) provisions concerning the term of the foundation and whether such term shall be for a definite or indefinite period of time.

(3) Subject to the provisions of this Act, the declaration of establishment of a foundation may, in addition to the particulars specified in subsection (2)—

(a) provide for the appointment, removal and term of office of the auditor, if any;

(b) provide for the appointment and removal of its guardian for the maintenance of the objectives and purposes of the foundation;

(c) specify the duties, functions, powers and rights (including rights to remuneration) of its guardian, if appointed;

(d) provide for the appointment of persons to act by power of attorney or otherwise to carry out particular duties on behalf of the foundation;

(e) provide for the transfer to the foundation of supplementary assets in addition to the initial assets;

(f) specify any named beneficiary; and

(g) make any other lawful provision that the founder or founders may deem appropriate.

Purposes of foundation

5. (1) Subject to subsection (2) and the terms of its declaration of establishment, a foundation may be established for any purposes which are capable of fulfilment and are not unlawful, immoral or contrary to public policy.

(2) The purposes for which a foundation may be formed shall not include—

(a) the carrying out of any activity prohibited from being carried on, in or from within Anguilla; and

(b) any financial services business, unless and until such licence as may be required to conduct such financial services business has been granted.

(3) A foundation may, in the course of the management of its assets, do all such things as are necessary for the proper administration of its assets including, but not limited to, buying and selling of such assets and engaging in any other acts or activities which are not prohibited under any law of Anguilla.

(4) In this section, the expression "financial services business" shall have the meaning assigned to it in the Financial Services Commission Act.

Language of declaration of establishment

6. The declaration of establishment of a foundation and any amendment thereto may be written in any language but, where such declaration is not written in the English language, it must include a certified translation into the English language.

Amendment of declaration of establishment

7. (1) Any amendment to the declaration of establishment of a foundation, when permitted, shall be made in accordance with the provisions of subsection (2).

(2) The declaration of establishment of a foundation established pursuant to section 3(2)(a) may, subject to the terms of that declaration of establishment, be amended or revoked in writing—

(a) in the case of a foundation established by one founder, by the founder during his lifetime; or

(b) in the case of a foundation established by 2 or more founders, by the founders jointly during their joint lifetimes;

if such right is personal to the founder or, as the case may be, the founders and is non-assignable.

By-laws

8. (1) A foundation established under this Act may adopt by-laws, and such by-laws may include regulations—

(a) concerning distributions or applications of property endowment;

(b) naming beneficiaries, defining classes of beneficiaries or providing for additional beneficiaries of the foundation;

(c) providing for the identification of the residual beneficiary on a dissolution of the foundation;

(d) providing guidelines, policies and procedures for the Foundation Council; or

(e) providing for any other lawful matter compatible with the purposes of the Foundation.

(2) Any such by-laws shall be in writing and shall be signed by at least one Foundation Council member.

(3) The Foundation Council of a foundation may, subject to the terms of the declaration of establishment of the foundation, amend or replace the by-laws of the foundation.

Foundation name

9. (1) The name of a foundation—

(a) must end with—

(i) the word "Foundation" or its abbreviation "Fdn.", or

(ii) the foreign language equivalent of the word "Foundation" or its recognised abbreviation in that language;

(b) may contain the name of a founder or Foundation Council member;

(c) must not be the same as or similar to the name of any other legal entity registered or deposited under the laws of Anguilla or reserved under this or any other Act, unless such other legal entity consents in writing to the use of that name; and

(d) must not be a name prohibited by regulations made by under this Act or by any other law in force in Anguilla.

(2) Notwithstanding subsection (1) and subject to the approval by the Registrar, one or more words, or an abbreviation thereof that, in the opinion of the Registrar, denote in a jurisdiction other than Anguilla the existence of an entity having the characteristics of a foundation, may be used in place of the word or words or abbreviation specified in that subsection.

(3) Where any word or its abbreviation approved by the Registrar under subsection (2) is used in the name of a foundation, such word or abbreviation shall be placed in such position within the name of the foundation as the Registrar may direct.

Reservation of name

10. (1) The exclusive right to the use of a name may be reserved by—

(a) any person intending to establish a foundation under that name;

(b) any foundation that proposes to change its name to that name; or

(c) any overseas foundation, by whatever name called, intending to continue under this Act as a foundation having that name.

(2) The reservation of a specified name shall be made by filing with the Registrar an application executed by the applicant in the prescribed form specifying the name to be reserved.

(3) If the Registrar approves the name and determines that it is available for use by such foundation, the Registrar shall reserve the name for the exclusive use of the applicant for a period of 120 days.

(4) A name reserved under subsection (3) may, by application made under subsection (2), be reserved for successive periods of 120 days.

(5) The prescribed fee shall be paid—

(a) upon the filing of an application to reserve a name under subsection (2); and

(b) upon the filing of each application to renew the reservation of a name under subsection (4).

Change of name

11. (1) Subject to the terms of its declaration of establishment and to the provisions of section 9, a foundation may, by resolution of its Foundation Council, amend its declaration of establishment to change its name at any time.

(2) Where a foundation is established or continued, or changes its name to a name that—

(a) is reserved for another entity under section 10;

(b) does not comply with section 9; or

(c) is, in the opinion of the Registrar, for any other reason objectionable;

the Registrar may, by serving a written notice on the foundation, direct it to change its name within such period of time as he may stipulate.

(3) If a foundation which has been served a notice pursuant to subsection (2) does not change its name to a name that complies with section 9 within such time as the Registrar specifies in that notice, the Registrar—

(a) may assign a new name to the foundation; and

(b) shall enter such assigned name in the Register or, as the case may be, in the schedule of deposited foundations maintained under this Act.

(4) Where the name of a foundation has been changed, pursuant to this section, the Registrar must—

(a) in the case of a registered foundation, issue a certificate of registration on change of name to the foundation; and

(b) in the case of a deposited foundation, issue a certificate of deposit on change of name to the foundation;

specifying the new name and the reason for the change of name.

(5) After the issue to a foundation of a certificate of registration on change of name under paragraph (4)(a) or a certificate of deposit on change of name under paragraph (4)(b), any other foundation (except one already registered under the former name) that uses the former name of the foundation commits an offence and is liable to such penalty as may be prescribed by regulations.

Assets

12. Where a person contributes assets as property endowment of a foundation, such assets shall—

(a) irrevocably become assets of the foundation upon the vesting of such assets in the foundation; and

(b) cease to be assets of the contributor.

Registration of foundation

13. (1) The Registrar shall maintain a Register of Foundations.

(2) Unless section 14(1) applies to a foundation, the registered agent of the foundation shall apply to the Registrar to enter the name of the foundation on the Register.

(3) For the purpose of registering a foundation under this Act, the declaration of establishment of the foundation shall be delivered to the Registrar together with the prescribed fees.

(4) If the Registrar is satisfied that all the requirements of this Act in respect of the registration of a foundation have been complied with, he shall register on the Register the declaration of establishment delivered to him.

(5) Upon the registration of the declaration of establishment, the Registrar shall—

(a) allocate to the foundation a registration number in accordance with section 56(1);

(b) issue to the registered agent a certificate of registration in respect of the foundation stating—

(i) the date of registration of the foundation,

(ii) the name of the foundation, and

(iii) the registration number of the foundation; and

(c) issue to the registered agent an extract of the declaration of establishment of the foundation stating—

(i) the full names and addresses of the Foundation Council members,

(ii) the name and address of that registered agent,

(iii) the purposes of the foundation, and

(iv) the initial property endowment of the foundation.

(6) Each certificate of registration shall be signed and sealed by the Registrar.

(7) The certificate of registration shall be conclusive evidence of the registration of the foundation.

Deposit of foundation documents

14. (1) The Foundation Council may decide not to register a foundation, not being a foundation that has a commercial purpose, and in any such case the declaration of establishment of the foundation must be deposited by the registered agent with the Registrar together with the prescribed fees, and the Registrar shall record such declaration of establishment in a schedule of deposited foundations.

(2) If, upon such deposit, the Registrar is satisfied that all the requirements of this Act in respect of the deposit of the declaration of establishment of the foundation have been complied with, the Registrar shall—

(a) allocate a deposit number to the foundation in accordance with section 56(2); and

(b) issue to the registered agent a certificate of deposit stating—

(i) the date of deposit of the declaration of establishment of the foundation,

(ii) the name and deposit number of the foundation, and

(iii) the name and address of the registered agent.

(3) In such case, the Registrar shall only disclose information on the foundation—

(a) as provided for in section 59;

(b) upon an order of the High Court; or

(c) upon a written request from the Commission or any other body duly authorised under any other enactment.

(4) For the avoidance of doubt, any foundation to which subsection (1) does not apply, including any foundation that has a commercial purpose, must be registered pursuant to section 13(2).

Acquisition of legal personality of foundation

15. (1) A foundation shall, from the date of its registration pursuant to section 13 or, as the case may be, the date of acceptance of its deposit pursuant to section 14, have the status of a separate and independent legal person in its own right.

(2) A foundation shall be invalid and unenforceable—

(a) if it is not registered pursuant to section 13 or deposited pursuant to section 14;

(b) in the case of a registered foundation, if it has been struck off the Register; or

(c) in the case of a deposited foundation, if it has been struck off the schedule of deposited foundations pursuant to section 46 or 49.

Notice of change of registered or deposited particulars

16. (1) Where the declaration of establishment of a foundation is amended or a change occurs in any of the particulars specified in section 4(2)—

(a) the foundation shall, within 14 days of the amendment or occurrence of such change or within 14 days of becoming aware of such amendment or occurrence, file or deposit with the Registrar a notice, signed by the registered agent, containing details of the amendment or change, together with the prescribed fees; and

(b) the Registrar shall—

(i) in the case of a registered foundation, retain such notice and file it in the Register, and

(ii) in the case of a deposited foundation, retain such notice, cancel the certificate of deposit and issue to the registered agent a new certificate of deposit indicating such amendment or change.

(2) Where such amendment constitutes a change of name of a registered foundation, the Registrar must issue a new certificate of registration indicating the change of name.

(3) Any amendment of the declaration of establishment of a foundation and any change in the particulars specified in section 4(2) shall come into effect—

(a) in the case of a registered foundation, from the date when notice of the such amendment or change has been filed in the Register; and

(b) in the case of a deposited foundation, from the date on which the Registrar issues to the registered agent the new certificate of deposit indicating such amendment or change.

(4) Any interested person or the Registrar may apply to the High Court for an order to require a foundation to comply with subsection (1), and the High Court may so order and make any further order it thinks fit.

Part 3

THE BODIES OF THE FOUNDATION

Registered agent

17. (1) Every foundation shall, at all times, have a registered agent in Anguilla.

(2) The registered agent must be a regulated person.

(3) The first registered agent of every foundation shall be as specified in the declaration of establishment of that foundation.

(4) A foundation may change its registered agent by filing a notice for that purpose in the prescribed form with the Registrar.

(5) The change of the registered agent takes effect upon the notice being registered or deposited by the Registrar.

(6) If the registered agent ceases to be a regulated person, the foundation shall, within 14 days of becoming aware of that fact, change its registered agent to a person who is a regulated person.

(7) If, pursuant to a notice given under section 18, a person ceases to act as the registered agent of a foundation, the foundation shall appoint a new registered agent immediately upon the effective date of the first mentioned registered agent ceasing to so act.

(8) If a person ceases to act as the registered agent of a foundation for any other reason, the foundation shall, within 14 days of becoming aware that the person concerned has ceased to act as its registered agent, change that registered agent to another person who is a regulated person.

(9) A foundation that contravenes subsections (6), (7) or (8) commits an offence and is liable to such penalty as may be prescribed by regulations.

(10) Subject to subsection (11), a person who, not being a regulated person, acts as the registered agent of a foundation, commits an offence and is liable to such penalty as may be prescribed by regulations.

(11) If a person who acts as the registered agent of a foundation ceases to hold a relevant licence, he does not commit an offence under subsection (10) if, upon ceasing to hold such licence, he forthwith notifies the foundation that he is no longer a regulated person and that the foundation must change its registered agent in accordance with subsection (6).

Registered agent ceasing to act for foundation

18. (1) If the registered agent of a foundation intends to cease to act as its registered agent, he must give not less than 30 days written notice of his intention to do so in accordance with subsection (2).

(2) A notice given under subsection (1) must be sent to any Foundation Council member at the address of the Foundation Council member last known to the registered agent.

Foundation Council

19. (1) A foundation shall, at all times, have a Foundation Council, whose duties and responsibilities shall be set out in the declaration of establishment of the foundation or in its by-laws.

(2) The Foundation Council may comprise one or more persons, whether corporate entities or individuals.

(3) No person shall be a Foundation Council member of a foundation if the person is—

(a) a minor; or

(b) an incompetent; or

(c) the guardian of the foundation; or

(d) disqualified from being—

(i) a Foundation Council member of a foundation under this Act, or

(ii) a director of a company under any law of Anguilla.

Duties and obligations of Foundation Council

20. (1) The Foundation Council of a foundation shall have the responsibility of carrying out the objectives and purposes of the foundation.

(2) Subject to the terms of the declaration of establishment of the foundation or its by-laws and without prejudice to the generality of subsection (1), the Foundation Council shall have the following general obligations and duties—

(a) to direct the administration of the assets of the foundation;

(b) to exercise the powers of the foundation, directly or indirectly, through the employees and agents of the foundation;

(c) to enter into any transactions, contracts or lawful business that may be suitable or necessary to fulfil the purposes of the foundation;

(d) to provide information relating to the property endowment to the beneficiaries of the foundation and the guardian, if any;

(e) to make distributions or applications of all or any part of the property endowment or the income of the foundation; and

(f) to do all such other acts as may be provided for by this Act.

Duty of care of Foundation Council members

21. (1) A Foundation Council member shall, in the exercise and discharge of his powers and duties—

(a) act honestly and in good faith with a view to the interests of the foundation, its beneficiaries or its purposes; and

(b) exercise the care, diligence and skill which a reasonably prudent person would exercise in comparable circumstances.

(2) Subject to the provisions of this Act and notwithstanding any provision to the contrary in the declaration of establishment or by-laws of a foundation or in any agreement entered into by the foundation, a Foundation Council member who commits or concurs in committing a breach of the duties imposed by subsection (1) (hereafter referred to in this section and in sections 22 and 23 as a "breach") is liable for—

(a) any loss or depreciation in value of the property endowment resulting from the breach; and

(b) any profit that would have accrued to the property endowment had there been no breach.

(3) A Foundation Council member may not set off a profit accruing from one breach against a loss or depreciation in value resulting from another breach.

(4) A Foundation Council member is not liable for a breach committed by another person prior to his appointment or for a breach committed by another Foundation Council member unless—

(a) he becomes or ought to have become aware of such breach; and

(b) he actively concurs in or conceals such breach, or fails within a reasonable time to take proper steps to protect or restore the property endowment or to prevent the continuance of the breach.

(5) Where 2 or more Foundation Council members are liable for a breach, they are liable jointly and severally.

(6) A Foundation Council member who becomes aware of a breach shall take all reasonable steps to remedy the breach or cause the breach to be remedied.

Indemnification

22. (1) Subject to subsection (2) and to the terms of its declaration of establishment or its by-laws, a foundation may indemnify against all expenses, including legal fees, and against all judgments, fines and amounts paid in settlement and reasonably incurred, in connection with legal, administrative or investigative proceedings, any person who—

(a) is or was a party or is threatened to be made a party to any threatened, pending or completed proceedings, whether civil, criminal, administrative or investigative, by reason of the fact that the person is or was a Foundation Council member or guardian of the foundation; or

(b) is or was, at the request of the foundation, serving as a Foundation Council member, guardian or liquidator of, or in any other capacity is or was acting for, another foundation.

(2) Subsection (1) only applies to a person referred to in that subsection if the person acted honestly and in good faith with a view to the interests of the foundation and, in the case of criminal proceedings, the person had no reasonable cause to believe that his conduct was unlawful.

(3) The decision of the Foundation Council, with the written concurrence of the guardian, if any, as to whether the person—

(a) acted honestly and in good faith and with a view to the interests of the foundation; or

(b) had no reasonable cause to believe that his conduct was unlawful;

is, in the absence of fraud, sufficient for the purposes of this section unless a question of law is involved.

(4) The termination of any proceedings by any judgment, order, settlement, conviction or the entering of a *nolle prosequi* does not, of itself, create a presumption that a person—

(a) did not act honestly and in good faith with a view to the interests of the foundation; or

(b) had reasonable cause to believe that his conduct was unlawful.

(5) If any person referred to in subsection (1) has been successful in defence of any proceedings referred to in that subsection, the foundation shall indemnify such person in respect of such proceedings as therein mentioned.

(6) The High Court may relieve a Foundation Council member of liability, in whole or in part, for a breach where it appears to the High Court that the Foundation Council member has acted honestly and reasonably and ought fairly to be excused for the breach or for omitting to obtain the directions of the High Court in the matter in which the breach arose.

Limitation of liability

23. (1) The declaration of establishment of a foundation or its by-laws may provide that the Foundation Council or the Foundation Council members of the foundation may only exercise certain powers by obtaining prior authorisation of its guardian, if any.

(2) Where such authorisation for the exercise of a power has been duly obtained from the guardian of the foundation, a Foundation Council member of that foundation is not liable for—

(a) any loss or depreciation of the property of the foundation; or

(b) any damages or prejudice caused to the foundation;

resulting from the exercise of the power, unless the exercise of that power is a breach within the meaning of section 21(2).

Capacity of Foundation Council to bind foundation

24. (1) Any person dealing with a foundation in good faith may assume that the Foundation Council of the foundation has the power to bind the foundation or to authorise others to do so.

(2) Subject to subsection (3), subsection (1) shall not affect the right of the foundation or its guardian, if any, or any Foundation Council member of the foundation to bring proceedings to restrain the doing of an act which is beyond the powers of the Foundation Council.

(3) Subsection (1) shall not affect any liability of a Foundation Council member or any other person who has acted beyond his powers.

Information concerning foundation

25. (1) The Foundation Council of a foundation shall, so far as is reasonable and within a reasonable time from the date of receipt of a request in writing to that effect, provide full and accurate information as to the nature and amount of the assets of the foundation and the conduct of their administration—

(a) subject to the terms of the declaration of establishment of the foundation and its by-laws—

(i) to the founder of the foundation,

(ii) to the guardian of the foundation, if any, and

(iii) to any beneficiary of the foundation; or

(b) pursuant to an order of the High Court.

(2) Subject to the provisions of this Act, the terms of the declaration of establishment of a foundation and its by-laws and any order of the High Court, neither the Foundation Council nor the guardian of the foundation shall be required to produce and make available to any person any document which—

(a) discloses their deliberations as to the manner in which they have exercised or have not exercised a power or discretion or performed a duty conferred or imposed on them or on the guardian; or

(b) relates to, or discloses the reason for, any particular exercise or non-exercise of the power or discretion or performance or non-performance of any duty or the material on which such reason was or might have been based.

Meetings of Foundation Council

26. (1) Subject to the terms of the declaration of establishment or by-laws of a foundation, the Foundation Council of the foundation shall meet at such times and in such manner and places within or outside Anguilla as it may determine.

(2) A Foundation Council member of the foundation shall be deemed to be present at a meeting of the Foundation Council if he participates in the meeting by telephone or any other electronic means and all the Foundation Council members participating in the meeting are able to hear each other.

(3) Decisions of the Foundation Council may be taken by way of written resolutions signed by all the Foundation Council members.

Removal and appointment of Foundation Council members

27. The removal and appointment of new or additional Foundation Council members of a foundation shall be effected in accordance with the terms of the declaration of establishment and by-laws of the foundation, but the full names and address of any Foundation Council member appointed shall be notified to the registered agent within 14 days of his appointment and every Foundation Council member shall have a duty to notify the registered agent of any change of his address within 14 days of the occurrence of such change and the provisions of section 16 shall apply.

Judicial removal of Foundation Council members

28. (1) Where the declaration of establishment of a foundation or its by-laws do not provide for the right to remove members of the Foundation Council of the foundation and the causes for such removal, the founder, any beneficiary, the guardian, or any Foundation Council member of the foundation may apply to the High Court for the removal of one or more Foundation Council members, for any of the following causes—

(a) when the interest of any such Foundation Council member is incompatible with the interests of the beneficiaries of the foundation or the founder or with the objectives and purposes of the foundation;

(b) if the administration of the assets of the foundation lacks the diligence of a reasonably prudent person;

(c) if any such Foundation Council member is charged with and convicted of an indictable offence;

(d) for incapacity or inability to carry out the objectives of the foundation, from the time such cause arises; or

(e) for the insolvency of, or in the event of bankruptcy proceedings against, any Foundation Council member.

(2) Without prejudice to paragraph (1)(c), where a Foundation Council member of a foundation is charged with an indictable offence, the High Court may, while the criminal proceedings in respect of that offence are in progress, suspend such Foundation Council member.

(3) Subject to the provisions of this Act, the High Court may appoint a person to replace the Foundation Council member suspended or removed.

Secretary

29. (1) Every foundation shall, unless its Foundation Council includes at least one person who is permanently resident in Anguilla and is a regulated person, have a Secretary who—

(a) must be a person residing in Anguilla;

(a) must be a regulated person; and

(c) may be the registered agent of the foundation.

(2) No foundation shall have as its Secretary a person who is the sole Foundation Council member.

(3) The Secretary of a foundation shall be responsible to the Foundation Council of the foundation for the implementation of the decisions and policies of the Foundation Council in compliance with the laws of Anguilla and for due compliance with the provisions of this Act.

Register of Foundation Council and Secretary

30. Each foundation shall keep, at its registered address, a register in which shall be recorded and maintained the identification particulars of its Foundation Council members and of its Secretary, if any.

Part 4

THE GUARDIAN

Appointment of guardian

31. (1) The declaration of establishment of a foundation may provide for the appointment of a person to be the guardian of the foundation.

(2) Where more than one person is appointed as the guardian of a foundation, such persons shall act jointly unless the declaration of establishment or by-laws of the foundation provide otherwise.

(3) Subject to the terms of the declaration of establishment or by-laws of a foundation, the guardian of the foundation shall be appointed in the following manner—

(a) if appointed on the establishment of the foundation, by the founder;

(b) if appointed after the establishment of the foundation, by the founder or such other person as may be empowered by the founder in the declaration of establishment or by-laws;

(c) by an outgoing guardian on his resignation; or

(d) if any case other than a case specified in paragraph (a), (b) or (c), by the Foundation Council.

(4) A guardian of a foundation duly appointed under the terms of the declaration of establishment or the by-laws of the foundation and this section shall cease to be a guardian in the event of—

(a) his or its resignation;

(b) his or its removal in accordance with the terms of such declaration of establishment or by-laws;

(c) if the guardian is an individual, his death, incapacity or bankruptcy;

(d) if the guardian is a legal entity, its winding up or dissolution; or

(d) the dissolution of the foundation.

Duties and powers of guardian

32. The guardian of a foundation shall have such powers, rights and duties as may be specified in the declaration of establishment and by-laws of the foundation and in this Act.

Part 5

DISPUTED RIGHTS

Exclusion of foreign law

33. (1) No foundation governed by the laws of Anguilla, and no transfer of property to a foundation which is valid under the laws of Anguilla, shall be void, voidable, liable to be set aside or defective in any manner by reference to the law of a foreign jurisdiction.

(2) The capacity of a founder of a foundation or any other person who transfers property to a foundation shall not be questioned, nor shall any beneficiary or other person be subjected to any liability or deprived of any right by reason that—

(a) the laws of any foreign jurisdiction prohibit or do not recognise the concept of a foundation; or

(b) the transfer of property to the foundation, or any terms of its declaration of establishment or its by-laws—

(i) avoids or defeats rights, claims or interests conferred by any law of a foreign jurisdiction on any person by reason of a personal relationship to the founder or a subsequent transfer or by way of heirship rights, or

(ii) contravenes any rule of law or judicial or administrative order or action of a foreign jurisdiction intended to recognise, protect, enforce or give effect to any rights, claims or interests referred to in sub-paragraph (i).

Restriction against alienation

34. (1) Notwithstanding any rule of law or equity to the contrary, no beneficiary, object or purpose of a foundation shall have any right in specie against the property endowment of the foundation irrespective of the nature of any right to enforce the due administration of the foundation, and, subject to the terms of its declaration of establishment or by-laws, any assets of the foundation available for distribution to a beneficiary shall not be—

(a) capable of being alienated or passed by bankruptcy, insolvency or liquidation; or

(b) liable to be seized, sold, attached, or otherwise taken in execution by process of law.

(2) Where any of the assets of the foundation is subjected to a restriction against alienation, the right to derive income from that property shall not be alienable for as long as that restriction remains in force.

(3) Any restriction applicable pursuant to this section may at any time be removed in accordance with any provisions in the declaration of establishment or by-laws for such removal.

Enforcement of terms

35. (1) Notwithstanding the provisions of section 34(1), any beneficiary of a foundation may enforce the due administration of the foundation in accordance with the terms of its declaration of establishment and by-laws, and any claim for such purpose shall constitute a claim *in personam*.

(2) For the avoidance of doubt, a claim referred to in subsection (1) shall not constitute a claim *in rem*.

Forfeiture of benefits

36. The declaration of establishment or by-laws of a foundation may provide that any beneficiary of the foundation shall forfeit any benefit or right under it in the event that he challenges—

(a) the establishment of the foundation;

(b) the transfer of any assets to the foundation; or

(c) its declaration of establishment or by-laws or any provision of such declaration or by-laws.

Part 6

ACCOUNTS AND RECORDS

Accounts and records

37. (1) A foundation shall keep or cause to be kept—

(a) such accounts and records as its Foundation Council considers necessary or desirable in order to reflect the financial position of the foundation;

(b) a copy of its declaration of establishment and by-laws and any amendment or change to its declaration of establishment or by-laws;

(c) minutes of all meetings of its Foundation Council and copies of all resolutions consented to by its Foundation Council.

(2) The Secretary of the foundation or, if there is no Secretary, its registered agent, shall keep or cause to be kept a register in which is recorded the identification particulars of the Foundation Council members, guardian and beneficiaries and auditors, where applicable, and any persons having power of attorney granted by the foundation.

(3) The accounts, records, minutes, resolutions, copy documents and register required by this section (hereafter referred to in this section as the "books") shall—

(a) be kept at the registered address of the foundation or, subject to subsection (4), at such other place as the Foundation Council of the foundation may designate; and

(b) at all reasonable times, be open to inspection by the registered agent and the Foundation Council members of the foundation and, where applicable, its Secretary, guardian or auditor.

(4) If the books are kept at a place other than the registered address, whether within or outside Anguilla, the registered agent of the foundation shall—

(a) be notified of the location of such place where such books are kept within 14 days after the designation of such location; and

(b) upon request, be furnished with such books or, as the case may be, notarially certified copies of such books, within a reasonable time for the purpose of inspection by the registered agent and the Foundation Council members of the foundation and, where applicable, its Secretary, guardian or auditor.

(5) Where the accounting records of a foundation are kept outside Anguilla, the foundation must ensure that it keeps at its registered address—

(a) accounts and returns adequate to enable the Foundation Council members to ascertain, on a quarterly basis, the financial position of the foundation with reasonable accuracy; and

(b) without prejudice to subsection (4), a written record of the place or places outside Anguilla where its accounting records are kept.

(6) Every record required to be kept under this section shall be preserved for a period of not less than 6 years after the end of the period to which it relates.

(7) A foundation that contravenes subsection (5) or (6) commits an offence and is liable to such penalty as may be prescribed by regulations.

Part 7

CONTINUANCE OF FOUNDATIONS

Continuance in Anguilla

38. (1) An overseas foundation may apply to the Registrar for a certificate of continuance under this Act.

(2) An application under subsection (1) must be made in the prescribed form as specified by the Registrar.

(3) Articles of continuance may, without so stating, effect any amendment to the organisational instruments of an overseas foundation which applies for continuance under this section if the amendment—

(a) is authorised in accordance with the law applicable to the overseas foundation before continuance under this Act; and

(b) is an amendment that a foundation established under this Act is entitled to make.

Articles of continuance

39. (1) Articles of continuance of an overseas foundation and any amendment thereto may be written in any language but, where such articles or amendment is not written in the English language, they must be accompanied by a certified translation into the English language.

(2) Articles of continuance of an overseas foundation shall—

(a) declare the intention of the overseas foundation, pursuant to a resolution in writing of its governing body, to continue its legal existence in Anguilla as a foundation;

(b) state the name of the overseas foundation and the name under which it is being continued;

(c) state the jurisdiction in which the overseas foundation is established and, if different, the jurisdiction in which it was originally formed;

(d) state the date on which the overseas foundation was formed;

(e) state whether the overseas foundation will be registered or its documents deposited;

(f) state such other provisions as are required to be included in the declaration of establishment of a foundation under this Act; and

(g) be duly signed by all the members of the governing body or Foundation Council of the overseas foundation.

Certificate of continuance

40. (1) Upon receipt of the application and articles of continuance, the Registrar shall issue a certificate of continuance if he is satisfied that the application and articles of continuance are in compliance with the requirements of sections 38 and 39.

(2) On the date shown in the certificate of continuance—

(a) the overseas foundation becomes a foundation to which this Act applies as if that foundation had been established under this Act; and

(b) the articles of continuance shall be deemed to be the declaration of establishment of the foundation which is continued under this Act.

Preservation of foundation

41. When an overseas foundation is continued as a foundation under this Act—

(a) the property of the overseas foundation continues to be the property of the foundation;

(b) the foundation continues to be liable for the obligations of the overseas foundation;

(c) any existing cause of action, claim or liability to prosecute is unaffected;

(d) any civil, criminal or administrative action or proceedings pending by or against the overseas foundation may be continued by or against the foundation; and

(e) any conviction against, or any ruling, order or judgment against or in favour of, the overseas foundation is enforceable by or against the foundation.

Continuance in foreign jurisdiction

42. (1) Subject to its declaration of establishment and by-laws, a foundation may, pursuant to a resolution of its Foundation Council or as otherwise provided, apply to the appropriate official or public body of a foreign jurisdiction to be continued as an entity in the foreign jurisdiction as if it had been established under the laws of that foreign jurisdiction, in the manner provided by such laws.

(2) Subject to the provisions of this Act, a foundation that continues as an entity under the laws of a foreign jurisdiction does not cease to be a foundation unless the laws of the foreign jurisdiction permit such continuation and the foundation has complied with such laws.

Conditions applicable to continuance in foreign jurisdiction

43. Where a foundation is continued as an entity under the laws of a foreign jurisdiction—

(a) the property of the foundation continues to be the property of such entity;

(b) such entity continues to be liable for the obligations of the foundation;

(c) any existing cause of action, claim or liability to prosecution in respect of the foundation is unaffected;

(d) any civil, criminal or administrative action or proceeding pending by or against the foundation can be continued by or against such entity; and

(e) any conviction against or ruling, order or judgment against, or in favour of, the foundation is enforceable by or against such entity.

Discontinuance and effect

44. (1) Every foundation departing Anguilla must file a certificate of departure containing the prescribed information in the prescribed form with the Registrar.

(2) A foundation which—

(a) has filed a certificate of departure under subsection (1); and

(b) has been continued under the law of a foreign jurisdiction;

may apply to the Registrar for a certificate of discontinuance.

(3) An application under subsection (2) must be accompanied by evidence, acceptable to the Registrar, that the foundation has been continued under the laws of a foreign jurisdiction.

(4) If the Registrar is satisfied that—

(a) all fees payable under this Act have been paid;

(b) all returns and notices required to be filed under this Act or regulations made under this Act have been filed; and

(c) the requirements of this section have been complied with;

the Registrar must issue to the foundation a certificate of discontinuance in the prescribed form and strike it off the Register or, as the case may be, the schedule of deposited foundations.

(5) The Registrar must, in the case of a registered foundation, publish a notice of the discontinuance and striking off in the *Gazette*.

(6) Subject to subsection 42(2), from the date of the certificate of discontinuance, the foundation ceases to be a foundation domiciled in Anguilla.

Part 8

IRREVOCABILITY AND DISSOLUTION

Foundation to be irrevocable

45. Subject to section 7(2), a foundation established under this Act or continued in Anguilla shall be irrevocable and any transfer of assets made to a foundation under this Act as an addition to its property endowment shall be irrevocable by whosoever made such transfer.

Dissolution

46. (1) A foundation shall be dissolved where—

(a) the foundation has been established for a definite period and that period has expired;

(b) any term of its declaration of establishment or by-laws or of this Act so requires;

(c) its Foundation Council has so resolved; or

(d) the High Court orders its dissolution.

(2) The Registrar shall, immediately after the completion of the dissolution of a foundation pursuant to this section—

(a) strike the foundation off the Register or, as the case may be, the schedule of deposited foundations; and

(b) in the case of a registered foundation, publish a notice of the striking off and dissolution in the *Gazette*.

Voluntary dissolution

47. (1) Before a foundation is dissolved pursuant to section 46(1)(a), (b) or (c), a statement of intent to dissolve the foundation must be filed with the Registrar in the prescribed form.

(2) If the Registrar is satisfied that the relevant requirements of this Part have been complied with, the Registrar shall, upon receipt of a statement of intent to dissolve the foundation, issue a certificate of intent to dissolve the foundation.

(3) When a certificate of intent to dissolve the foundation is issued by the Registrar, the foundation shall cease transacting business except to the extent necessary for its dissolution, but its legal personality continues until the Registrar issues a certificate of dissolution of the foundation.

(4) After the issue of a certificate of intent to dissolve a foundation, the foundation shall—

(a) immediately cause notice of its intent to dissolve to be sent to each of its known creditors;

(b) proceed to—

(i) collect its property,

(ii) dispose of its properties that are not to be distributed in kind,

(iii) discharge all its obligations, and

(iv) do all other acts required to liquidate its assets; and

(c) after giving the notice required under paragraph (a) and adequately providing for the payment or discharge of all its obligations, distribute any residuary assets in accordance with section 52.

Dissolution by High Court

48. (1) The High Court may order the dissolution of a foundation upon the application of the Registrar or the guardian, a beneficiary, a Foundation Council member or a creditor of the foundation if the High Court is satisfied that—

(a) the declaration of establishment or any by-law of the foundation or any term of this Act entitles the applicant to demand dissolution of the foundation after the occurrence of a specified event and that event has occurred;

(b) the objectives of the foundation have been fulfilled or have become incapable of being fulfilled and it is just and equitable that the foundation be dissolved;

(c) the foundation is insolvent or unable to pay its debts; or

(d) it is in the public interest to order the dissolution of the foundation.

(2) Where the High Court orders the dissolution of a foundation under this section, the High Court shall appoint a person to supervise the dissolution of the foundation and may, from time to time, direct the manner in which the dissolution is to be conducted.

(3) Where a foundation is dissolved pursuant to the provisions of subsection (1), its residuary assets, if any, shall be distributed in accordance with section 52.

Striking off

49. (1) If a foundation fails—

(a) to pay the prescribed annual fees within the time specified by this Act;

(b) to maintain a registered agent pursuant to section 17; or

(c) to file with the Registrar any return, notice or document required to be filed under this Act or regulations made under this Act;

the Registrar may strike it off the Register or, as the case may be, the schedule of deposited foundations.

(2) Where the Registrar intends to strike—

(a) a registered foundation off the Register; or

(b) a deposited foundation off the schedule of deposited foundations;

the Registrar shall give the foundation notice of his intention and a reasonable opportunity to show cause why the foundation should not be struck off the Register or, as the case may be, the schedule of deposited foundations.

(3) After the expiration of time mentioned in the notice, being not less than 90 days, the Registrar may, unless the foundation shows cause to the contrary, strike the foundation off the Register or, as the case may be, the schedule of deposited foundations.

(4) Without prejudice to sections 46, 47 and 48, a foundation is dissolved when it is struck off the Register or the schedule of deposited foundations under subsection (3) and the Registrar shall publish a notice of its striking off and dissolution in the *Gazette,* but the striking off and dissolution of the foundation shall take effect from the date of publication of the notice in the *Gazette*.

(5) Where a foundation is struck off the Register or the schedule of deposited foundations under this section, the provisions of sections 48(2) and 48(3) shall apply as if the High Court had ordered the dissolution of the foundation.

Appeal

50. (1) Any person who is aggrieved by the striking or proposed striking of a foundation off the Register or the schedule of deposited foundations under section 49 may, within 90 days from the date of publication of the notice in the *Gazette*, appeal to the High Court against the decision of the Registrar.

(2) Notice of an appeal to the High Court under subsection (1) must be served on the Registrar who shall be entitled to appear and be heard at the hearing of the appeal.

(3) Where any person who is aggrieved by the striking or proposed striking of a foundation off the Register or the schedule of deposited foundations files an appeal under subsection (1), the Registrar may suspend the operation of the striking off, upon such terms as he considers appropriate, pending the determination of the appeal.

Restoration of name to Register or to schedule of deposited foundations

51. (1) Where a foundation has been struck off the Register or the schedule of deposited foundations, the Registrar may, upon receipt of an application in the prescribed form to restore a foundation to the Register or the schedule of deposited foundations and upon receipt of payment of the prescribed fee and any outstanding fees, restore the foundation to the Register or the schedule of deposited foundations, as the case may be, and issue a certificate in a form adapted to the circumstances.

(2) An application to restore a foundation to the Register or the schedule of deposited foundations under subsection (1) must be made within 20 years of the date of publication of the notice in the *Gazette* under section 49(3).

(3) The foundation or a creditor, beneficiary or liquidator of the foundation may, within 90 days from the date of the refusal of the Registrar to restore the foundation to the Register or the schedule of deposited foundations, appeal to the High Court against that refusal and, the High Court may, if it is satisfied that it is just for the foundation to be restored to the Register or, as the case may be, the schedule of deposited foundations, direct the Registrar to do so upon such terms and conditions as the High Court may consider appropriate.

(4) Notice of an appeal to the High Court under subsection (3) must be served on the Registrar who shall be entitled to appear and be heard at the hearing of the appeal.

Distribution of residuary assets

52. (1) Subject to subsection (2), the residuary assets of a foundation shall be the property of the person who, according to the declaration of establishment or by-laws of the foundation, is entitled to receive the residuary assets.

(2) Where—

(a) there is no person entitled to receive the residuary assets as provided in subsection (1); or

(b) the person entitled to receive such assets refuses to accept its transfer;

and there is no relevant provision in the declaration of establishment or by-laws respecting the distribution of such assets, the residuary assets shall vest in the Crown.

Part 9

EXEMPTION FROM TAXES

Exemption from taxes

53. (1) For the purposes of this Act, a foundation shall be entitled to the exemptions specified in subsection (2) if—

(a) the founder or any person who has contributed assets to the foundation otherwise than for full consideration is not resident in Anguilla;

(b) none of the beneficiaries of the foundation is resident in Anguilla; and

(c) the property endowment does not include any land situated in Anguilla or the shares of any company beneficially owning any land situated in Anguilla other than property—

(i) for use as an office for the purpose of the administration of the foundation, or

(ii) where books and records of the foundation are prepared or maintained.

(2) Subject to this Act, any foundation to which subsection (1) applies shall not be subject to any income tax, withholding tax, asset tax, gift tax, profits tax, capital gains tax, distributions tax, inheritance tax, estate duty or any other like tax based upon or measured by assets or income originating outside of Anguilla or in connection with matters of administration that may occur in Anguilla.

(3) Notwithstanding any provisions of the Stamp Act, but subject to subsection (4), an instrument relating to a transfer of property to or by a foundation to which subsection (1) applies is exempt from the payment of stamp duty.

(4) Subsection (3) does not apply to an instrument relating to a transfer of property situated in Anguilla, including any interest in land in Anguilla or in shares in a company incorporated under the Companies Act.

Part 10

REGISTRAR

Registrar and other officers

54. (1) The Registrar of Companies shall be the Registrar of Foundations.

(2) Any functions of the Registrar under this Act may, to the extent authorised by him, be exercised by any officer on his staff.

Official seal

55. The Registrar shall procure that an official seal be prepared for use by the Registrar in the authentication or other issue of documents required under this Act

Official registration and deposit number

56. (1) The Registrar shall allocate—

(a) to every registered foundation a number, which shall be the registration number of that registered foundation; and

(b) to every deposited foundation a number, which shall be the deposit number of that deposited foundation.

(2) The registration numbers of registered foundations shall be in such form, consisting of one or more sequences of figures or letters or any combination thereof, but distinct from the sequence or sequences applicable to deposited foundations, as the Registrar may, from time to time, determine.

(3) The deposit numbers of deposited foundations shall be in such form, consisting of one or more sequences of figures or letters or any combination thereof, but distinct from the sequence or sequences applicable to registered foundations, as the Registrar may, from time to time, determine.

Form of documents to be delivered to the Registrar

57. (1) Where this Act requires a document or any information to be delivered to the Registrar, and the form of the document or information has not been prescribed, it shall be sufficient compliance with the requirement if—

(a) in the case of a document, it is delivered in a form which is acceptable to the Registrar and is accompanied by the prescribed fee; or

(b) in the case of information contained in a material other than a document, it is delivered in a manner acceptable to the Registrar and is accompanied by the prescribed fee.

(2) In this section, the reference to "a document or any information to be delivered" shall be construed to include any notice to be served or given.

Certificate of good standing in case of registered foundations

58. The Registrar shall, on request by the registered agent of a foundation and on receipt of payment of the prescribed fee, certify that the registered foundation is of good standing, if the Registrar is satisfied that—

(a) the name of the foundation is on the Register;

(b) the foundation has filed with the Registrar all documents required by this Act to be filed; and

(c) the foundation has paid all fees and penalties required by this Act to be paid.

Official confirmation in case of deposited foundations

59. The Registrar shall, on request by the registered agent of a deposited foundation and on receipt of payment of the prescribed fee, certify that the details of a confirmation prepared by the registered agent and delivered to the Registrar are true and correct if the Registrar is satisfied that this is the case according to the deposited declaration of establishment of the foundation and any further evidence produced by the registered agent, if necessary.

Inspection of documents kept by the Registrar

60. (1) Subject to the provisions of this Act, no inspection or production of documents kept by the Registrar under this Act shall be permitted other than by the registered agent, except that any of the Foundation Council members of a foundation may, by notice in writing to the Registrar, authorise the person named in the notice—

(a) to inspect, or obtain a copy of, a document of the foundation delivered to the Registrar under this Act ; or

(b) to require a certificate of registration of the foundation or a copy or part, certified or otherwise, of any other document referred to in paragraph (a);

and a certificate given under paragraph (b) shall be signed by the Registrar and sealed with the official seal.

(2) A copy of or an extract from a record kept by the Registrar, certified in writing by the Registrar to be an accurate copy or extract, shall, in all legal proceedings, be admissible in evidence as of equal validity with the original record and as evidence of any fact stated in the copy or extract of which direct evidence would be admissible.

Enforcement of duty to deliver documents or notices to the Registrar

61. (1) Where a foundation—

(a) fails to comply with a requirement to deliver to the Registrar any document or to give notice to the Registrar of any matter; and

(b) does not make good such failure within 14 days after the service of a notice on the foundation requiring it so to do;

the High Court may, on an application made to it by a Foundation Council member or the guardian of the foundation or by the Registrar, make an order directing the foundation to make good the failure within a time specified in the order.

(2) The order of the High Court may provide that all or any part of the costs of and incidental to the application shall be—

(a) borne by the foundation or by any Foundation Council member or members responsible for such failure; or

(b) apportioned between the foundation and any Foundation Council member or members so responsible.

(3) Nothing in this section shall prejudice the application of any provision imposing penalties on the foundation or its Foundation Council in respect of a failure mentioned in subsection (1).

Part 11

INVESTIGATION OF FOUNDATIONS

Investigation order

62. (1) A founder, beneficiary or guardian of a foundation, or the Registrar may, without notice or upon such notice as the Court may require, apply to the Court for an order directing that an investigation be made of the foundation or any foundation or company affiliated with it.

(2) If, upon an application under subsection (1), it appears to the Court that—

(a) the affairs of the foundation or any of its affiliates are being or have been carried on with intent to defraud any person;

(b) the foundation or any of its affiliates was established for a fraudulent or unlawful purpose or is to be dissolved for a fraudulent or unlawful purpose; or

(c) persons concerned with the establishment, business or affairs of the foundation or any of its affiliates have in connection therewith acted fraudulently or dishonestly; or

(d) it is in the public interest that an investigation of the foundation or any of its affiliates be made;

the Court may make any order it thinks fit with respect to an investigation of the foundation or any of its affiliates by an inspector.

(3) If a founder, beneficiary or guardian makes an application under subsection (1), he shall give the Registrar reasonable notice of it, and the Registrar is entitled to appear and be heard at the hearing of the application.

Contents of order and copies of reports

63. (1) An order made under section 62(2) shall include an order to investigate and an order appointing an inspector, who may be the Registrar, and fixing his remuneration and may include an order—

(a) replacing the inspector;

(b) an order determining the notice to be given to any interested person, or dispensing with notice to any person;

(c) an order authorising an inspector to enter any premises in which the Court is satisfied there might be relevant information, and to examine anything, and to make copies of any documents or records, found on the premises;

(d) an order requiring any person to produce documents or records to the inspector;

(e) an order authorising an inspector to conduct a hearing, administer oaths or affirmations and examine any person upon oath or affirmation, and prescribing rules for the conduct of the hearing;

(f) an order requiring any person to attend a hearing conducted by an inspector and to give evidence upon oath or affirmation;

(g) an order giving directions to an inspector or any interested person on any matter arising in the investigation;

(h) an order requiring an inspector to make an interim or final report to the Court;

(i) an order determining whether a report of an inspector should be published, and, if so, ordering the Registrar to publish the report in whole or in part, or to send copies to any person the Court designates; and

(j) an order requiring an inspector to discontinue an investigation.

(2) An inspector shall file with the Registrar a copy of every report made by the inspector under this section.

(3) A report received by the Registrar under subsection (2) must not be disclosed to any person other than in accordance with an order of the Court made under paragraph (1)(i).

Inspector's powers

64. An inspector—

(a) has the powers set out in the order appointing him; and

(b) shall upon request produce to an interested person a copy of the order.

Hearing *in camera*

65. (1) An application under this Part and any subsequent proceedings, including applications for directions in respect of any matter arising in the investigation, must be heard *in camera* unless the Court orders otherwise.

(2) A person whose conduct is being investigated or who is being examined at a hearing conducted by an inspector under this Part may appear or be heard at the hearing.

(3) No person shall publish anything relating to any proceedings under this Part except with the authorisation of the Court.

Incriminating evidence

66. No person is excused from attending and giving evidence and producing documents and records to an inspector appointed by the Court under this Part by reason only that the evidence tends to incriminate that person or subject him to any proceeding or penalty, but the evidence may not be used or received against him in any proceeding thereafter instituted against him, other than a prosecution for perjury in giving the evidence.

Absolute privilege

67. An oral or written statement or report made by an inspector or any other person in an investigation under this Part has absolute privilege.

Part 12

MISCELLANEOUS MATTERS

Compliance inspections

68. (1) The Commission may, for the purpose specified in subsection (2)—

(a) inspect the accounts and records of a relevant person, whether in or outside Anguilla, including the systems and controls of the relevant person;

(b) inspect the assets of a relevant person, including cash, belonging to or in the possession or control of the relevant person; and

(c) examine and make copies of documents belonging to or in the possession or control of a relevant person;

that, in the opinion of the Commission, relate to a foundation established under this Act.

(2) A compliance inspection may be undertaken, in the case of a person specified in paragraphs (1)(a), (b) and (c), for the purpose of monitoring and assessing such person's compliance with his obligations under the Money Laundering Reporting Authority Act, Anti-Money Laundering Regulations and any other Acts, Regulations, Guidelines or Codes relating to money laundering or the financing of terrorism.

(3) The powers and duties conferred or imposed on the Commission by this section are in addition to, and not in derogation of, any other powers and duties conferred or imposed on the Commission by any other Act.

Registration and annual fees

69. (1) Every foundation, whether registered or deposited, must pay a fee upon registration or deposit and the annual fee and any applicable penalties as may be prescribed by regulations.

(2) The Foundation Council members of a foundation shall be personally liable—

(a) to pay any outstanding fees in respect of the foundation; and

(b) to such penalties as may be prescribed by regulations in respect of any failure or default mentioned in section 49(1).

Legal professional privilege

70. Where any proceedings are instituted under this Act, nothing in this Act is to be taken to require a person to disclose any information which the person is entitled to refuse to disclose on grounds of legal professional privilege.

Powers of the High Court

71. (1) Subject to the provisions of section 73, the High Court has jurisdiction in respect of any matters concerning any foundation established under this Act.

(2) A Foundation Council member, guardian or registered agent of a foundation may apply to the High Court for directions as to how he should or might act in any of the affairs of the foundation, and the High Court may make such order as it thinks fit.

(3) If a person does not comply with an order of the High Court under this Act requiring him to do any thing, the High Court may, on such terms and conditions as it thinks fit, order that the thing be done by another person nominated for the purpose by the High Court at the expense of the person in default or otherwise, as the High Court directs, and a thing so done has effect in all respects as if done by the person in default.

(4) The High Court may order the costs and expenses of, and incidental to, an application to the High Court under this Act to be paid from the property endowment of the foundation or in such manner and by such persons as it thinks fit.

Arbitration tribunal

72. (1) The declaration of establishment or by-laws of a foundation may—

(a) provide that any controversy arising in respect of the foundation shall be resolved by arbitration;

(b) make provision for the arbitration procedure that should be followed; and

(c) stipulate that, to the extent specified, the arbitration tribunal shall interpret such declaration of establishment and by-laws according to their terms and to the principles of civil law, without regard to the principles of common law and equity otherwise applicable thereto.

(2) Subject to any specific provisions in the declaration of establishment or by-laws of a foundation, any reference in this Act to “High Court” shall be construed to include a reference to the arbitration tribunal within or outside Anguilla provided for in the declaration of establishment and by-laws of the foundation.

Service of process, etc. on foundation

73. (1) Any summons, notice, order, document, process, information or written statement required to be served on a foundation may be served—

(a) by leaving it, or by sending it by registered mail addressed to the foundation, at its registered address; or

(b) by leaving it with, or by sending it by registered mail to, the registered agent of the foundation.

(2) Service of any summons, notice, order, document, process, information or written statement to be served on a foundation may be proved by showing that the summons, notice, order, document, process, information or written statement—

(a) was mailed in sufficient time as to admit to it being delivered, in the normal course of delivery, within the period prescribed for service; and

(b) was correctly addressed and the postage was prepaid.

Regulations

74. (1) The Governor in Council may, on the advice of the Commission, make regulations providing for any matter contemplated by this Act or as may be necessary or convenient for carrying out or giving effect to this Act and its administration.

(2) Without limiting the generality of subsection (1), the Governor in Council may, on the advice of the Commission, make regulations—

(a) prescribing anything required or permitted to be prescribed by this Act;

(b) exempting any person from any provision of this Act;

(c) prescribing annual returns to be made;

(d) prescribing forms to be used;

(e) prescribing the format for any filings to be made under this Act;

(f) prescribing or amending the fees payable under this Act;

(g) prescribing or amending the penalties for offences committed under this Act;

(h) prescribing standards of foundation governance to which foundations shall be subject.

Citation and commencement

75. This Act may be cited as the Anguilla Foundation Act, 2008 and shall come into force on such day as the Governor may, by notice published in the *Gazette,* appoint.

PROTECTED CELL COMPANIES REGULATIONS

Regulations made by the Governor, on the advice of the Commission, under section 25 of the Protected Cell Companies Act, R.S.A. c. P107.

Interpretation

1. In these Regulations—

“Act” means the Protected Cell Companies Act, R.S. A. c. P107;

“Commission” means the Financial Services Commission established by the Financial Services Commission Act, R.S.A. c. F28;

“Registrar” means the Registrar of Companies;

“$” means the currency of the United States of America.

Application to be registered as a protected cell company to operate protected cell accounts

2. An application for registration to operate protected cell accounts shall be made in the form as set out in Schedule 1.

Application to be authorised as a protected cell account of a protected cell company

3. An application to be authorised as a protected cell account of a protected cell company shall be made in the form as set out in Schedule 2.

Application for approval of a protected cell account representative

4. An application for the approval of a protected cell account representative shall be made in the form of a letter addressed to the Commission as set out in Schedule 3.

Application for directions of the Commission to modify provisions of the Act

5. An application to the Commission to modify the provisions of sections 3, 5, 8 and 12 of the Act made by a protected cell company, or any company intending to file a notice pursuant to section 3 of the Act, shall be in the form of a letter accompanied by the information required in sections 24(1) and 24(4) of the Act as set out in Schedule 4.

Fees

6. The payment of fees and late payment penalties by applicants are as set out in Schedule 5.

Notice of payments conditions imposed by the Commission under section 4(3) of the Act

7. The Commission makes it a condition of registration of each protected cell company so registered and each protected cell account formed by each protected cell company that the payment of fees as detailed in schedule 5 is complied with within the deadlines set therein.

Citation

8. These Regulations may be cited as the Protected Cell Companies Regulations, 2005.

Made this 24th day of March, 2005

Alan Edden Huckle

GOVERNOR of Anguilla

SCHEDULE 1

(Section 2)

APPLICATION TO BE REGISTERED AS A PROTECTED CELL COMPANY TO OPERATE PROTECTED CELL ACCOUNTS

Notes

Complete all sections and attach supplementary sheets where appropriate.

Completed forms should be submitted to:-

FINANCIAL SERVICES COMMISSION

P.O. BOX 1575

THE VALLEY

ANGUILLA

Tel: 1 264 497 5881

Fax: 1 264 497 5872

And be accompanied by the non-refundable Application Fee set out in Schedule 5.

---

1. State the name of the company (which shall include the expression "Protected Cell Company" or "PCC")

2. Address of the registered office of the company.

3. Address of the applicant's place of business in Anguilla (if different from 2 above).

4. Name and address of the protected cell account representative and if different, the name and address of the person (s) (individual) resident in Anguilla who is/are authorized to represent the applicant and to accept service of documents on its behalf.

5. Address of any place (s) of business that the applicant may have outside of Anguilla.

6. Date of incorporation of the company, if already incorporated.

7. Please provide a statement verifying that the company has made provision to account for protected cell accounts in the manner as set out in section 12 of the Act. Explain any matters regarding the statement which you think the Commission should be aware of.

8. Has the company included a statement in its articles of incorporation that the company is a protected cell company? Please provide a copy of that statement or verification from the Companies Registry that it is so included.

9. State the proposed business of the protected cell company to be registered and of the subsequent protected cell accounts to be administered (if known at the time).

10. If the proposed business of the protected cell company and of the underlying protected cell accounts is insurance, mutual fund business or another business licensed by the Commission, the appropriate application form to conduct such business should be completed and submitted to the Commission, unless the proposed company already has the appropriate licence.

11. Where the company applying to become a protected cell company has conducted business prior to this application, Attachment A of Schedule 1 of these Regulations should also be submitted, together with the appropriate attachments.

Application is hereby made for the registration of the protected cell company specified above and the undersigned it is certified that all the particulars contained in the Application and in the documents accompanying it or otherwise furnished in the support hereof are true and correct and that any change to the information submitted will be communicated to the Commission forthwith.

Dated this day of 20

____

Name of Applicant

By its Director (s)

Signed ____________________

Attachment A to Schedule 1

To be completed by the applicant where the applicant company has conducted business prior to this application

Date:

Financial Services Commission

P.O. Box 1575

The Valley

Anguilla

Dear Sir

Re:

We confirm that the company has conducted business prior to its registration and we apply in the name of .... ("the company") to be registered as protected cell company under section 4 of the Protected Cell Companies Act, R.S. A. c. P107.

We hereby include the following information as attachments and make the following declarations.

i) The attached statutory declaration signed by ourselves which sets out a true and accurate description of the information required in section 3(2)(a)(i) through to section 3(2)(a)(v) of the Act.

ii) The attached evidence in writing that section 3(2) (b) of the Act has been complied with.

Please refer to sections 3(3) through to section 3(10) of the Act for further explanatory information on complying with the above declarations.

Yours faithfully,

____________________ ____________________

Director of the Company Director of the Company

____________________ ____________________

Signature Signature

Cc: Registrar

SCHEDULE 2

APPLICATION BY A PROTECTED CELL COMPANY TO BE AUTHORISED TO FORM A PROTECTED CELL ACCOUNT

Date:

Financial Services Commission

P.O. Box 1575

The Valley

Anguilla

Dear Sir/Madam:

Re:

We apply in the name of ....(“the Company”) to register the following protected cell account (s)

....

....

....

....

....

....

....

....

....

....

....

....

We hereby confirm that:

1. We have done all the requisite due diligence on the protected cell account owners and source of

funds in line with the Anti-money Laundering Regulations 2000, the Guidance Notes, and all

applicable laws currently in force in Anguilla.

2. The governing instrument which details the rights, interests and obligations of the owners of

the proposed protected cell account as specified in section 8(1) of the Act has been created and that it has been signed by all protected cell account owners.

3. Copies of any contract (s) which detail the rights, interests and obligations of counter parties as

specified in section 8(1) of the Act has/have been created and that the contract (s) has/have been signed by all relevant counter parties.

4. The above protected cell account (s) will not be undertaking insurance or mutual fund business

or any other business which would require a licence from the Commission.:

OR

5. The above protected cell account(s) will be undertaking ....business which is

an activity licensed by the Commission. An application to undertake such business is attached to this letter.

Application is hereby made for the authorization for the creation of the abovementioned protected cell account (s). The undersigned certify that all the particulars contained in the Application and in the documents accompanying it or otherwise furnished in the support hereof are true and correct and that any change to the information submitted will be communicated to the Commission forthwith.

Dated this day of 20

....

Name of Applicant

....

Director of Applicant

....

Signature

SCHEDULE 3

APPLICATION FOR APPROVAL OF A PROTECTED CELL ACCOUNT REPRESENTATIVE

Date:

Financial Services Commission

P.O. Box 1575

The Valley

Anguilla

Dear Sir,

Re:

We hereby apply for approval to appoint...

of *(state physical address)*..

as a protected cell account representative in Anguilla.

Yours faithfully,

....

Director of the Company

....

Signature

SCHEDULE 4

APPLICATION FOR DIRECTIONS OF THE COMMISSION TO MODIFY PROVISIONS OF THE ACT

Date:

Financial Services Commission

P.O. Box 1575

The Valley

Anguilla

Dear Sir,

Re: ("The name of the company")

We hereby apply in accordance with section 24 of the Act for the *(delete as appropriate)* disapplication/ modification of the following sections of the Act. *(delete as appropriate - Section 3, Section 5, Section 8 and or Section 12).*

We have attached a letter setting out the reasons why we believe these sections should be disapplied or modified.

Yours faithfully,

....

Director of the Company

....

Signature

SCHEDULE 5

(Section 30 of the Act)

FEES

Where the Protected Cell Company is applying for registration to conduct insurance business

Application fee $500

Licence fee $1,500

Annual fee $1,500

For the approval of each cell account $350

For the annual fee for each cell account $350 up to a maximum of $3,500 per annum

Where the Protected Cell Company is applying for registration to conduct mutual fund business

Application fee $350

Licence fee $350

For the approval of each cell account $350

For the annual fee for each cell account $350 up to a maximum of $3,500 per annum

Where the Protected Cell Company being registered is applying to conduct a non-licensed activity*

For the approval of each cell account $100 each for the first 10 cell accounts

For the annual fee for each cell account $100 each for the first 10 cell accounts

*For a protected cell company which conducts a non-licensed activity, a maximum of 15 cell accounts can be formed unless an exemption is granted by Commission upon receipt of a request in writing from the protected cell company directors or authorized agents. The first 10 cell accounts will be required to pay both an approval and annual fee. The remaining 5 cell accounts will be exempted from this requirement.

The normal registration/incorporation fee and annual filing fee for a company incorporated under the Companies Act 2000 is paid to the Registrar.

Date by which Annual Fees must be paid

The annual fee must be paid on or before every 31st of December during the currency of the registration of the protected cell company or approval of the protected cell account.

If the annual fee is not paid on or before every 31st December but is paid on or before the 31st March in the same year, a late payment penalty of 25% of the annual fee will be additionally payable.

If the annual fee is not paid on or before every 31st March in the same but is paid on or before the 30th June in the same year, a late payment penalty of 50% of the annual fee will be additionally payable.

If the annual fee is not paid on or before every 30th June in the same year, the protected cell company will be in breach of the Act and the Commission will invoke section 29 to have the company removed from the register. If the non-payment of the annual fee for an individual cell account is not paid by this date, the Commission will require the protected cell company to remove the protected cell account from within the terms of its governing instrument.

A NEW TELECOMMUNICATIONS REGULATORY FRAMEWORK FOR ANGUILLA

I. OBJECTIVES OF THIS POLICY

The objective of this Policy is to create an open market for the provision of facilities and services and conditions in Anguilla's telecommunications sector in support of the continued development of tourism, financial services and information-based services on the Island, including the processing and secure storage of all types of data, encryption, software development, web hosting and back office services in the information technology sector, and international finance, trust and company management, insurance, and company registration in the financial services and insurance sectors

While Anguilla can be proud of a highly developed and ubiquitous telecommunications network, it often comes up short of being able to satisfy the requirements for the reliable, high quality and affordable telecommunications of sufficient capacity to transmit the ever increasing quantities of information needed for the production of these quickly evolving servicesA

It is the Government's opinion that certain constraints, which impede the rapid development of these and other services, can be overcome by encouraging additional investment in telecommunications and by facilitating the entry of those who wish to invest in the telecommunications sector in AnguillaA

In order to achieve the objectives of this Policy, a central goal of the Government is to encourage the development and widespread use of broadband network infrastructureA

There are also important social reasons for promoting the development of telecommunications in Anguilla, which because of its limited resources is dependent on outside revenue sources to support education and health servicesA Reliable, good quality, efficient, and affordable telecommunications services are essential to ensure that all citizens and residents can access these essential social servicesA

Development of the information-based and financial services industries in Anguilla will require a highly specialized and trained workforceA With its limited resources Anguilla is unable to provide all the needed training on its ownA Implementation of high-speed data networks easily accessible to all citizens and residents will facilitate access to the best and most up-to-date training availableA

Improved communications and information technology will also make government more efficient through electronic processing, storage, and retrieval of information related to rates, taxes, licence fees, filing and copy fees, for court documents, citizens records, infrastructure planning and organization, budgets and expendituresA Improved communications and information technology will also give added support to the emergency measures currently in place to facilitate preparedness for hurricanes and other disastersA

The Government recognizes the important role that the British Government and the incumbent operator, Cable & Wireless, have played in the development and operations of telecommunications networks on the IslandA It is the sincere desire of the Government that Cable & Wireless continue to participate alongside other new operators and service providers in making Anguilla's information and communications technology sector the most developed and vibrant of the regionA

This Policy proposes a new institutional and legal structure, with conditions to ensure fair competition for the telecommunications sector in Anguilla and a timetable for its implementation

II. THE CURRENT LEGAL AND REGULATORY

FRAMEWORK FOR TELECOMMUNICATIONS IN ANGUILLA

The existing legal and regulatory framework for telecommunications in Anguilla is outdated and not appropriate for promoting the economic and social objectives of the Government and those sectors dependent on telecommunicationsA

The Telecommunications Act and Telecommunications Rules, which were adopted 50 years ago, regulate the various types of wireless equipment used by radio amateurs, ships, aircraft, and broadcastersA The Telecommunications Ordinance, which allows Cable & Wireless to establish telecommunications within the Island and authorizes the issuance of an external operating licence, was introduced in 1973, and the Telecommunication Operating Licence that was granted to Cable & Wireless dates back to 1988A Taken together, the present framework did not foresee nor does it adequately cater for modern telecommunications systems and servicesA Indeed, even the most recent of these documents, the licence granted to Cable & Wireless in 1988, did not foresee the provision of access to the Internet as a specific serviceA The current framework requires the licensing of anyone that establishes any telecommunications station, that installs and operates any telecommunications apparatus (including a simple telephone set), or that sells or leases any telecommunications apparatusA

The sector consists today of a single operator and service provider, Cable & Wireless (Anguilla), and a Government department, the Ministry of Transport and Communication, which sets policy, supervises the sector, and manages the radio frequency spectrumA

III. THE TELECOMMUNICATIONS NETWORK AND SERVICES IN ANGUILLA TODAY

There are currently in excess of 6,000 telephone customers connected to Cable & Wireless' fixed telephone network, which has been completely digitised since 1986A The penetration rate of over

50 main telephone lines per 100 population is similar to that of the developed economies and some other Caribbean countries such as Antigua, Barbados and StA Kitts & NevisA Indeed, penetration is continuing to increase and it is estimated that there are only about 350 households on the island that do not have a telephoneA The penetration rate is significantly higher than that of Jamaica and Trinidad & TobagoA The current exchange line capacity for the Island is about 8, 00A

Anguilla is currently connected to the outside world through a STM (565 Mbitls) spur on the Eastern Caribbean Fiber Optic System and through a 36 km microwave link to the 1 0 Mbitls Digital Eastern Caribbean Microwave System in SabaA When this link is taken out of service at the end of this year, it will be replaced by a new microwave system between Anguilla and StA MartinlStA MaartenA This will provide continued redundancy on Cable & Wireless' international networkA

Anguilla is not currently connected to the rest of the world via satelliteA

Cable & Wireless operates the only cellular mobile system in AnguillaA It is a TDMA system with a limited amount (10%) of AMPS capacity to serve the few remaining analogue customersA There are close to 2,200 subscribers, equivalent to a penetration of about 19 wireless telephone subscribers per 100 populationA This is up from about 7% penetration two years agoA This level is a third to one-half of that found in European countries that have similar fixed telephone penetration ratesA In July 2001 Cable & Wireless began to offer limited inbound and outbound roamingA Tariffs for the mobile wireless telephone service are based on the principle of Calling Party Pays (CPP); that is, the wireless telephone subscriber does not pay for incoming callsA The person making the call doesA

Cable & Wireless also offers various data services including frame relay and XA25 as well as paging, Internet and leased line servicesA It has over 1,000 Internet customers of which about 10 are connected to dedicated leased linesA

Weblinks has established a Wireless Local Area Network (WLAN) that supplies high speed Internet access to its customersA The WLAN operates in the 2A to 2A5 GHz frequency band and provides a 11 Mbitls access serviceA Weblinks had initially provided its customers access to the Internet through a 128 Kbitsls leased circuit connection provided by Cable & WirelessA This service was terminated by Cable & Wireless in February 2001A This termination and the legality of the Weblinks service are presently the subject of litigation between the partiesA This course of events is predicated on the lack of clarity in the legal and regulatory frameworkA Currently Weblinks provides access to the Internet by way of a leased microwave link service provided by a supplier located in StA MaartenA

There are three licensed radio broadcast stations and one television broadcasterA All Island Cable TV provides a cable television service using coaxial cable, which serves close to 3,000 subscribers or almost 100% of all households in AnguillaA

IV. THE TELECOMMUNICATIONS SECTOR IN ANGUILLA TODAY: THE IMPEDIMENTS TO GROWTH

IV.1 INTRODUCTION

As in other countries in the region and elsewhere, where there is only one supplier of telecommunications services, quality of service in Anguilla is perceived to require improvement to meet international standards, and prices, particularly for international services, are considered to be too highA Consumers have no choice and the incumbency of the operator is generally perceived to be contrary to best interests of the people and the economy of the IslandA This Policy seeks to establish a framework and propose legislation that will remedy this situationA

IV.2 Quality of Service

There is some dissatisfaction among business and residential customers with the quality of telecommunications services being provided by Cable & WirelessA There are complaints of poor sound quality in the fixed telephone service, long service outages in the data services including Internet, and lack of prompt response in repairing faultsA A particularly disturbing complaint concerns the difficulty that overseas clients of businesses in Anguilla have in completing calls to the IslandA It has not been determined if the source of this problem is with the originating operator, Cable & Wireless, or some transit pointA

IV.3 Investment

There is evidence that Cable & Wireless is not investing sufficiently to maintain and expand its network, and to introduce technologies to meet the growing demand for existing and new telecommunications servicesA The decline in the level of investment between 1995 and 2000 bears this outA

IV.4 Prices

One of the main objectives of this Policy is to create the means and the incentives for all users to be able to benefit from the technical advances and structural changes in the sector, which have caused a significant impact not only on the quality and quantity of services that are available but also on their pricesA While comparison of prices of individual service offerings can be misleading, the general perception of users in Anguilla is that the price of international services (for example, international switched telephone and leased circuit services) are high when compared to other countries with a competitive market environmentA Accordingly, the objective of this Policy is to reduce prices through the promotion of competition and by regulation, where competition alone is inadequate to lower pricesA

V. THE NEW LEGAL AND REGULATORY FRAMEWORK

V.1 Introduction

This Policy calls for the implementation of a new legal and regulatory framework that will create a stable, predictable, institutional environment for the development of telecommunications in AnguillaA The new framework will create a climate which is conducive to private investment and which will contribute to overall economic development of the territory and, in particular, to the development of financial services, tourism, and information technologyA It will create an open market for the provision of telecommunications networks and services under conditions of fair competitionA It will promote the development of telecommunications for the social, economic, and cultural wellbeing and the safety and security of all people living in AnguillaA It will ensure universal access to essential telecommunications services and will protect consumersA

Under the new framework, only public telecommunications networks and public telecommunications services that provide real time voice and data communications services will be subject to a licence and, therefore, to the conditions attached to those licencesA The provision of value added services will not require a licence or other authorization but may be subject to regulation if provided under conditions of exclusivity or dominance, nor will telecommunications networks and services for private or restricted use be regulated (except if they use spectrum or public rights of way)A The regulations may require, however, that certain types of service providers that are not otherwise subject to licensing or authorization register their services.

The new framework relies on an independent telecommunications regulatory capability (an independent regulator) with responsibility for supervising the proper functioning of the sector and ensuring that the Government's policy for the sector is implementedA This capability will be incorporated into the Public Utilities Commission ("PUC"), which is soon to be established by enactment of the Public Utilities Commission ActA

Given the limited resources available in Anguilla to supervise the telecommunications sector, it is intended that regulation will be light-handed and confined to the essential requirements to ensure the optimal implementation of this Policy and the smooth and efficient functioning of the sectorA The regulatory function will encompass the granting of licences and authorizations, and ensuring compliance with their terms and conditions; monitoring the sector and regulating to promote competition; protecting consumers; ensuring the fulfilment of and funding for universal service obligations; managing and administering the use of scarce resources such as frequencies, domain names and numbers; and preparing regulations as necessary to accomplish all of the foregoingA

The respective roles of the Minister and the PUC as they relate to these functions are described in Sections VA2 and VA3 belowA

Under the new regulatory framework, the development and implementation of the Government's telecommunications policies and the implementation of laws and regulations will be transparent; that is, any decisions, rules, guidelines and procedures affecting the sector will be developed through a process of open, public consultation, where all stakeholders will be able to express their views, with the assurance that these views are taken into accountA All such decisions, rules, guidelines and procedures will be set forth in writingA

The following sections describe the roles of the Minister and the regulator and the proposed policies with respect to licensing, convergence, interconnection, management of scarce resources, prices, consumer protection, quality of service, the terminal equipment market, and ensuring fair competitionA

V.2 Role of the Minister

The Minister responsible for the telecommunications sector will continue to develop sector policy, prepare legislation, manage the radio frequency spectrum, and administer numbers and other scarce resources in a nondiscriminatory, fair and transparent manner, and represent the international interests of the Government of AnguillaA

The Minister will not be able to interfere with the functions committed by legislation to the regulator, including decision-making as it relates to

supervision and regulation of the telecommunications sector in AnguillaA

V.3 Role of the Regulator

The newly established regulator will be responsible for implementing the Government's policy for the sector, issuing licences and authorizations, collecting licence and spectrum usage fees, ensuring compliance with terms and conditions of licences and authorizations, enforcing competition rules for the sector, protecting consumers, including the regulation of prices, where this in necessary, monitoring compliance with and, where necessary, establishing standards for telecommunications services and equipment, recommending policy to, and formulating legislative proposals for, the Minister, ensuring that universal service obligations are met and that Anguillians have easy and ready access to emergency communications, and ensuring that Anguilla's international obligations with respect to the sector are metA

The new legislation will ensure that the new regulator is able to function effectively and independentlyA

The new regulator will be independent of any operator, service provider or user of telecommunications services in Anguilla or elsewhereA It will also be independent of the MinisterA The Governor-in -Council will appoint and may remove members of the PUC and may issue written policy directions to the regulatorA

The head of the PUC will be a highly qualified professional with relevant experience, such as in regulation, law, economics or administration, and with an appointment based on his or her integrity and professional qualifications, and not on political or other allegiancesA It will be possible to remove the him or her for criminal reasons, incapacity or malfeasanceA The division of the PUC responsible for telecommunications will be staffed with suitable professionals and other support personnelA

The law will provide that the Commissioners of the Public Utilities Commission will be subject to strong and effective conflict of interest rules, including the requirement that they declare their interest, and that all senior officers also be subject to those rulesA The statute will provide that decisions of the regulator can be appealed to the High Court in certain circumstancesA The standard of review that the High Court will apply will be limited, such as where the regulator has made an error in law, or where the decision is not supported by the factsA Finally, the regulatory process will be completely transparent and, to the extent possible, the regulator will be financed independently of the Government's revenuesA

The regulator will also be empowered to arbitrate in disputes between users, on the one hand, and network operators and service providers, on the other, and among the latter if invited to do soA It will have the power to resolve disputes in cases where the parties involved in a dispute are unable to agreeA

The regulator's actions and proceedings applicable to the regulation of the sector including the regulations identified in this Policy will be developed in an open and transparent way and subject to public consultationA In addition, the PUC's relationship with the Minister and the Governor-in-Council generally will be openA This does not, however, mean that the regulator will divulge sensitive or commercially confidential information, which regulated network operators and service providers will have provided as part of their licensing conditionsA

The regulator's operating (and to the extent necessary) capital expenses will be funded through a levy on all licensed operators and service providersA This levy will be fair, proportionate, and will be kept to the minimum required for the functioning of the regulatorA

The funding formula and precise amounts to be imposed on each licensed operator and service provider will be established once the new regulatory framework has been put into placeA Funding obligations from the telecommunications sector will, to the extent possible, be limited to funding the administration and supervision activities of the PUC and the Ministry as they relate to telecommunicationsA In other words, regulatory activities of the PUC that are specific to other sectors, or that may fall under the responsibility of other government departments, will not be funded through licence fees imposed on regulated operators and providers in the telecommunications sectorA The Government measures that will set out the licence fee obligations will be subject to public consultation when they are being draftedA In practical terms, establishing an independent regulatory capability for telecommunications will require the new Public Utilities Commission to develop or hire a few telecommunications specialists, who will be supported by the cross-sectoral legal, economic, financial, and consumer protection specialists in the CommissionA It is also expected that the help of outside experts will be sought during peak work periods, especially during the transition period described below and during the early stages of liberalization of the telecommunications sectorA

The regulator's annual accounts will be publicly available and be subject to audit by the Auditor General and scrutiny by the GovernmentA

V.4 Licensing

The objective of this Policy is to promote market entry, competition and investment in a wide range of existing and future telecommunications servicesA In order to encourage maximum participation in the telecommunications sector in Anguilla there will be a simple, nondiscriminatory, transparent and light-handed licensing schemeA

A licence (concession) will be required to operate a public telecommunications network (whether terrestrial, mobile or satellite-based), to provide public telecommunications services that offer real time voice or data services , and to operate any system that uses the radio frequency spectrumA Licence holders will be subject to a certain number of conditions, which will be described in their licencesA These include, *inter alia*, the obligation to pay an annual licence fee based on a percentage of annual revenues in an amount needed to fund the regulator's operating and capital expenses on a pro rata basis to pay an annual spectrum usage fee according to a formula established by the Minister, to contribute to funding universal and emergency services, to refrain from anti-competitive behaviour, to provide services on a non-discriminatory basis to all users (including other service providers and end users, without regard to their use of the services being provided), to use scarce resources effectively and efficiently, to provide certain information to the regulator so as to enable it to supervise the sector, to make interconnection available to competing operators and service providers, and to protect consumers' rights and their confidentialityA

The number of licences that will be issued for any particular type of service may be limited if scarce resources, such as frequencies, are unavailable or for economic reasonsA

Licences to operate networks, provide services and for the use of spectrum will be granted by the regulatorA Licences will be for a fixed term and will be subject to renewal where the licence holder has not breached the terms and conditions of its licenceA

Licences issued for particular networks or services will be nondiscriminatory; that is similarly situated providers will have identical licence conditionsA Where a network or service provider is dominant, certain licence provisions will applyA No licence will be required to provide information or value-added servicesA Value-added services are services, other than public telecommunications services, that modify the form, content, code, protocol, or other similar aspect of the communication, restructure, add or supply information or permit user interaction with informationA

For the purposes of the new regulatory framework in Anguilla, access to the Internet, other online services, access to Web sites and similar services all will be considered as value-added services and, therefore, not subject to a licence; however, any entity in Anguilla offering voice services generally to the public, be it over the Internet or by other means, will be considered to be offering a public telecommunications service and, therefore, subject to a licence and the conditions incumbent on licensed service providersA

No licence will be required for the establishment of telecommunications networks and telecommunications services that are private or otherwise restricted, except to the extent that they may make use of the radio frequency spectrum or cross public rights-of-wayA

All licence holders will be subject to licence and annual spectrum usage fees, which will be established to cover only the costs of administering and regulating the sector and the spectrum used not bring in additional amounts for the TreasuryA In addition all licensed operators and service providers may be required to contribute to funding universal access and emergency servicesA All such fees and contributions will be will be fair, reasonable and proportionateA

V.5 Convergence

Voice, data and images are indistinguishable when transmitted over modern digital networksA This convergence of technologies of transmission has created certain regulatory uncertaintiesA For example, access to the Internet allows not only the transmission of e-mail messages or voice but also the downloading of recorded music and moviesA

The new framework created by this Policy recognizes this convergence of technologies, which allows previously distinct services to be delivered over the same medium, be it a simple telephone line, a coaxial or fibre optic cable connection to the home, a satellite link, or a fixed or mobile wireless linkA Under the new framework, the means by which this information is transmitted is covered, irrespective of the technological medium used; however, regulation of content is outside the scope of this Policy and this new framework, and falls under the jurisdiction of the Ministry responsible for information and broadcastingA

The new telecommunications framework will regulate radio and television over-the-air broadcasting only if and the extent to which these require the use of a scarce resource, namely, the radio frequency spectrumA Furthermore, under this framework, other content delivery services that may make use of other resources, such as public rights of way, may also be subject to some regulation under the new law or to the jurisdiction of the Planning DepartmentA

Convergence may also raise issues of fair competition where, for example, an operator of a telecommunications network merges with a provider of contentA To the extent that convergence or market concentration raise issues of potential or actual anti-competitive behaviour, they will be dealt with under the competition rules that will be developed separatelyA (See Section VA12 below)

V.6 Interconnection and Access to Infrastructure

Anyone who is licensed to operate a public telecommunications network or to provide public telecommunications services will be obliged to provide interconnection for the purposes of transmitting public telecommunications traffic between subscribers of different networksA

In the first instance, operators seeking to interconnect their networks will be required to negotiate interconnection arrangements on a commercial basisA The regulator will only intervene in these negotiations if invited to do so by the negotiating parties or if they are not able to come to agreement within a specified, reasonable time periodA The regulator will have the authority to resolve disputesA Interconnection agreements will be made publicA

In order to facilitate such negotiations and to ensure that interconnection is based on fair, non-discriminatory and transparent terms, the regulator will establish general rules, guidelines, conditions and procedures for interconnectionA These will be issued after a process of public consultation(s) governing interconnectionA

Prices for interconnection must be based only on the cost of providing the required interconnectionA Such cost-based pricing means that the operator providing interconnection services must base its prices on the proportionate costs of the elements of its network and services used by the operator seeking such interconnectionA

Any operator in a dominant position will be required to publish an offer that sets out the terms and conditions of interconnection to its networkA This offer must include all financial, technical, commercial and informational elements in a clear and unambiguous mannerA These terms and conditions will be available equally to all operators and service providers seeking to interconnect their networks and services with those of the dominant operator(s)A Dominance will be defined in the same way as it is defined for the purposes of price regulationA (See Section VA9 below)A

To ensure that new entrants will have access to facilities, that may be technically or commercially essential, operators (and public utilities) will be required to provide access to their infrastructure (such as towers, poles, conduits and other facilities) to other operators on the basis of fair and nondiscriminatory terms and conditions, and on a timely basisA Access may be denied only for specified reasons, such as safety, interference or lack of spaceA Disputes among operators may be mediated or be subject to arbitration by the regulatorA

V.7 Regulation of Scarce Resources

Scarce resources in the telecommunications sector include the electromagnetic spectrum and the space segment, numbers, rights-of-way and Internet domain namesA Fair, open and non-discriminatory treatment of these scarce resources is essential in supporting effective competitionA This is reflected, for example, in the World Trade Organization's principles pertaining to competition in the telecommunications sectorA

Accordingly, the Minister will be responsible for Anguilla's radio frequency spectrumA He will do this on behalf of and in co-operation with all users of spectrum in Anguilla, including broadcasters, public security, civil aviation, maritime transport, Government services and, of course, the telecommunications sectorA

Government Policy and implementing regulations will determine the specific process for allocating and licensing use of spectrumA The Government reserves the right to charge for the use of a national resource, such as spectrum, based on the value of that resource (as determined for example, by the price paid at auction)A

Access to public, rights-of-way for licensed operators and service providers will be made available through the Planning DepartmentA Any major infrastructure development, including the erection of towers and the laying of terrestrial and submarine cables on Anguillian territory, will be subject to applicable environmental regulationsA

Given that there are competing uses of scarce resources, all planning, policy, and regulations related to such resources will be developed through consultation with all stakeholdersA

It will also be the responsibility of the Minister to co-ordinate spectrum use regionally with the other countries and regional organizations, such as Eastern Caribbean Telecommunications Authority (ECTEL) and the Inter-American Telecommunications Commission (CITEL) of the Organization of American States, and globally within the framework of the International Telecommunication UnionA

The Minister will also ensure that there is transparent and nondiscriminatory access to space segment through any fixed or mobile satellite service, be it Intelsat or any other global and regional satellite systemA

The Minister will be responsible for administering Anguilla's (264) numbering plan in a fair, non-discriminatory and transparent manner; the numbering plan will be based on the numbering plan currently being used in Anguilla The Minister may assign this task to a neutral, non-governmental organisationA

As competition in the sector develops, the Government and the regulator will consider whether to require number portability, whereby any customer who wishes to change telecommunications providers is able to maintain the number that he or she has been assignedA The Government recognizes that number portability is an important goal that will facilitate competitionA The Government and the PUC will evaluate the possible future number portability requirement in light of economic and technical considerationsA

Anguilla's "Top Level Domain" (*.ai*) will be administered by the Minister, who may, however, assign this task to a neutral, non-governmental organisationA In any case the Minister will be responsible for ensuring that administration of this scarce resource is open, transparent and non-discriminatoryA

V.8 Consumer Protection

The legislation and implementing regulations and licences will require that public telecommunications network operators and service providers directly respond to complaints addressed to them by their customersA The regulator will monitor compliance with these requirements to ensure that these operators and service providers respond properly, adequately, and rapidly to each of these complaintsA The regulator will not normally be expected to intervene but will be available at the request of either party to either arbitrate or mediate in any such disputeA (See Section VA10 below)A

The regulator will publish guidelines on consumer protection, including the procedures to be followed in dealing with customer complaints and standards for customer contracts and billsA These will be developed in consultation with consumers, industry groups, operators and service providersA

V.9 Regulating Prices for Users

This Policy and the implementing legislation will establish the principle that prices for telecommunications networks and services, in an open and competitive market, will not be regulatedA Instead, they will be freely determined by the principles of supply and demand in the marketA Nevertheless, in the following limited circumstances, the regulator will be able to regulate prices: where there is only one operator or service provider supplying a particular facility or service (monopoly supplier); where an operator or service provider is in a dominant position as the supplier of the particular facility or service; where, in the regulator's opinion, there is no fair and open competition to establish prices; or where there is evidence of anti-competitive pricing practicesA

Increasingly, an incentive-based approach is being adopted internationally as the standard for regulating the prices of dominant providersA Such an approach places caps on certain prices, to assure end users that prices will not increase above a ceiling; instead, this approach generally requires certain price decreases, and allows a provider to retain profits if it increases its efficiencyA The Government and the regulator will consider this approach with respect to regulating those services of Cable & Wireless, where it is dominantA

The regulator will establish rules and procedures for regulating prices of networks and services in the above-described casesA This will be done through a process of public consultationA Prices for the supply of all regulated services and facilities will be publishedA

The regulator will also determine what constitutes dominance of a facility or service in a market for the purposes of regulating a dominant provider's pricesA One of several possible tests of dominance is whether an operator or service provider is able to raise prices without its customers moving away to other suppliersA In addition, as the telecommunications sector and particular services become competitive, an operator or service provider that had been dominant may no longer be soA The PUC, upon petition, may determine that it is no longer warranted to treat such entity as dominantA

The Government undertakes to determine the extent to which current prices for the supply of certain services and facilities are provided either below or above their cost of productionA It is the intention of the Government to allow prices, which do not reflect the cost of supplying the particular service or facility, to evolve toward cost in a transition period to full liberalization of the marketA This should prevent "cream skimming", where new entrants may be tempted to enter only market segments, where current prices are above costA This process of rate rebalancing, by which prices of services will be aligned more closely with costs, will need to take place before any price cap formula is fully implementedA

An analysis of prices being currently charged may reveal that Cable & Wireless is subsidizing the supply of certain non-profitable services and facilities with the benefits derived from market segments, where it is able to price its services or facilities above costA The regulator will determine to what extent it is currently not possible to supply these subsidized facilities and services on a commercial basis and develop a program to ensure that these are made available at affordable prices to the extent it is considered that they are essentialA (see Section VIA Universal Access to Communications, below)

V.1□ Quality of Service

As competition develops, it can be expected that competitors will improve their service to maintain and obtain customersA Nevertheless, because quality of service for licensed services is an important policy goal, ongoing oversight by the regulator will be importantA

Licensed service providers will be required to develop quality of service procedures and processes for handling of customer complaintsA

In addition the regulator will establish a list of quality of service performance indicators for all licensed servicesA

Public telecommunications network operators and service providers will be required to report regularly on their performance as measured against these indicatorsA The regulator will have the power to verify the reported results through independent investigationsA Performance indicators and results obtained will be published at regular intervalsA

Public telecommunications network operators and service providers will have to respond quickly and adequately to customer complaints related to quality of serviceA The regulator will have the power to intervene in disputes between the customer and an operator or service providers, if they are not able to satisfy the customer regarding his or her complaint in a reasonable time, or if the regulator is requested to intervene by either partyA

V.11 TERMINAL E□UI□MENT AND TECHNICAL STANDARDS

The market for the supply of any telecommunications equipment that can be attached to a public telecommunications network will be open under the new regulatory framework; however, there will be provisions to ensure that such terminal equipment is compatible with and does not pose a risk of harm to any public telecommunications network, that it is not harmful to the environment or to the health and safety of anyone and, if it uses the radio frequency spectrum, that it does not interfere with other users of the spectrumA

The new regulator will define standards for such equipmentA It will do so generally by adopting internationally approved standards, in consultation with the public telecommunications network operatorsA One approach is for the regulator to recognize approval of telecommunications equipment by other jurisdictions, such as the European Union or the United StatesA No licence or any permission will be required to install, own and operate any equipment that has been approved by the regulator for attachmentA There will, furthermore, be no restrictions on building, importing and selling such equipment as long as it has been approved by the regulator for attachment to a public telecommunications networkA

The Government intends to liberalise the ownership of inside wiringA The regulator will establish a procedure and timetable for such liberalisationA In addition, the provision of customer premises equipment will be unbundled from telecommunications servicesA

V.12 REGULATING TO ENSURE FAIR COM□ETITION

One of the main functions of the regulator will be to ensure that there is fair competition, that services and facilities are made available to consumers and interconnecting operators and service providers at cost-based prices, and that operators and service providers that are in a position of monopoly or dominance do not discriminate against existing or potential new competitors by subsidizing their competitive business with the benefits of their non-competitive businesses or through other anti-competitive practices, such as predatory pricingA

Other types of anti-competitive practices will also be proscribedA The regulator, for example, will have the principal responsibility for ensuring that operators and service providers comply with the law, applicable regulations and their licences, if anyA That is, operators and service providers may not take it upon themselves to determine whether a person to whom they are providing service is complying with applicable law and regulations; instead the regulator and the law enforcement authorities will have this responsibilityAA Accordingly, except for reasons relating to billing, public safety and other specified circumstances, an operator or service provider should not be able to disconnect the service of a competitor on the ground of non-compliance absent a determination of the regulatorA

Over time, particular networks and services will be subject to full competition, which will supplant the need for regulatory intervention to ensure fair competition or to protect the interests of usersA Accordingly, the new law will provide that the regulator may forbear from imposing regulatory obligations when and as they are no longer justifiedA

The Government will separately be developing a policy and legislation to ensure fair competition in all sectorsA

VI. UNIVERSAL ACCESS TO COMMUNICATIONS

The Government considers that it is a fundamental right of each citizen, resident, social and community organisation, and business establishment to have access to the basic means of communicationA This access has to be of good quality and affordable for all usersA

The definition of what constitutes basic means of communication will evolve with time but must today include basic voice telephone service, a free telephone directory and operator assisted information services, free emergency services access, and special voice telephone services for the handicappedA This list will be reviewed from time to time in consultation with all stakeholders and revised as necessaryA

Before implementation of the new regulatory framework the Government will undertake a study of the availability and prices of these essential services todayA Such a study will have three elementsA First, the Government will determine to what extent these services would continue to be unavailable, if they are currently unavailable, or would no longer be available, after the telecommunications market in Anguilla is liberalizedA Secondly, if the Government and, subsequently, the newly established regulator determine that not all these services would be universally available under the new regime for the sector at prices that people on the Island can afford, they will establish a program designed to ensure that anyone who wants and needs these services can obtain them at affordable pricesA Such a program will consist of methods of funding and realizing universal access, including by establishing obligations to provide universal services and determining a service provider of last resortA Thirdly, the Government will determine the costs associated with providing universal service based on appropriate costing methodologiesA

If it is determined that a funding mechanism does need to be established, all licensed public telecommunications network operators and service providers will be obliged to contributeA The new regulator will develop regulations establishing a fair, non-discriminatory, and proportionate formula for determining contributions to universal access for each licensed public telecommunications network operator and service providerA Contributions may be based on a percentage of gross revenues less settlement paymentsA

Regulations will also define the functioning of the universal access fund and how universal access objectives are to be achievedA The new regulator will have responsibility for administering the program of universal access to the extent that it is considered to be necessaryA Its administration will be transparentA

VII. REGIONAL COOPERATION

Development of the information and technology sector will not succeed in Anguilla if it is treated on the scale of the Island aloneA The Government recognizes that the economics of developing this highly capital intensive sector will require regional cooperation and that there is a need to share the few, very specialized human resources, which each of the small economies in the region can offerA Consequently, the Government will explore the possibility of developing cooperative arrangements initially with the other Overseas Territories to share the expertise and burden of regulating this highly specialized sectorA The goal is to agree with the Overseas Territories on a common regulatory framework for the information and communications technology sector and to establish a single regulatory capability, which can share the function of regulating the sector among all the territoriesA Indeed, the Government of Anguilla will welcome an initiative to have all Overseas Territories adopt common legislation designed to promote information and communication technologiesA

In addition, the new regulator will look into the possibility of entering into a cooperative agreement with the newly established Eastern Caribbean Telecommunications Authority (ECTEL) with the objective of cooperation, and harmonization of the regulatory framework of countries and territories in the Caribbean and of eventually joining this organizationA

VIII. IMPLEMENTATION

On approval of this Policy by the Executive Committee, the Government will initiate the process of drafting new legislation to give effect to this PolicyA Concurrently, the Government will be negotiating with Cable & Wireless with a view to reaching agreement on modifications required to its present licence in order that the Policy, once implementing legislation is adopted, can be put in place as quickly as possibleA

The Government will consult with interested stakeholders and provide an opportunity for public comment on the new legislationA The Government's timetable for implementation of this Policy is set out in Attachment AA

Liberalisation of the telecommunications sector in Anguilla will begin immediately on passage of the new law; however, in order to ensure a smooth transition from monopoly provision of telecommunications services to full competition, there will be a period of transition of one year to permit:

• • prices for services and facilities to be adjusted so that they are cost-based in order to minimize the possibility of cross-subsidization of competitive services with potential benefits gained from services being provided under non-competitive circumstancesA The Government undertakes to carry out a study of prices of services and facilities to determine the extent to which they may currently be above or below their cost of productionA It will subsequently negotiate with Cable & Wireless a formula for adjusting or re-balancing of prices, if this should prove necessary;

• • the putting into place of an adequate regulatory framework necessary for competition to workA This includes required provisions for interconnection of competing networks and services (including all pricing, technical, accounting and informational aspects), authorization of the existing operator and new entrants, tariffs and quality of service regulations, and essential regulations pertaining to the use of scarce resources such as frequencies and numbersA During this period, the Government will establish the required telecommunications regulatory capability within the PUC and give the Minister the power he requires to fulfil his duties under the new legislationA

• • the Government to determine the extent to which the provision of essential services will be affected by the introduction of competition and the liberalization of prices and to design a program to ensure universal access is available to these services at affordable pricesA

On passage of the new law, it will be possible for anyone, including the incumbent, to provide all services and networks that do not require licences, including the establishment of private networks, the provision of value added services, access to the Internet, and the provision, acquisition and installation of terminal equipmentA In addition, public data networks will be permitted to operate under a provisional licence upon the passage of the new lawA Finally, international satellite-based mobile service providers will be licensed to provide service as of the effective date of the new lawA

Any entity that is operating a network or providing a service under the current legal and regulatory framework that would require a licence under the new framework will be able to operate that network and provide that service until it has a licence under the new regime, or until a licence is finally deniedA During a transitional period, existing operators and service providers, that will be required to obtain a licence under the new framework will be given an opportunity to file applications; However, During this one-year transition period only Cable & Wireless will be able to operate a public telecommunications network for voice services or offer a public telecommunications voice service, except as provided in the last sentence of the preceding paragraphA

The Government will also confirm any current licences for the operation of public telecommunications networks and the provision of services during the transition period.

The Government will, after passage of the new law, open a tender process for a second cellular operator licenceA This licence will permit the licensee to offer both domestic and off-Island services for its customers immediately; until the end of the one-year transition, the licensee will be required to offer off-Island services only by using the international facilities of Cable & Wireless, which will be required to make its services available at wholesale ratesA

In connection with the transition to competition in international services, the regulator will have to develop and implement the mechanism by which subscribers will chose their provider for these international services, when there is more than oneA In addition, such rules will have to ensure that any domestic provider of telecommunications services provides equal access to all competing operators and service providers, who offer an international serviceA

Anyone wishing to provide a public telecommunications network or service will be free to apply for a licence; the Government may, however, initially limit the number of licences it will issue for the use of scarce resources such as the radio frequency spectrumA Applications can be submitted before the end of the transition period to full liberalization; however, new entrants who are granted licences may not begin operations or provide services before the end of that periodA

During the period of transition and before the new regulator is fully functional, the Government will do everything to ensure a smooth passage to a fully liberalized telecommunications marketA In particular, the Government will monitor the sector to ensure that no providers engage in anti-competitive practices that would inhibit any new operator or service provider from entering the marketA It will also ensure that all the necessary implementing regulations are in place before the market is fully liberalizedA These include regulations governing interconnection, the funding and provision of universal services, prices and rate rebalancing (where required), licensing, cost accounting and internal, public comment and other administrative proceduresA To engage in this activity, the Government will, to the extent, necessary, seek outside assistance and supportA

ANGUILLA TRUST COMPANIES AND OFFSHORE BANKING ACT

An Act to make provision for the regulation of trust companies and offshore banking in Anguilla

ENACTED by the Legislature of Anguilla

PART 1 PRELIMINARY PROVISIONS

1. (1) In this Act —

Interpretation

"attorney-at-law" means an attorney admitted to practice before the Eastern Caribbean Supreme Court in Anguilla;

"auditor" means a person who is in good standing as a member of an association of chartered or public accountants or other similar body approved by the Governor as a reputable auditing association;

"authorized agent" means an authorized agent referred to in section 20;

"bank" means a person carrying on banking business

"banking business" means -

(a)

the business of receiving funds through the acceptance of money deposits payable on demand or after a fixed period or after notice or any similar operation through the frequent sale or placement of bonds, certificates, notes or other securities, and the use of such funds either in whole or in part for loans or investment for the account and the risk of the person doing such business; and

(b)

any other activity prescribed by the Governor as constituting customary banking practice that a bank engaged in activities described in paragraph (a) may additionally be authorized to do;

"company" means a company incorporated or continued under the Companies Ordinance, 1994; "Court" means the High Court; "dollar" or "$" means a dollar in the currency of the United States of America;

"domestic bank" means a person holding a licence under the Banking Ordinance, 1991; "foreign company" means a foreign company registered under Division C of Part III of the Companies Ordinance, 1994;

"foreign regulatory authority" means an authority in a jurisdiction outside Anguilla which exercises functions corresponding or similar to those exercised by -

(a)

the Inspector appointed under this Act;

(b)

the Inspector of Company Managers appointed under the Company Management Ordinance, 1994; or

(c)

the Registrar of Insurance appointed under the Insurance Act, 1968;

“Inspector” means the Inspector of Offshore Banks and Trust Companies appointed under section 30; “international business company” means a company incorporated or continued under

the International Business Companies Ordinance, 1994. “offshore banking business” means banking business carried on in or from within

Anguilla in a currency other than Eastern Caribbean dollars with a non-resident of Anguilla. “offshore banking licence” means a licence issued under section 6; “prescribed” means prescribed by regulations made by the Governor under section 38; “trust” means trust as defined in the Trusts Ordinance; “trust business” means the business of acting as trustee of property; “trust company licence” means a licence issued under section 12;

(2)

Subject to subsection (3), for the purposes of this Act, the following are regarded as non-residents of Anguilla -

(a)

an international business company;

(b)

a company or an LLC formed or continued under the Limited Liability Company Ordinance, 1994 that, at the relevant time does not engage in any revenue generating activities in Anguilla.

(3)

An LLC or a company shall not be regarded as engaging in a revenue generating activity in Anguilla in respect of -

(a)

any offshore banking business conducted with it by a person holding an offshore banking licence; or

(b)

any activity which the Governor may prescribe as exempt from subsection (2)(b)(ii).

(4) For greater certainty -

(a)

a company;

(b)

an international business company; or

(c)

an LLC formed or continued under the Limited Liability Company Ordinance, 1994;

that carries on banking business or trust business outside Anguilla carries on banking business or trust business, as the case may be, from within Anguilla.

2. (1) This Act does not apply to the Caribbean Development Bank.

Application

(2) For greater certainty

(a)

a person, including a domestic bank, that holds an offshore banking licence-

(i)

is exempt from the provisions of the Banking Ordinance, 1991 in respect of offshore banking business; and

(ii)

is subject to the provisions of the Banking Ordinance, 1991 in respect of banking business other than offshore banking business.

(b)

a person holding an offshore banking licence or a trust company licence, other than a domestic bank, does not require a licence under the Trades,

Businesses, Occupations and Professions Licensing Ordinance 1977 in respect of its offshore banking or trust business.

PART 2 OFFSHORE BANKING BUSINESS

In this Part -

Interpretation "licence" means an offshore banking licence; "licensee" means a person holding an offshore banking licence.

(1) No person, including a domestic bank, shall carry on offshore banking

Licence required

business unless he holds a licence that is not suspended under section 16.

(2) A person who contravenes subsection (1) commits an offence and is liable on conviction to a fine of $25,000, to a term of imprisonment of two years or to both.

5. (1) A company or a foreign company may apply to the Governor for a licence.

Application for licence

(2) An application under subsection (1) must -

(a)

contain the information and be in the form prescribed; and

(b)

be accompanied by the documentation prescribed.

6. If the Governor is satisfied -

Issuance of licence

(a)

that an applicant is

(i)

a fit and proper person, and

(ii)

is qualified to carry on offshore banking business;

(b)

that the persons having any share or other interest, whether legal or equitable, in the applicant and its directors and officers are fit and proper persons to have an interest in or be concerned with the management of a licensee, as the case may be;

(c)

that the applicant intends, if issued with a licence, to commence offshore banking business;

Restrictions on business that may be carried on by licensee

Maintenance of Capital

(d)

that the applicant satisfies the requirements of this Act in respect of the application and will, upon issuance of the licence, be in compliance with this Act in respect of licensing; and

(e)

that issuing the licence is not against the public interest;

he may issue a licence to the applicant subject to such terms and conditions as he thinks fit.

7. A licensee that is not a domestic bank may not -

(a)

invest in any asset that represents a claim on any person resident in Anguilla except a claim resulting from—

(i)

a transaction with another licensee, or

(ii)

the purchase of bonds or other securities issued by the Government, a statutory corporation or a company in which the Government is the sole or majority beneficial owner; or

(b)

without the written approval of the Governor carry on any offshore banking business other than that for which the licence has been issued.

8. (1) A licensee, other than a domestic bank, must ensure that its paid up share capital is maintained in an amount not less than $250,000, or the equivalent in another currency, or such greater sum as may be ordered under subsection (2).

(2)

The Governor may, on the recommendation of the Inspector, order a licensee to increase its fully paid up capital to such greater amount as he may determine having regard to the nature of the offshore banking business being, or sought to be, undertaken.

(3)

A company that contravenes subsection (1) commits an offence and is liable on conviction to a fine of $25,000.

(4)

Where an offence under this section is committed by a company, a director or officer of the company who knowingly authorized, permitted or acquiesced in the commission of the offence also commits an offence and is liable on conviction to a fine of $25,000, to a term of imprisonment for 6 months or to both.

PART 3 TRUST BUSINESS

In this Part -

Interpretation "licence" means a trust company licence; "licensee" means a person holding a trust company licence.

(1) Subject to subsection (2), no person shall carry on trust business in or from

Licence required

within Anguilla unless he holds a licence that is not suspended under section 16.

(2) Subsection (1) does not apply to

(a)

a domestic bank that holds an offshore banking licence that is not suspended; and

(b)

an attorney-at-law in so far as he is engaged in trust business solely in the practice of law.

(3) A person who contravenes subsection (1) commits an offence and is liable on conviction to a fine of $25,000, to a term of imprisonment of two years or to both.

11. (1) A company, a foreign company or, subject to section 13(2), an international

Application for

business company may apply to the Governor for a licence. licence

(2) An application under subsection (1) must -

(a)

contain the information and be in the form prescribed; and

(b)

be accompanied by the documentation prescribed.

12. If the Governor is satisfied -

Issuance of licence

(a)

that an applicant is

(i)

a fit and proper person, and

(ii)

is qualified to carry on trust business;

(b)

that the persons having any share or other interest, whether legal or equitable, in the applicant and its directors and officers are fit and proper persons to have an interest in or be concerned with the management of a licensee, as the case may be;

(c)

that the applicant intends, if issued with a licence, to commence carrying on trust business in or from within Anguilla;

(d)

that the applicant satisfies the requirements of this Act in respect of the application and will, upon issuance of the licence, be in compliance with this Act in respect of licensing; and

(e)

that issuing the licence is not against the public interest;

he may issue a licence to the applicant subject to such terms and conditions as he thinks fit.

13. (1) A licence shall be in one of the following classes:

Class and extension of licence

(a)

a general trust company licence; or

(b)

a restricted trust company licence.

(2) A general trust license must not be issued to an international business company.

(3)

A restricted trust company licence is subject to the restriction that the licensee does not undertake trust business on behalf of persons other than those listed in the undertaking accompanying the application for the licence or any amendment to the list filed with the Inspector.

(4)

An applicant for a general trust company licence may apply for the licence to extend to a wholly owned subsidiary of the applicant.

(5)

An application under subsection (4) must be made in writing to the Governor accompanied by -

(a)

the name of the subsidiary;

(b)

documentary proof sufficient to establish that the subsidiary is wholly owned by the applicant;

(c)

a description of the type of trust business being, or to be, carried on by the subsidiary; and

(d)

any other information or documentation that the Governor considers necessary.

(6)

The Governor may, upon granting a general trust company licence to the applicant, extend the licence to include any subsidiary referred to in subsection (4), subject to such terms and conditions as he thinks fit.

14. (1) A licensee, other than a domestic bank, must ensure that its paid up share

Maintenance of

capital is maintained in an amount not less than $250,000, or the equivalent in another Capital currency, or such greater sum as may be ordered under subsection (2).

(2) The Governor may, on the recommendation of the Inspector

(a)

order a licensee to increase its fully paid up capital to such greater amount as he may determine having regard to the nature of the trust business being, or sought to be, undertaken; or

(b)

in respect of a licensee holding a restricted trust licence, permit the licensee to maintain a lower amount of share capital than that specified in subsection (1).

(3)

A company that contravenes subsection (1) commits an offence and is liable on conviction to a fine of $25,000.

(4)

Where an offence under this section is committed by a company, a director or officer of the company who knowingly authorized, permitted or acquiesced in the commission of the offence also commits an offence and is liable on conviction to a fine of $25,000, to a term of imprisonment for 6 moths or to both.

PART 4

MATTERS APPLICABLE TO TRUST BUSINESS AND OFFSHORE BANKING BUSINESS

15. In this Part -

Interpretation

“licence” means an offshore banking licence or a trust company licence ;

“licensed business” means the trust business or offshore banking business, as the case may be, that the licensee is licensed to carry on;

“licensee” means a person holding an offshore banking licence and a person holding a trust company licence.

REVOCATION, SUSPENSION AND SURRENDER OF LICENCE AND VARIATION OF TERMS OF LICENCE

16. (1) The Governor may at any time revoke or suspend a licence if it appears to him -

Revocation or suspension of licence

(a)

that the licensee -

(i)

is not a fit and proper person or is not qualified to carry on the licensed business;

(ii)

is carrying on the licensed business in a manner detrimental to the public interest or to the interests of any of its creditors or, in the case of a holder of an offshore banking licence, of any depositors or, in the case of a holder of a trust company licence, of any beneficiary of a trust of which it is a trustee;

(iii) is insolvent;

(iv)

has contravened or is in contravention of any provision of this Act or of the Anti-Money Laundering Regulations, 2000;

(v)

has breached or is in breach of any term or condition of its licence;

(vi)

has ceased to carry on the licensed business;

(vii) has furnished the Governor or the Inspector with any false, inaccurate or misleading information whether on making application for a licence or subsequent to the issue of the licence; or

(b)

that any person having a share or interest in the licensee, whether equitable or legal, or any director or officer of the licensee is not a fit and proper person to have an interest in or to be concerned with the management of a licensee, as the case may be.

(2)

The Governor shall revoke a licence if the licensee fails to pay the prescribed annual fee together with the appropriate late payment penalty in full on or before 31st March in the year following the year in which the annual fee was due.

(3) Subject to subsection (4), the period of suspension of a licence under subsection

(1)

shall not exceed 30 days.

(4)

If it is satisfied that is in the public interest to do so, the Court may, on the application of the Inspector, extend the period of suspension of a licence under this section for one or more further periods not exceeding 30 days each.

17. (1) If a licence is or is about to be suspended or revoked under section 16, the

Appointment of Inspector may apply to the Court - adminstrator by the Court

(a)

for the appointment of an administrator to take over and manage the licensed business then carried on by the licensee or carried on by it immediately prior to the revocation or suspension of its licence, as the case may be; or

(b)

for an order that the licensee be wound up by the Court or subject to the supervision of the Court under the Companies Ordinance, 1994.

(2) An application made under subsection (1) may be made on an ex parte basis.

(3) On an application made under subsection (1), the Court may make such order as it considers necessary to safeguard -

(a)

in the case of a holder of an offshore banking licence, the interests of any depositors; or

(b)

in the case of a holder of a trust company licence, the interests of any beneficiary of a trust of which the licensee is a trustee.

(4) Without limiting subsection (3), an order made under that subsection may -

(a)

grant an administrator the powers of a licensee under this Ordinance;

(b)

require the administrator to provide security;

(c)

fix the remuneration of the adminstrator;

(d)

require such persons as it considers necessary to appear before the Court for the purposes of giving information concerning the licensed business; and

(e)

make any order that could be made by a Magistrate on an application made under section 31.

18. (1) A licensee that ceases to carry on the licensed business may apply to the

Surrender of Governor to surrender its licence. licence

(2)

An application under subsection (1) must -

(a)

contain the information and be in the form prescribed; and

(b)

be accompanied by the documentation prescribed.

(3)

If the Governor is satisfied that

(a)

the licensee has ceased to carry on the licensed business and that

(i)

in the case of a person holding an offshore banking licence, the licensee has repaid all deposits accepted by it; or

(ii)

in case of a person holding a trust company licence, the licensee has properly distributed, transferred or otherwise dealt with all trust assets that were held or administered by it; or

(b)

if the licensee is being wound up, that it is solvent and is able on demand -

(i)

in the case of a company holding an offshore banking licence, to repay all deposits accepted by it; or

(ii)

in the case of a person holding a trust company licence, to properly distributed, transfer or otherwise deal with all trust assets that are or were held or administered by it;

the Governor may approve the surrender.

(4) In the case of a surrender of a licence under subsection (3)(b), the Attorney General or the Inspector may apply to the court for an order that the licensee be wound up by the court or subject to the supervision of the court under the Companies Ordinance, 1994.

19. The Governor may, upon giving reasonable notice to the licensee -

Variation of terms or conditions of licence

(a)

vary or cancel any terms or conditions imposed on the issue of a licence or under the extension of a licence under section 13(4); or

(b)

impose new terms or conditions.

PRINCIPAL OFFICE AND AUTHORIZED AGENT

20. (1) A licensee must have -

Principal office and authorized agent

(a)

a principal office in Anguilla; and

(b)

two authorised agents who comply with subsection (2).

(2) Each authorised agent -

(a)

must be an individual resident in Anguilla; and

(b)

must, prior to his appointment

(i)

have consented in writing to act as an authorised agent; and

(ii)

be approved in writing as an authorised agent by the Inspector.

(3)

The licensee must appoint its first authorised agents not later than the day of the issue of its licence and shall forthwith notify the Inspector that the approved appointments have been made.

(4)

A licensee may not change the address of its principal office or appoint an authorised agent without the prior written approval of the Inspector.

(5)

The Inspector in his discretion may in writing revoke an approval given under this section.

(6)

Subject to subsection (7), a licensee that contravenes this section commits an offence and is liable on summary conviction

(a)

in respect of a breach of subsection (1) to a fine of $25,000;

(b)

in respect of a breach of subsection (3) or subsection (4), to a fine of $10,000;

(7)

A licensee does not contravene subsection (1) when an authorized agent dies or resigns or has his approval revoked under subsection (5) if

(a) the licensee forthwith submits to the Inspector for approval the name of a person to replace the authorised representative; and

(b)

appoints an authorised agent forthwith after he is approved; so long as the licensee has at least one authorised agent.

(8) This section does not apply to a domestic bank.

(9)

The authorized agents of a licensee shall reside in Anguilla and in their capacity as representatives of the licensee ensure compliance with any statutory requirements under this Act.

21. (1) A licensee must not operate a branch, agency or office outside Anguilla

Operation outside without the prior approval of the Inspector. Anguilla

(2) A licensee who contravenes subsection (1) commits an offence and is liable on summary conviction to a fine of $25,000.

Restrictions on use of certain terms

Change of name

RESTRICTIONS ON AND CHANGE OF NAMES

22. (1) No person other than a licensee shall, except with the authority of the Governor or under the authority of any other written law -

(a)

use, whether in the name under which he is registered or in the description or title under which he carries on business in or from within Anguilla and whether in English or in any language -

(i)

the words "bank", "savings" or "trust" or any derivative; or

(ii)

any word that, in the opinion of the Governor, suggests trust business or offshore banking business; or

(b)

make any representation in any document or in any other manner that is likely to suggest that he is carrying on trust business or offshore banking business.

(2) The Governor may, by written notice, require a licensee who carries on offshore banking business or trust business under a name that is-

(a)

identical to that of any other person, whether within or outside Anguilla, or which so nearly resembles that name as to be likely to deceive;

(b)

likely to suggest falsely the patronage of or connection with some person whether within or outside Anguilla; or

(c)

likely to suggest falsely that he has special status in relation to or derived from the Government or has the official approval of, or acts on behalf of, the Government or of any of its departments or officials,

forthwith to change the name and in default of compliance may revoke the licence.

(3)

A person who contravenes subsection (1) commits an offence and is liable on summary conviction to a fine of $25,000, to a term of imprisonment of 1 year or to both.

(4)

A licensee who fails to change his name within 7 days of the date of receipt of a written notice under subsection (2) commits an offence and is liable on summary conviction to a fine of $10,000 and to a daily default fine of $500.

A licensee shall not change its name without the prior written approval of the Inspector.

TRANSFER OF SHARES AND APPOINTMENT OF DIRECTORS

(1) No share or other interest, whether legal or equitable, in a licensee shall be

Transfer of shares

issued, transferred or otherwise disposed of without the prior written approval of the Governor.

(2) The Governor may exempt any company from the provisions of subsection (1), subject to such terms and conditions as he thinks fit.

25. (1) A licensee shall have not less than two directors.

Number and appointment of directors

(2)

Subject to subsection (3), no appointment of a director or other senior officer of a licensee shall be made without the prior written approval of the Inspector.

(3)

Subsection (2) does not apply to a licensee that is exempted in writing by the Inspector.

(4)

An exemption under subsection (3) may be granted subject to such terms and conditions as the Inspector considers fit and may be revoked by the Inspector in writing.

26. Sections 24 and 25 do not apply to a domestic bank.

Exemption for domestic bank

OBLIGATIONS OF LICENSEE

27. (1) A licensee shall pay the prescribed annual fee on or before 31st December of

Annual fee

each year.

(2)

If a licensee fails to pay the annual fee in full on or before 31st December in any year, it is liable to pay a late payment penalty calculated as follows -

(a)

if the annual fee is paid in full on or before 15th January of the following year, $100

(b)

if the annual fee is paid in full after 15th January but on or before 14th February of the following year, 25% of the annual fee; or

(c)

if the annual fee is not paid in full on or before 14th February of the following year, 50% of the annual fee.

(3)

A licensee that fails to pay the prescribed annual fee on or before 31st December in any year is deemed not to have contravened subsection (1) if -

(a) he pays the annual fee and the appropriate late payment penalty in full on or before 31st March of the following year; and

Display of licence

Accounts

Inspector

(b) at the time of payment his licence is not revoked or suspended.

(4) The annual fee and any late payment penalty payable by a licensee remains payable notwithstanding that his licence has been suspended.

A licensee must prominently display its licence on the premises where its licensed business is carried on.

(1) Every licensee shall have its accounts audited by an auditor annually or at such other periods as the Governor or the Inspector may require.

(2)

The licensee shall forward the audited accounts to the Inspector within six months from the end of the financial year of the licensee unless prior written approval for an extension has been granted by the Inspector.

(3)

Where a licensee changes its auditor, the licensee shall, when required by the Inspector, authorize the former auditor to disclose the circumstances that gave rise to the change, and when so authorized, the auditor shall disclose such circumstances.

ADMINISTRATION

30. (1) There is established the office of Inspector of Trust Companies and Offshore Banks as a public office to which appointments are to be made in accordance with section 66 of the Constitution of Anguilla.

(2)

Under the general supervision of the Governor, the Inspector is responsible for ensuring the proper administration of this Act.

(3) The functions of the Inspector include -

(a)

monitoring trust business and offshore banking business;

(b)

advising the Governor on all matters concerning the regulation and supervision of trust business and offshore banking business;

(c)

examining and evaluating all applications for

(i)

trust company licences, and

(ii)

offshore banking licences, and making recommendations to the Governor concerning such applications;

(d)

examining and, if he thinks fit, reporting to the Governor upon returns made and documents filed by licensees under this Ordinance;

(e)

where he thinks fit or when required by the Governor, the examination in such manner as he considers necessary, the affairs or business of any licensee for the purpose of satisfying himself that the provisions of this Act are being complied with and that the licensee is in a sound financial position and is carrying on its business in a satisfactory manner; and

(f)

the provision of assistance in the investigation of any offences under the laws governing banking and other commercial activities committed by the licensee, his director agent or officers;

(g)

reporting to the Governor regarding the examination of any documents produced to him in the course of the performance of his functions.

(4)

For the purposes of performing his functions under subsection (3), the Inspector shall be entitled -

(a)

to have access to and take copies of such books, records, vouchers, documents, cash and securities and all other financial instruments of any licensee;

(b)

to request such information, matter or thing from any person who, he has reasonable grounds to believe, is carrying on offshore banking business or trust business in contravention of any part of this Ordinance; and

(c)

to call upon the authorized agent, or manager, of the licensee for such information or explanation,

as the Inspector may reasonably require for the purpose of enabling him to perform his functions under this Ordinance.

(5)

Where the Inspector is satisfied that there is *prima facie* evidence of illegal activity carried on by any licensee and for any reason is unable to obtain the information required from such licensee the Inspector may apply to the Magistrate for an order of the Magistrate directing such licensee to provide information to the Inspector, as appropriate, as to -

(a)

the name and title of an account of a depositor or settlor;

(b)

the name and title of a trust; or

(c)

any other matter he may require.

(6)

Where the Magistrate is satisfied that the Inspector has adduced prima facie evidence of illegal activity carried on by a licensee and that the Inspector is unable to obtain

Power of search

such information as is referred to in subsection (5), the Magistrate shall, on application made by the Inspector, issue an order directing the licensee to provide to the Inspector such information.

(7)

Any licensee who contravenes the order of the Magistrate commits an offence and is liable to a fine of $25,000, to a term of imprisonment for one year or to both.

(8)

With the written approval of the Governor, the Inspector may authorize in writing any person to assist him in the performance of his functions under this Act.

(9)

If the Magistrate is satisfied by information on oath given by the Inspector or by a person authorized by the Governor to assist the Inspector that there is reasonable ground for suspecting that an offense against this Ordinance has been or is being committed by a licensee the Magistrate shall, on application made by the Inspector, issue an order authorizing him to take such action as the Magistrate may consider necessary in the interest of the depositors or of the beneficiaries of any trust or other creditors of the licensee and to preserve any assets of the licensee.

31. (1) If the Magistrate is satisfied by information on oath or affirmation given by the Inspector or by a person authorized by him -

(a)

that a licence has been revoked or suspended under section 16;

(b)

that there are reasonable grounds for believing that an offence under this Act has been or is being committed and that evidence of the commission of the offence is to be found on any premises or in any vehicle, vessel or aircraft specified in the information; or

(c)

that any document that ought to have been produced under section 30(4) and has not been produced is to be found at any premises or in any vehicle, vessel or aircraft specified in the information,

he may grant a search warrant authorizing the Inspector, together with any other person named in the warrant, to enter the premises or any premises upon which the vehicle, vessel or aircraft may be located at any time within one month from the date of the warrant and to search the premises or the vehicle, vessel or aircraft.

(2)

The Inspector or any other person authorized by a warrant to search any premises or any vehicle, vessel or aircraft

(a)

may search every person who is found in or whom he has reasonable grounds to believe to have recently left, or to be about to enter, those premises or that vehicle, vessel or aircraft; and

(b)

may seize any document found on the premises or in the vehicle, vessel or aircraft that he has reasonable grounds for believing ought to have been produced under section 30(4).

(3)

Where under this section a person has any power to enter any premises or a vehicle, vessel or aircraft, he may use such force as is reasonably necessary for the purpose of exercising that power.

32. Where a licensee or a person who has at any time been a licensee is being wound

Attorney General up voluntarily, the Attorney General may, when being requested by the Inspector, apply may apply to Court to the Court for leave to intervene on behalf of any interested party if he considers that the winding up is not being conducted in the best interests of its depositors, the beneficiaries of any trust, or other creditors and the Court shall make such order as it shall consider appropriate.

MISCELLANEOUS

33. (1) The Inspector may by written notice require a licensee to effect a policy of

Insurance insurance with an approved insurance company and maintain it.

(2) The policy of insurance shall insure against

(a)

losses arising out of claims of negligence or breach of duty by the licensee or by an employee;

(b)

the dishonesty of employees or of the licensee;

(c)

loss of documents; and

(d)

such other risks as the Inspector may stipulate,

in such amount and of such nature as the Inspector determines having due regard to the nature and type of business carried on by the licensee.

(3)

The licensee shall effect the policy of insurance within the time specified in the notice or any extension of the time given by the Inspector.

(4) The licensee shall without delay give notice to the Inspector in writing if -

(a)

he is unable to obtain insurance as required by the Inspector; or

(b)

he ceases to maintain the insurance.

(5)

A licensee who contravenes this section commits an offence and is liable on conviction to a fine of $10,000 or to a term of imprisonment of one year or to both.

34. (1) For the purposes of this section, "protected person" means

Confidentiality

(a)

a person who has applied for a licence under this Ordinance;

(b)

a licensee;

(c)

a customer of a licensee; and

(d)

a company managed by a licensee.

(2)

Subject to subsection (3), the Inspector, a person acting under the Inspector's authority, and a person appointed by the Governor under section 30(7) to assist the Inspector must not disclose to any person information concerning the affairs of a protected person that he has acquired in the course of his duties or in the exercise of his functions under this Ordinance.

(3) Subsection (2) does not apply to a disclosure

(a)

required or permitted by any Court of competent jurisdiction in Anguilla;

(b)

to the Governor;

(c)

to any person for the purpose of discharging any duty or exercising any power under this Ordinance;

(d)

in respect of the affairs of a protected person made with the consent of that person;

(e)

if the information disclosed is or has been available to the public from any other source;

(f)

where the information disclosed is in a summary or in statistics expressed in a manner that does not enable the identity of a protected person to which the information relates to be determined; or

(g)

made by the Inspector to a foreign regulatory authority upon the written request of that authority.

(4)

The Inspector may not disclose information concerning the affairs of a protected person to a foreign regulatory authority under subsection (3)(g) unless he is satisfied

(a)

that the foreign regulatory authority is subject to adequate legal restrictions on further disclosure; and

(b)

that the information disclosed is reasonably required by the authority for the purposes of its regulatory functions.

(5)

The Governor may issue guidelines to the Inspector concerning the discharge of his functions under this section.

(6)

Any person who contravenes the provisions of this section commits an offence and is liable on summary conviction to a fine of $10,000.

35. No liability attaches to the Governor, the Inspector or any person acting under the

Immunity

authority of the Governor or the Inspector for an act done in good faith in the discharge or purported discharge of his functions under this Act.

36. (1) The Governor shall cause notice of the issue, revocation or suspension of a

Gazette notices

licence to be published in the *Gazette*.

(2) A notice of issue of a licence published in the *Gazette* must specify the terms and conditions, if any, to which the licence is subject.

37. (1) A decision of the Governor under section 7, section 13(5), section 14(2) or

Appeals

section 19 is final and conclusive and shall not be called into question in any court of law

(2)

An appeal lies to the court from a decision of the Governor to suspend or revoke a licence under section 16.

(3)

Unless the Court otherwise orders, an appeal made under subsection (2) does not operate to suspend the decision of the Governor.

38. The Governor-in-Council may make regulations generally for giving effect to the

Regulations

provisions of this Act and specifically

(a) requiring the payment of fees under this Act and prescribing them, including -

(i)

fees for filing an application;

(ii)

fees for the issuance of a licence; and

(iii) annual fees;

(b) controlling the form of advertising undertaken by licensees; and

Code of Practice

Offences

(c) prescribing any thing required or permitted to be prescribed by this Act.

39. (1) The Inspector may issue a Code of Practice with respect to the procedures to be followed by and the conduct expected of a licensee in the operation of its licensed business.

(2) The Code of Practice may include -

(a)

due diligence procedures;

(b)

record keeping requirements; and

(c)

audit requirements.

(3)

The Code of Practice may make different provision in relation to different persons, circumstances or cases.

(4)

The Inspector must publish the Code of Practice and any amendments thereto in the *Gazette*.

40. (1) A person who with intent to deceive, or for any purpose of this Act makes any representation that he knows to be false or does not believe to be true commits an offence and liable on conviction to a fine of $25,000 or to imprisonment for a term not exceeding one year or to both.

(2) A person who

(a)

assaults or obstructs the Inspector or other person in the performance of his functions under this Act;

(b)

uses any insulting language to an Inspector or other person in the performance of his functions under this Act;

(c)

by the offer of any gratuity, bribe or other inducement prevents or attempts to prevent an Inspector or other person from performing his functions under this Act; or

(d)

contravenes any provision of this Act or regulations, for which no penalty is specifically provided,

commits an offence and is liable on summary conviction to a fine of $5,000, to imprisonment for a term of one year or to both.

(3)

A licensee that carries on business contrary to the terms or conditions of its licence or, in the case of the holder of a restricted trust licence, in contravention of the restriction commits an offence and is liable on summary conviction to a fine of $25,000.

(4)

Where an offence under this Act is committed by a company, a director or officer of that company who knowingly authorized, permitted or acquiesced in the commission of the offence also commits the offence and is liable on conviction to

(a)

a fine of the amount specified for the offence; or

(b)

to a term of imprisonment as specified for the offence, if any; or

(c)

to both a fine and imprisonment.

(5)

Notwithstanding the Criminal Code, offences committed under the following sections may be proceeded with summarily or by indictment -

(a)

section 4(2);

(b)

section 8(3);

(c)

section 8(4);

(d)

section 10(3);

(e)

section 14(3);

(f)

section 14(4);

(g)

section 21(2);

(h)

section 33(5);

(i)

section 40(1); and

(j)

section 40(4), where the offence committed by the company is an offence referred to in paragraphs (a) to (f).

41. The Offshore Banks and Trust Companies Ordinance, 1991 is repealed.

Repeal of Offshore Banks and Trust Companies Ordinance, 1991

42. (1) A person holding a licence under the Offshore Banks and Trust Companies

Transitional

Ordinance, 1991 immediately before the commencement of this Act is deemed to have provisions been granted a licence under this Act subject to such terms and conditions as may have been imposed on the granting of the licence under that Ordinance.

Citation and commencement

(2)

The Governor may make regulations providing for such further savings and transitional provisions to have effect in connection with the coming into operation of this Act as he considers necessary or expedient.

(3)

Regulations made under subsection (2) may be given retrospective operation to a day not earlier than the date that this Act comes into operation.

43. This Act may be cited as the Trust Companies and Offshore Banking Act, 2000 and shall come into operation on such day as the Governor may appoint by notice published in the Gazette.

TRAVEL TO ANGUILLA

Language	English
Government	British Dependent Territory
Capital	The Valley
Size	35 sq. miles, 16 mi. long & 3 mi. wide at widest point
Location	Eastern Caribbean, most northerly of the Leeward Islands
Temperature	80°F Monthly Mean Temperature
Rainfall	35 inches per year
Electricity	110 Volts AC
Currency	Eastern Caribbean Dollar (US currency widely accepted)
Driving	On left, license required
Rentals	Car, jeeps, scooters & bikes
Airports	Wallblake Airport: American Eagle, WINAIR & LIAT, Caribbean Star Local Air Charter Services: Tyden Air, Air Anguilla & Trans Anguilla Nearest International Gateways: San Juan & Antigua (1 hr. flight); St. Martin, (7 minute flight).
Ferry	From Marigot Bay, St. Martin to Blowing Point, Anguilla, 20 minute crossing, half hour intervals. Ferry service available from Blowing Point to Juliana via Link Ferry.
Entry	Passport preferred OR official photo ID accompanied by birth certificate w/raised seal, plus onward/return ticket.
Dress Code	Casual, in good taste. (Short-shorts, bikinis, bra-type tops and topless in both men and women are undesirable in public places; nude and topless swimming and/or sunbathing are not permitted.) All beaches are public.

PUBLIC HOLIDAYS FOR 2003

New Years Day	Wednesday, 1 January
Good Friday	Friday, 18 April
Easter Monday	Monday, 21 April
Labour Day	Thursday, 1 May
Anguilla Day	Friday, 30 May
Whit Monday	Monday, 9 June
Celebration of the Birthday of Her Majesty the Queen	Monday, 16 June
ALHCS/VSS Day	Thursday, 31 July
August Monday	Monday, 4 August
August Thursday	Thursday, 7 August
Constitution Day	Friday, 8 August
Separation Day	Friday, 19 December
Christmas Day	Thursday, 25 December
Boxing Day	Friday, 26 December

GENERAL TRAVEL TIPS

- US currency is widely accepted throughout the island. Prices on menus, in hotels and for activities are generally quoted in US dollars.
- ATMs on Anguilla accept international bank cards. Currently there are five ATMs located conveniently throughout the Island: one each at National Bank of Anguilla (NBA), Scotia Bank, Caribbean Commercial Bank, and Ashley & Sons Grocery.
- Driving is on the left. To rent a car on the island, a valid driver's license from the resident country is needed to obtain a local driver's license. Local driver's licenses are available at car rental agencies and cost $20. Rental cars are readily available; however reservations for 'in season' car rentals and children's car seats should be made in advance.
- Electricity is 110 AC voltage, the same as in the US.
- Water is potable; however, bottled water is available at hotels and convenience stores.
- Dress is casual. It is generally advisable to bring a light sweater or wrap for evenings.
- There are no nude beaches on Anguilla; topless sunbathing is not permitted.
- There are no casinos.

- There is very little crime in Anguilla; however, travelers should take normal precautions such as locking doors and securing valuables.
- Anguilla is a dry island with an average annual rainfall of 35 inches and average monthly temperature of 80ºF. The island is continually cooled by prevailing trade winds, with little change of temperature in the summer.
- Water temperatures are in the upper 70ºs to lower 80ºs. Optimum diving conditions are in the summer months when visibility is at its highest and there are little or no ground seas.

GETTING THERE

Transportation
Anguilla is located in the Eastern Caribbean, (18º North Latitude and 63º West Longitude) just one-hour east of Puerto Rico and seven minutes north of Dutch St. Maarten by air; and 20 minutes north from French St. Martin by ferry.
There are a number of options available for getting to this idyllic island. Visitors can fly directly into Anguilla's Wallblake Airport from Puerto Rico via American Eagle/American Airlines and LIAT, or opt to fly directly to St. Maarten, Antigua, St. Thomas or St. Kitts for easy transfer to Anguilla:

- San Juan via American Eagle and LIAT
- St. Thomas via American Eagle, LIAT, TransAnguilla and WINAIR
- St. Maarten/Martin: St. Maarten via scheduled and chartered air with WINAIR, LIAT,
- TransAnguilla and Island Charters. St. Martin (Marigot Bay) via regularly scheduled ferries.
- Antigua via LIAT and Caribbean Star
- St. Kitts via LIAT and Caribbean Star

Airline reservation numbers/websites:		
American Eagle/American Airlines	1-800-433-7300	www.aa.com
LIAT	1-264-497-5002	www.liatairline.com
TransAnguilla	1-264-497-8690	-
Caribbean Star	1-264-497-8690	www.flycaribbeanstar.com
WINAIR	1-264-497-2748	www.fly-winair.com
Island Charters	1-264-497-4064	-

Ferries: Anguilla / St. Martin
Ferries are a popular way to travel between Anguilla and St. Martin. No reservations are necessary. Between 7:30AM and

GETTING AROUND

Sixteen miles long and three miles wide, Anguilla is an easy island to explore on your own. One major road runs from the East End to the West End, with smaller roads branching off. Whether you're seeing the island by taxi, bike, scooter or car, 'right around the bend' there's always a beautiful beach; a restaurant, café or barbecue with sumptuous fare; an interesting museum, art gallery or boutique; a harbour dotted with brightly colored 'Anguilla' boats; a breathtaking vision of architectural resort styles that include stunningly white Moorish, Mediterranean, and modern designs just 'up the road' from charming, colorful and quaint West Indian hotels, resorts, and private homes. Grab an Anguilla map at www.skyviews.com and take off on your own when you get here! If you do get lost, friendly and helpful Anguillians will get you 'back on the road in no time!

Driving
Driving is on the left and the speed limit is 30 mph. To rent a car you'll need your valid driver's license from your resident country, and $20 to purchase a temporary Anguilla driver's license. Temporary Anguilla driver's licenses are available through car rental agencies. Well-maintained rental cars and jeeps are readily available. Car seats are available at rental agencies or through www.travellightanguilla.com.

Car Rental Services	
APEX Car Rental	264-497-2642
AVIS Rent A Car	264-497-2642
Budget Rent-A-Car	264-497-5871
Caribbean Rentals Ltd.	264-497-4662
Connor's Car Rentals	264-497-6433
High-Way Rent A Car	264-497-2183
Island Car Rentals	264-497-2723
Rodco's Car Rental	264-497-2773
Summer Set Car Rental	264-497-5278
Thrifty Car Rental	264-497-2656
Triple K Car Rental	264-497-5934
Uncle Ernie's Car Rentals	264-497-2542

Bikes and Scooters

Bicycles © Carol Lee

Our flat land persuades many visitors to sightsee on a bike or scooter. Bikes are available from about $10 per day, scooters from about $20 per day.

Bike and Scooter Rentals	
A&S Scooter Rentals	264-497-8803
Exotic Plus	264-497-8528
Flambayo Health Depot	264-497-5370

Taxis You'll find our taxi drivers knowledgeable, friendly, courteous -- and always willing to relate one or two great Anguilla stories! Island taxi tours are reasonable -- why not learn about Anguilla from an expert! Ask your concierge, villa rental agency, or call the Anguilla Tourist Board to arrange a taxi tour for you.

FESTIVALS

February

St. Gerard's Garden Party at the Church grounds (TBA)

Anguilla Cultural Education Festival (TBA)
A week of Activities coordinated by the Anguilla National Trust Office to showcase Our culture and heritage.

15-16 Anguilla Beautification Club Annual Flower & Garden Show

March

Wallblake House Fundraising Auction (TBA)

14-16 3rd Annual Jazz & Arts Festival

14-16 Moonsplash Annual Music Festival
Occurs on the weekend of the full moon in March. The festival showcases Caribbean and International talent at the Dune Preserve, Rendezvous Bay.

April

National Arts & Crafts ExhiBition & Demonstration (TBA)
At The Anguilla Craft Shop (TBA)
19-20 Kiddie's Easter Extravaganza
Activities catering to children.
21 Easter Monday/Easter Monday Boat Racing
Fun day rallies, sports meets, family gatherings & picnics.

May

23-31 Festival Del Mar
Anguillian sea festival reflecting all aspects of sea life including fishing tournament, yacht regatta, sea related activities, local culinary food, etc.

30 Anguilla Day

Commemorates the beginning of the Anguillian Revolution, which took place on May 30th, 1967. Parade, Around-the-island boat race starts and ends at Sandy Ground. Sport meets, bicycle races & tennis competitions.

30 May -- 1 June 2003 Anguilla Yacht Regatta
Friday, May 30, yachts and local boats race around the island. On Saturday, May 31, yachts race around the buoys. Sunday, June 1, is mix-up 'Friendly Racing" day when the crews of yachts and local boats 'mix up' and race for fun. You can learn more at the Anguilla International Yacht Club.

June

16 Celebration of Her Majesty Queen Elizabeth's Birthday
8:00 am parade at the Ronald Webster's Parks

July

27 Miss Anguilla Swim Suit Competition
A pre-Summer Festival event that showcases the contestants of Miss Anguilla Pageant.

31 Opening of Summer Festival '03

August

1 Anguilla Summer Festival
Colorful expressions of the Anguillian culture through dance, song, parades & boat racing!

Heineken Cup Boatrace
At Sandy Ground

4 August Monday
Jouvert Morning's at the crack of dawn,People from all over the island dance in the streets of the Valley until noon.

August Monday Boatrace
At Sandy Ground

7 August Thursday
August Thursday Boat Race - the national sport of the island. Handmade racing boats compete everyday of carnival for the grand prize. Great party also!

Miss Anguilla Pageant
At the Landsome Bowl cultural center. The crowning event of carnival festivities - talented young ladies compete for the title of "Miss Anguilla"

8 Parade of Troupes
Colorful parade of troupes through The Valley.

November

14 -17 Tranquility
A rejuvenation of the body, mind & soul by the sounds of Jazz at some of Anguilla's top resorts & beaches. Event will feature regional and international jazz musicians!

16-22 Tourism Week

December

1 Optimist Race Against Aids
Public awareness campaign to raise funds for AIDS related services.

DAYTIME ACTIVITIES

Snorkling
Snorkels and fins are available at most hotels, dive shops, on most charters and at some beaches where either beach operators or casual, beachfront restaurants are located.

Cruising & Sailing
Cruising and sailing to many of Anguilla's offshore cays or secluded beaches can be a great way to experience some of the island's most pristine spots. Picnics on board or ashore, sunset cocktail cruises, secluded snorkeling trips and excursions to sand cay restaurants are just some of the fun itineraries available.

Motorboats

. Island Yacht Charter Company	264-497-3743
. Sandy Island Enterprises	264-497-5643
. Gotcha	264-497-2956
. No Mercy	264-235-6383

© Jackie Cestero

Sailboats

. Chocolate	264-497-3394
. El Tigre/Sail Anguilla	264-497-3304
. Eros	264-497-3743
. Sail My Way	264-235-6655

Fishing

Wahoo, Marlin, Tuna, Swordfish, Yellow fin and Black fin Tuna are just some of the game fish found off the shores of Anguilla.

Charters	
Gotcha	264-497-2956
Johnno's	264-497-2728
Sandy Island Enterprises	264-497-5643
No Mercy	264-497-6383

Parasailing & Paddleboats
Anguilla Watersports located on Shoal Bay, offers a class act parasailing excursion to visitors. Rides at 400 and 600 feet above Shoal Bay are available. Also for rent are paddleboats, windsurfers and sailboats.

Windsurfing, Sunfishing, Catamaran Sailing & Water Skiing
These activities can be arranged through individual accommodations, hotel concierges or front desk personnel.

Nighttime Diversions

For a small island, Anguilla has a number of nightlife options and musical entertainment to offer its visitors. Classical pianists and guitarists, a quiet saxophone, reggae, steel drum and calypso bands are just a few options. What We Do in Anguilla and Anguilla Life list 'what, where and when' for night owls. These publications are available from the Anguilla Tourist Board and most properties.

Many resorts and hotels offer nightly entertainment and an incredibly romantic ambience of candle light, moonlight and the music of a classical pianist, guitarist or one of Anguilla's acclaimed reggae, soca, steel drum or calypso bands.

Local hot spots offer an opportunity to dance barefoot to Caribbean tunes that move your body and shake your soul. Generally, Sandy Ground is the "Hotspot" on Fridays and Saturdays, while Sundays and Wednesdays the crowds move to Shoal Bay East. There is music and entertainment almost every night of the week somewhere on the island.

Hotspots and Hangouts

Sandy Ground

Johnno's	Dancing: soca, calypso, reggae, jazz
Pumphouse	Historic salt factory turned barefoot bar. Dancing: soca, calypso, reggae.
Ripples	Dinner and convivial bar

www.gov.ai/angstamp

South Hill

Rafes	Late night barbecue, music
Red Dragon Disco	Variety of dance music on weekends. The last Friday of every month is "Over 30s."

Rendezvous Bay

The Dune Preserve	Aesthetic reggae beach bar roost manned by Anguillla's own renowned entertainer, Bankie Banx

Shoal Bay

Hardbroke	Sunday soca dancing
Madeariman Reef	Open air beach bar/grill
Uncle Ernie's	Open air beach bar/grill
Le Beach	Open air beach bar/grill
Elodias Beach	Bar Open air soca parties on Sunday/grill

Mead's Bay

CoCo-Mo's Lounge	Sonido Latino Band Wednesdays through Sundays

(Cocoloba
Beach Resort)

Some names to look for: Sleepy and the Allstars; Dumpa, Sprocka, Bankie Banx & Dune People, Reggae Groovers, Boss and Friends, Happy Hits String Band, Clement Lake and his quiet sax, Mitch, The Mussingtons, Mighty Springer, Keith Gumbs, Steel Vibration, Montana Pam, Kingsley (on the keyboard), High Tension.

ANGUILLA'S RESTAURANT SPECIALTIES, CHEFS AND "MORSELS OF INSIDE INFO"

A cross-section sampling includes 30 of Anguilla's 70+ Restaurants

© Carol Lee

Anguilla's dining scene offers visitors a variety of gastronomic diversions and a choice of dining ambiance and cuisine specialties. With over 70 restaurants, visitors can choose a dining experience based on an appetite impulse, a desire for a romantic or convivial setting, or their pocketbook.

There are as many chef and restaurant cuisine specialties as there are restaurants on this small island, ranging from Caribbean to Mediterranean, French, Continental, Creole, Italian, American and Indo-Chinese. From seafood to Black Angus Steak to Rack of Lamb to barbecued ribs, chicken and hamburgers, there's a palatable dish for the pickiest of diners and those with a desire for an international oddity.

Anguilla's 5-star dining establishments boast internationally-acclaimed chefs from every corner of the globe, including those Anguilla-born and bred. International chefs blend their specialty cuisine with Caribbean regional and indigenous Anguilla spices and herbs to create award-winning fare. Still, most visitors don't leave the island without enjoying a famous Anguillian stalwart – a hearty breakfast of fried fish and johnny-cakes.

Depending on the time of day and dining mood, Anguilla vacationers choose from elegant and intimate gourmet seaside restaurants to casually chic beachfront bistros and festive, affordable beachside and roadside grills. An intimate dinner for two, a quiet table for introspection, an opportunity to meet a convivial group of fellow diners and visitors, dancing to Caribbean beats, or time-out for ribs at a roadside grille are choices for some visitors and a 'to do' list for others.

Here is a brief profile of 30 Anguilla restaurants including restaurant and chef specialties, and morsels of known, and not so known, information about each:

Altamer Restaurant ~ French and Caribbean Fusion
Chef Maurice Leduc, whose experience encompasses 40 years at Maxim's Restaurant in Paris, offers a first class menu featuring dishes such as Boned Quail flambéed with Brandy and Calvados Marinated Grapes and Tenderloins of Black Angus Beef flambéed with Brandy, Dijon Mustard and Pinot Noir Demi Glaze presented on a Bed of Caramelised Bermuda Onions. Guests view activities in the kitchen through a glass wall. Found at the exclusive Altamer Resort, this unique dining experience combines the highest standards of cuisine and service with a magnificent setting at Shoal Bay West.

The Barrel Stay Restaurant ~ Alfresco By The Seashore
Specializing in French and Creole cuisine, this small alfresco restaurant overlooking the ocean at Sandy Ground has been serving choice meals in a relaxed setting for more than 20 years, achieving rave reviews on a regular basis. Famous for Chef Marvilla Carty's fish soup, other specialties include grilled fish prepared with blackened garlic or mustard seed sauce.

Blanchard's at Meads Bay ~ Stylish Sophistication
A regular winner of the Wine Spectator 'Award of Excellence', Blanchard's offers visitors style and sophistication, combined with an excellent Caribbean menu developed by Chef Melinda Blanchard. Fine china, hand-made crystal glasses and crisp white linen adorn the tables at this classic restaurant, which offers panoramic views of the Caribbean Sea at Meads Bay.

The Cocoloba Restaurant ~ Romantic Dining Room, Dining Islands, an Aquarium
Open for breakfast, lunch and dinner, Cocoloba serves an array of International and West Indian cuisine. Views of the sea and soft candlelight provide a romantic dining ambiance. The restaurant's unique centerpiece is its aquarium, which features a spectacular display of local sea life. Five dining islands provide intimate settings both above and around the tank. Chef Jerome Vanterpool's specialties include filet mignon with roasted peppercorn sauce; ensemble of yellow-tailed snapper fillet topped with lobster sauce; and butterfly shrimp.

Covecastles ~ An Exceptional Culinary Experience in a Romantic Setting
Booking well in advance is essential if visitors are to secure one of the seven tables at this romantic hideaway restaurant in the exclusive Covecastles resort overlooking Shoal Bay West. Chef Dominique Thévent has compiled a small but unusual menu with several surprises. Highly recommended are the Crayfish Ravioli with Tamarind Broth, Gingerbread Crusted Roast Loin of Lamb and Vermouth-laced Crayfish Choucroute.

E's Oven ~ Colorful Cuisine
It's easy to be enticed into this attractive red, yellow and white building with wooden shutters, located in South Hill. Chef Peggy Hughes has established a reputation for excellent cuisine and great value since opening E's Oven in April 2000. The menu includes a wide variety of meals from sandwiches and salads to sirloin steak and more elaborate dishes such as Blue Fish in Basil Cream Sauce. Nothing on the menu exceeds $15.

The English Rose ~ Capital Dining
Located in The Valley, Anguilla's capital, The English Rose serves both lunch and dinner at affordable prices. With appetizers such as Chef Floyd Gumbs' Golden Fried Calamari and Buffalo Wings starting from around $3, plus light meals including Jerk Chicken Caesar Salad, Chicken and Chips, and Cheeseburgers available from $4 to $6, this restaurant pub is welcoming and easy on the budget. Diners enjoy gathering around the large-screen television for a pre-meal news update.

Fat Cat Gourmet ~ Picnics Prepared to Order
Vacationers wishing to take off for the day with a picnic, but not wanting to spend time shopping for and preparing it, can take advantage of the catering services offered by a number of delicatessen's on Anguilla, including Chef Valerie Banks' Fat Cat Gourmet. Salads, sandwiches, pasta dishes, patés, cold meats, cookies and cakes are all on the menu and picnic baskets are prepared to order.

Flavours ~ Fun and Excellent Fare
Opened just this year, this convivial restaurant overlooks Sandy Ground Harbour. Chef Rexford Fleming's garnered his expertise during his twelve years with Cap Juluca's Pimms restaurant, and his menu features West Indian cuisine with a 'twist' of creativity and ingenuity. Favorite dishes for many repeat diners include the pumpkin soup appetizer and Parrot fish entrée with local style fungi. Another favorite is Flavours' Punch, a 'secret' combination of limejuice, sugar syrup, strong and dark rum stirred together with a dash of amoretto floated on top.

George's at Cap Juluca Resort ~ Decidedly Casual, Carib/Mediterranean
Award-winning chef, George Reid, has acquired a well-earned reputation with a combination of Mediterranean and Caribbean cuisine at his restaurant located within the exclusive Cap Juluca resort. West Indian Buffets and Big Beach Barbecues are regular events, complete with live entertainment in an informal setting overlooking Maundays Bay.

Hemingway's ~ New at Cinnamon Reef
The Palm Court at Cinnamon Reef Resort has been transformed into a new restaurant called Hemingway's that serves a combination of local and international dishes. The menu is influenced by countries where Ernest Hemingway spent much of his time, and features dishes from destinations including Spain, Africa and America.

Hibernia
Guests enjoy peeking at the guest book when visiting this hot spot for the cogno-scenti. This small, intimate and elegant restaurant with 11 tables set in an open air West Indian house by the sea serves a light French cuisine with a far-eastern touch. Owners Raoul Rodriguez (Chef) and Mary Pat O'Hanlon (Hostess) take pleasure in presenting Raoul's innovative dishes such as Asian mushroom soup served warm and topped with a cream of cauliflower; grilled black angus beef tenderloin with parmesan gratin potatoes and whole shallots, stewed in red wine sauce; and Hibernia's rum & raisin ice cream with aged rum. Of course there's always a choice of fresh local seafood; duck and chicken creations.

Jacquie's Ripples Restaurant ~ A Fun Place To Be
Offering excellent food and a great atmosphere, Ripples is a lively spot where everyone talks to everyone else. Head Chef Kenrick Richardson joined the restaurant in 2001 after gaining a wealth of experience at some of Anguilla's five-star resorts. He has added tasty dishes to the menu, including coconut soup, jerk chicken with fresh mango sauce and fresh crab wontons.

Johnno's for Music and Local Seafood
Based at Sandy Ground, Johnno's is a classic Caribbean beach bar famous for its late night music and delicious seafood selection, much of which is caught by the proprietor himself and prepared by Chef Wesley Thompson. Grilled and barbecued lobster, kingfish and snapper are featured on the menu of this fun nightspot.

Kemia ~ Cap Juluca's Hors d'Oeuvrerie and Tapas Bar
The third restaurant to open at the luxury Cap Juluca Resort, Kemia – the African word for 'little tastes' - features a wide selection of appetizer size dishes from around the world. Open from noon to midnight, its menu boasts a huge array of international flavors such as Indonesian satay, South American ceviche, Japanese sushi and, of course, Spanish tapas prepared by Chef Tomas Bengtsson and his team. The average price of a dish is $12.50.

Le Bistro at Malliouhana ~ Lunch, Appetizers, Afternoon Tea at Meads Bay Beach
Le Bistro restaurant is located poolside next to Meads Bay beach and adjacent to the resort's adventure pirate ship playground for children. This daytime restaurant's is open to all hotel guests and island visitors. Le Bistro's delectable menu choices include lunch, snacks and afternoon tea.

Malliouhana Hotel & Spa ~ Five-star Dining; A Night and Meal to Remember
Michelin-starred consultant Chef Michel Rostang of Paris, and Head Chef Alain Laurent have gained international acclaim for the main restaurant of this luxurious spa hotel, which continues to be applauded for the excellent quality of its French cuisine blended with subtle flavors of the Caribbean. The resort provides a sophisticated yet informal alfresco setting where guests enjoy romantic evenings. From Wine Spectator - "Malliouhana has stacked the deck with stunning views, graceful architecture and some of the best cuisine found in the islands;" and Diversion Magazine - "You're taken to gastronomic heights rarely attained in this part of the world."

Mango's Seaside Grill ~ Casual Elegance on the Beach
This open-air restaurant offers casual but elegant dining on the beach at Barnes Bay, in the island's southwest corner. Candlelight and soft music accompany Chef David Corbourn's sumptuous cuisine which includes Conch Chowder, Barnes Bay Lobster Cakes and Whole Grilled Snapper, all made from the freshest ingredients.

Mediterraneo Café ~
Mid-Day Dining at CuisinArt, Just a Short Stroll From the Beach
CuisinArt's Café Mediterraneo, located poolside, is a short stroll from the beach. The Café is an ideal place to enjoy a mid-day meal from a menu selection of grilled items, pizza, fresh homegrown salads, seafood, desserts, drinks and specialty coffees.

CuisinArt Resort & Spa features the first hydroponic farm at a resort, which grows the majority of the fresh fruits, vegetables, edible flowers and herbs used in the resort's restaurants.

Oliver's Seaside Grill ~ Authentic Rock Oven by the Beach
This beachside restaurant uses an authentic Anguillian rock oven to create a selection of dishes combining both West Indian and European flavors. Host Oliver MacDonna urges visitors to call ahead for the house special: Home Style Rock Oven Baked Whole Free-Range Chicken, stuffed with Gingered Sweet Potatoes and served with a Rosemary Ginger Sauce. If that's not an option, guests can start with Gazpacho soup, move on to a fine wine and Crayfish or Lobster, and top the meal with a Creme Brulee and a brandy in the lounge.

Overlook ~ Fine Dining, Breathtaking View
Perched on the cliff overlooking Sandy Ground Bay, Chef Deon's Overlook combines fine dining with a breathtaking view. The menu here is contemporary, with a decided Caribbean flair. Chef Deon adds exotic accents to creative menu choices, including chilled Bosc pear soup with seared shrimp and rosemary oil, lobster pancakes, and his award-winning garlic encrusted snapper. For dessert, try Deon's Decadent Chocolate Rum Cake with Grand Mariner Chocolate soup. Dinner is served nightly, and lunch every day but Sunday.

Pimms at Cap Juluca Resort ~ Candle Light, Romance, Gustatory Delights
Pimms has created its enviable reputation with an outstanding five-star menu, featuring exotic tropical dishes such as Seared Black Sea Bass on Bamboo, Coconut and Kaffir, and Wok Charred Red Snapper with Pickled Daikon and Ver Jus. Anguillian born and bred Executive Chef George Reid and Cuisine Chef Vernon Hughes invite guests to partake in an extraordinary culinary experience in an idyllic environment. Visitors desiring Pimms' sought after tables over-looking the sea where jumping fish vie for attention are urged to make reservations in advance.

The Pumphouse American Grill ~ Lively Menu, Live Music
Located in the historic, old salt factory at Sandy Ground, The Pumphouse is described by some as a 'rocking roadhouse'. An American grill restaurant, it is known for live music, good service, great value meals, and the celebrities many visitors often find themselves 'bumping into' on the dance floor. The Pumphouse provides good times and enjoyable evenings for all merry-makers.

Santorini ~ CuisinArt Resort & Spa's "Piece d' resistance"
The resorts' fine dining and gourmet restaurant, Santorini, with an original French rotisserie, sets a new standard for epicurean kitchens. The kitchens are designed with glass walls to offer interested guests the opportunity to observe Chef Denis Jaricot of Lyon, France, and his team creating their Mediterranean and Caribbean cuisine specialties including appetizer Madagascar Prawns with "Romesco" Salsa and Charbroiled Rack of Lamb with Spice Crust. Music and dancing on Friday and Saturday evenings ensure a most romantic evening.

Sapphire ~ A Jewel at Maundays Bay
Created by a team whose pedigree includes a period at the luxurious Cap Juluca Resort, Sapphire combines a fantastic setting overlooking Maundays Bay, with an excellent Euro-Caribe menu and moderate pricing. Seafood plays a significant part in the menu with dishes created by Chef Payson Dennis including Lobster Ravioli served with a light bisque sauce and Anguilla Crayfish Salad in a dressing of capers, fresh lemon and tomatoes.

Scilly Cay ~ Private Island Lunches
Stand on Island Harbour's dock, give a wave of the arm and a motor boat comes to ferry you to the private island of Scilly Cay. In five minutes, visitors are enjoying this open-air restaurant where lunch is usually preceded by sunbathing, swimming and snorkeling in the clear waters of the Caribbean, followed by a glass of Scilly Cay's famous rum punch. Chef Sandrine Webster's fresh grilled lobster and crayfish are among the most popular dishes served on the tiny island, which can also be hired for private parties and wedding celebrations.

Smokey*s Restaurant ~ Romantic Beach Bistro
The latest restaurant to be opened by Alan and Lisa Gumbs, Smokey's offers a relaxed atmosphere during the day with a volleyball net set up outside on the beach at Cove Bay, and an interior decorated with colorful hammocks. At night, the restaurant is transformed into an intimate bistro for romantics, with tiki torches, candles, fine china and linen. Daytime and evening's gastronomic delights are prepared by Chef Leonard Sharplis.

Straw Hat ~ Restaurant on the Water
Straw Hat is the only restaurant on Anguilla situated above the water. Built on supports over the sea at Forest Bay, this stylish restaurant made a huge first impression when it appeared on Condé Nast Traveler's '50 Best New Restaurants in the World' list in 1999. Chef James Hassel's conch Spring Rolls with Citrus Glaze and Pickled Ginger followed by, for example, Saffron Laced Seafood Stew or Anguillian Spiny Lobster Sautéed in Pernod Cream Sauce, are just some of the creative dishes which appear on the Straw Hat's exciting and varied menu.

Tasty's ~ Home-Style Anguillian Cooking with a French Influence
Located on Anguilla's main road, friendly and reasonably-priced Tasty's is a delightful eatery serving indigenous Anguillian cuisine with a European flair gained from owner and Executive Chef Dale Carty's 13-year tenure with Malliouhana Hotel & Spa. Chef Carty's mastery of West Indian spices and his training under renowned French Chef Michel Rostang combine with Sous Chef Patrick Carty's innovative flair to create scrumptious dishes like marinated conch salad, grilled whole snapper with fungi, and trigger fish in island-flavored sauce. Not to be missed is Tasty's fried fish and johnny cakes breakfast!

Uncle Ernie's ~ Lively Shoal Bay West Beach's Famous BBQ Eatery
Good eats, good fun, any day of the week. Sunbathers and swimmers find their way from beach blankets to a table at Uncle Ernie's and enjoy cold drinks, BBQ ribs, chicken, fish, hamburgers, and lobster or crayfish; or just a Hagen Daz ice cream bar. Everyone

chats here – visitors meet local Anguillians and other visitors from all over the world. Live music on Sunday afternoons!

ANGUILLA'S 2003 ROMANCE PACKAGES INCLUDE MORE THAN GREAT RATE DEALS

Picnics for Two; Spa Treatments, Sunset Cruises Set the Stage for Romance

Romantic two-somes visiting tranquil Anguilla find more than uncrowded, pristine beaches; acclaimed and numerous gourmet dining experiences; a host of land and water activities; and the welcoming smiles of gracious citizens. Exceptional values and imaginative inclusions are available at all price ranges in the 2003 romance packages offered by Anguilla's resorts, hotels and villas, including:

Arawak Beach Inn
Island Adventure's 2003 weekly rates for this uniquely charming hotel are $849 until April 6; $674, April 7-June 1, Nov. 1-Dec. 22; and $599, June 2-Oct. 31 (per person, plus tax and service fee). Rates include an oceanfront double room, champagne upon arrival, full breakfast daily, four dinners at the Inn's Restaurant, a romantic lunch for two on a secluded island, full day excursion to Marigot, St. Martin (with transfer to/from the ferry), 3-day car rental and airport transfers.
800-4-ARAWAK; 264-497-4888; www.arawakbeach.com

Cap Juluca
This sophisticated romantic retreat on Maundays Bay offers couples a 7-night/8-day Romantic Rendezvous until Dec. 19 ranging from $3585 in a superior room (summer) to $7850 in a Junior Suite (winter), depending on time of year and accommodation chosen. Included: champagne and flowers on arrival, beachfront accommodation, four dinners for two, a trip to Prickly Pear with barbecue lunch, one-day car rental, and round-trip hotel transfers, tax and service fee. Wedding packages are also available. (Closed September/ October)
888-858-5822; 264-497-6666; www.capjuluca.com

Carimar Beach Club
Located on pristine Meads Bay beach, Carimar's Honeymoon Plan features 7 nights/8 days at $1125 per couple, plus $150 tax and service charge. The plan includes beach view accommodation in a one-bedroom apartment, champagne upon arrival, starter breakfast basket, one sunset cruise, 2-day car rental, one gourmet dinner for two with cocktails, snorkel equipment, tennis courts, fresh flowers daily, and a special honeymoon gift. The plan is available May 1-Nov. 15 (closed Aug. 24—Oct. 15).
800-235-8667; 264-497-6881; www.carimar.com

Covecastles
This resort's unique architecture and placement on beautiful Shoal Bay West beach make it a popular choice for destination weddings. From April 16–Dec. 16, the resort's five-night, $3750 per couple Wedding Plan includes beachside ceremony, license, minister, flowers, champagne, cake, one hour of music, photographer, pictures, wedding album, accommodation in a one-bedroom beach house, daily continental breakfast, one

dinner for two, RT airport transfers, sailing, biking, kayaking, snorkeling, tax and service fee (closed Aug. 31–Oct. 24). A 7-night honeymoon with romantic amenities and special inclusions is $3600 per couple.
800-223-1108; 264-497-6801; www.covecastles.com

Cocoloba Beach Resort
Cocoloba's tropical gardens mantel a coral bluff dividing two magnificent beaches. Individual beachfront & garden chalets provide an intimate world of romance. Per couple 7-night honeymoon rates are $2500 in a garden chalet & $2850 beachfront till April14; $1500 & $1850, April 15-Dec.14. Included: 7-day car rental, full breakfast daily, sunset cruise with beverage & hors d'oeuvres, 1 dinner for 2, 1-hour full massage for 2, champagne greeting, tennis, watersports, tax & service fee.
264-497-8800; www.cocolobaresort.com

CuisinArt Resort & Spa
A contemporary Spa and culinary artistry await couples opting for Sea of Love, a 7 night stay in a Junior Suite including wine & cheese upon arrival, 3 lunches at Café Mediterraneo, 3 dinners at Santorini, 1 'couples' massage, 1-day car rental, a day at Scilly Cay (lunch and transfers). Per couple rates are $5040 until March 30; $3100, May 1—Dec.16 (tax & service fee not included). Wedding plans are also available. (Closed Sept.2—Oct.15.)
800-943-3210; 264-498-2000; www.cuisinartresort.com

Frangipani Beach Club
Tropical gardens meeting beautiful Meads Bay's beach entice couples to opt for Frangipani's 7-night, $2700 Champagne & Love plan, available April 16–Dec. 16. Rate includes beachfront accommodation in a 1-bedroom suite, champagne with strawberries and cream on arrival, en suite daily continental breakfast, lunch daily, one champagne dinner for two, three-day car rental, snorkel excursion to secluded Little Bay, framed photo of the bride and groom, tax and service fee (closed September 4 – November 3).
800-892-4564; 264-497-6442; www.frangipani.ai

Malliouhana Hotel & Spa
This award-winning, sophisticated hotel & spa acclaimed for its cuisine and new spa facilities offers couples Romantic Interlude, available June 1–Aug. 31. Included: accommodation in an ocean view double with covered terrace, welcome bottle of French champagne, continental breakfast daily, 3-course dinner for two each evening, a daytime excursion to a deserted cay and sunset cruise on the hotel's 40' yacht, watersports, tennis lesson, tax and service fee. Rates per couple are $1995 for 4 nights, $3480 for 7 nights. Wedding plans are also available.
800-835-0796; 264-497-6111; www.malliouhana.com

Paradise Cove
Lush tropical gardens surround this intimate apartment resort hideaway where the Honeymoon in Paradise plan includes champagne and flowers on arrival, daily continental breakfast, one dinner served en suite, daily car rental, gourmet picnic for two, sunset cruise, bottle of Anguilla rum and two t-shirts. Until March 31, 5- and 7-night rates range from $2015 studio (5nts) to $5280 Super Deluxe Penthouse (7nts). From April 1 to

October 31 rates are $1505 studio (5nts) to $3810 Super Deluxe Penthouse (7nts). Tax and service fee included.
264-497-6603; www.paradise.ai

Rendezvous Bay Hotel
Rendezvous Bay Hotel's romantic couples enjoy long walks on deserted beaches, a luxurious beach villa double room and candlelit, gourmet dinners. The 7-night Honeymoon Plan per couple rates until March 31 are $2856 MAP (breakfast & dinner), $2448 breakfast only; April 1—Dec. 14, $2040 MAP and $1530 breakfast only. Rates include champagne on arrival, flowers, fruit basket, 5-day car rental, 2 t-shirts from the resort's boutique, airport transfers, tax and service charges. Wedding packages are also available.
800-274-4893; 264-497-6549; www.rendezvousbay.com

Splash! Villa
Romantic seclusion, luxurious appointments, and indulgent amenities await couples in this 3-bedroom private villa boasting a master suite Jacuzzi-for-two, outdoor pool, poolside dining and roof patio for sunset cocktails. The 2003 Honeymoon Package includes 7 nights accommodation, chilled champagne on arrival, two 30-minute deep tissue massages, starter breakfast, and selection of honeymoon amenities (massage oils, candles and other delights). Per couple rate (plus 10% tax & 10% service fee) until April 14 is $2599; $1699 from April 15-Dec. 14.
264-497-3666; www.splash.ai

For more information on Anguilla activities and the packages, rates, facilities and amenities offered by its properties, contact the Anguilla Tourist Board at 1-800-553-4939 or atbtour@anguillanet.com.

ANGUILLA RESORTS AND VILLAS:SETTING THE STANDARD FOR LUXURY AND SOPHISTICATION

A jewel of the Caribbean, the island of Anguilla, is home to 33 pristine beaches and shimmering sapphire water. Combining natural beauty and unsurpassed accommodations, Anguilla offers discerning travelers a wide variety of luxurious resorts and villas.

The newly opened **Temenos**, Greek for "sanctuary," is positioned on Long Bay Beach and consists of three lavish villas, Sand, Sea and Sky, which invite tranquility and seclusion. Temenos offers guests numerous amenities, including tennis courts; state-of-the-art fitness center and inspiring views that encourage yoga, stretching or self-meditation. The resort also provides guests with the use of a private 32-foot fiberglass boat. With a peak season rate of $50,000 a week, and a superior staff to fulfill every wish, Temenos' guests will undoubtedly experience the absolute ultimate in luxury.

Rich in design with the finest handpicked furnishings from Italy, Turkey and Russia, the **Altamer Resort**, on Shoal Bay West, is a luxurious five-bedroom beachfront villa designed by award-winning architect, Myron Goldfinger. A seven-night minimum stay ranges from $24,000-$38,000 depending upon the time of year. A private wine cellar, inviting pool, floodlit tennis court and custom designed silverware are just some of Altamer's exclusive features.

Situated on Barnes Bay, **Cerulean Villa** is extravagant with inlaid mosaics and imported limestone tiled floors and fountains. Covering over 13,000 square feet, the villa's furnishings are original – constructed by craftsmen in Mexico and Morocco. Cerulean Villa consists of seven large bedrooms, vaulted ceilings and French doors, which open to the clear Caribbean Sea. A seven-night minimum stay during peak season can cost up to $35,000. Guests can choose from a vast selection of water sports, dine elegantly on a private beach or simply relax in the sun.

The **CuisinArt Resort & Spa** on Rendezvous Bay exudes classic Caribbean style. Luxury suites and rooms are spacious yet private, airy and sunny, providing the ultimate setting for relaxation. Guests will enjoy the freshest fruits and vegetables grown in CuisinArt's own Hydroponic Farm. The Venus Spa offers an all-new health and wellness program using the resort's homegrown vegetation. During peak season, rooms are priced between $695 - $2,000 per night.

Cove Castles, located in Shoal Bay West is elegance at its best. Anguilla's first Myron Goldfinger creation, Cove Castles' striking structural design, sweeping staircases and cool white terra cotta interiors, create an atmosphere of sophisticated luxury. For those looking to avoid the crowds, Cove Castles offers a private haven that encourages guests to nap in hammocks, read books or play tennis day or night. Guests can dine at the resort, experiencing French /Caribbean cuisine, or have a gourmet selection brought right to the villa for private dining. Throughout the winter months, rates range from $795 - $2,995 per night.

Cap Juluca, occupying 179 acres of land and inland waters, rests on Maunday's Bay, celebrated for its 2.5 miles of white beach. This glorious property, encircled by vast ocean views is comprised of 18 individual Moorish-inspired beachfront villas. Some of Cap Juluca's luxurious accommodations include a fully-equipped fitness center, Main House library, lounge, 24-hour room service, scuba diving, live entertainment weekly, ultimate spa amenities and a Continental breakfast served intimately upon guest's private terrace. Cap Juluca offers three exquisite dining spots including Pimms, an internationally-acclaimed restaurant with award-winning chef, George Reid, who provides a light healthy French Asian cuisine. Depending on the type of room, rates are $825 - $5,400 per night during the winter months.

The **Malliouhana Hotel and Spa** is located on beautiful Meads Bay. In addition to a warm welcome, genuine hospitality and renowned service, guests are offered a choice of activities, such as water-skiing, sailing, and snorkeling. The Malliouhana is home to

Anguilla's only on-site 'Children's Place,' making this resort family friendly. A new full-service spa is set to open in November 2002. The Restaurant at Malliouhana merges Caribbean culinary tradition and authentic French cuisine. Malliouhana's Wine Cellar houses an impressive 20,000 bottles of wine and is a winner of the coveted Wine Spectator Grand Award. The rates at Malliouhana range from $550 - $2,600 per night in peak season.

ANGUILLA'S HIDDEN TREASURES

Travelers Will Discover Paradise on Anguilla is Real and Affordable

Though the island of Anguilla is known for its exclusive reputation, and luxurious properties, the island is home to a number of hidden treasures which combine to make a vacation accessible to any budget. 85% of the island's accommodations are available for $200 or less, during most of the year, and once on the island, visitors can enjoy moderately-priced island activities such as a glass-bottom boat ride at Shoal Bay, a visit to observe the dolphins and stingrays at Dolphin Fantaseas, or the luxury of a self-indulgent spa treatment available at both the island's award-winning spas or priced more modestly, through individually licensed practitioners. Ideal for travelers on any budget, Anguilla offers a wide variety of less expensive mid-luxury options for your special vacation experience.

Luxury for Less

During the summer months, incredible savings abound in some of Anguilla's intimate accommodation establishments. The Allamanda Beach Club, located near beautiful Shoal Bay, offers its studio rooms, with a pull out couch, for only $87 per night, while at The Anguilla Great House on Rendezvous Bay rooms begin at $140 and offer an intimate hideaway and uncrowded atmosphere. This property is also offering a special all-inclusive package this summer, starting at $170 per person, double occupancy. Yet another local jewel, Paradise Cove, is offering its 12 elegantly appointed, fully furnished, air-conditioned studio suites from $135 per night.

Family Fun

With competitively priced accommodations, Anguilla is a vacation haven for parents and children alike offering a best buy for families. La Sirena Hotel starts at $90 per night and includes either a garden or ocean view, balcony, ceiling fan and/or A/C. Each room provides direct-dialing telephone service, radio-alarm clock, room safe, mini-bar and daily maid service. The Shoal Bay Beach Hotel's one-bedroom apartments begin at $125 per night and include twin or queen-sized beds. Every room has a balcony overlooking the swimming pool and sea, a fully equipped kitchen, dining and living room area with cable TV and direct-dial phone. The Ferry Boat Inn offers two-bedroom apartments for $175 per night. The bedrooms offer two bathrooms, living room with a double sofa bed, dining room, kitchen and patio. At Shoal Bay Villas, parents can enjoy a "7 nights for the price of 5" package while up to two children stay free in a fully furnished 1 bedroom suite from $195 per night.

Romance on Anguilla

Anguilla is consistently ranked as a top destination of choice for those lucky in love. The

Arawak Beach Inn, with its Amerindian-inspired architecture, is located in Island Harbor. The friendly efficient staff can help organize an ideal romantic vacation at a reasonable rate. A double room accommodation is available year round priced competitively and ranges from $95 - $175 per night. A number of special romance packages are also available. The Rendezvous Bay Hotel, with full service accommodations ranging from $90 - $175, depending on the time of year, provides the ideal backdrop for couples to experience the romance of Anguilla, strolling hand in hand on stunning Rendezvous Bay. And for a truly intimate, romantic experience check out Blue Waters on Shoal Bay West, where a one bedroom, fully furnished beachfront apartment goes for $125 per day.

Courtney Devonish © C. Lee

EXPLORING ART AND ARTIFACTS ON ANGUILLA: SPLENDOR ON AND OFF THE BEACH

Growing Colony of Artists, Galleries, Museums and Historic Sites on Idyllic Caribbean Island

The world-renowned white sands of Anguilla's 33 unspoiled beaches, caressed by a brilliant turquoise sea and 80°F temperatures year round, lure travelers seeking rest and pampering in style. However, lazy days in the sun are only the start of an Anguillian idyll. Away from the beach, visitors will enjoy another side of Anguilla in the tranquil island's art studios and galleries, private museums and historic sites.

Anguilla is home to a veritable colony of artists who have come here from many parts of the world to pursue their creative muse. The diverse art forms include pottery, sculpture, handcrafts, paintings and woodcraft. There is also a growing collection of tribal artifacts, textiles, antiques, carvings and furniture from many exotic destinations, in the Caribbean and beyond, which can be found in art galleries and studios around the island.

A self-guided "Art Tour of Anguilla" brochure, available through the Anguilla Tourist Board, takes visitors to 15 galleries and studios across the island. Among these, Devonish Art Gallery, located on West End Rd., features Anguillian, Caribbean and international artists as well as the art of proprietor-artist, Courtney Devonish. Next to the Devonish Art Gallery one finds Cheddie's Carving Studio, a one-of-a-kind atelier where local, self-taught artisan, Cheddie, fashions intricate, unique designs out of driftwood, bronze and stone. The CuisinArt Resort & Spa Art Gallery at Rendezvous Bay displays a beautiful selection of original art from Italy by a variety of world-renowned artists, while The World Art & Antiques Gallery, in The Valley, hosts a collection of precious antiques, exotic collectibles and worldwide furnishings.

Italian artist, Gianni Bracciali and his working glass studio, Glass Island in The Old Manse, produce original platters, tiles, jewelry and decorative objects. In The Valley, Savannah Gallery is home to a variety of artwork from local and regional artists alike. Oils watercolors, inks, prints, sculpture and crafts are available.

If you are interested in exploring the island's past, then a visit to The Heritage Collection Museum is a great place to start your journey. As Anguilla's first privately owned museum, it houses an array of Anguillian artifacts, old records and photographs tracing the island's history from the golden age of the Arawaks to the present time. On display from the Arawak period are pottery shards, zemi idols and stone tools. The Plantation Era collection includes original documents and artifacts from the early 19th Century. Colville Petty, OBE, a historian and collector, is the curator-owner of the museum. He is widely regarded as an authority on Anguilla's history and has published three books on the subject.

If your interest takes you further back, you may already know that over 4,000 years ago, Amerindian peoples discovered Anguilla when they ventured from South America's mainland in hand dug canoes and rafts. The Arawak-speaking Amerindians called the lush rain forest "Malliouhana," which meant - arrow-shaped sea serpent. Settling inland, the Amerindians developed villages, began farming and left behind evidence along the eastern end of the island which centuries later historians identified as shell axes, flint blades and stone objects, over 3,300 years old.

Along the eastern end of the island, are two incredible cave sites, The Fountain at Shoal Bay and Big Springs at Island Harbour. Inside The Fountain one can find original petroglyphs, a large religious stalagmite, as well as offering bowls and other tribal artifacts. It is the island's most intact ceremonial site from the time of the Amerindians, and speaks of the importance of religion to this early people.

Big Springs is a limestone sinkhole, which contains a large petroglyph and a carved stalagmite as well as other historic artifacts. Though currently closed to the public, the National Parks System, administered by the Anguilla National Trust, is developing both sites into a historic attraction.

Turtle Cove ©M. Tichy

TRADE THE WHITE SNOW FOR THE WHITE SANDS OF ANGUILLA DURING WINTER 2002

After the rigors of the holiday season, enjoy the tranquility waiting to greet you on the island of Anguilla. The alluring combination of 80-degree sun-filled days, pristine white sand beaches, award-winning restaurants and resorts ranging from five-star to private guesthouses, has become even more enticing with the special rates and packages being offered by many of this Caribbean island's most luxurious resorts.

The Arawak Beach Inn, cast in calming pastels and providing a casual and relaxed, home-away-from-home atmosphere, is offering a number of multi-night stays beginning January 3 through April 6. These packages include oceanfront accommodations, full island breakfast daily, between one and four dinners at the Inn and a full-day, private excursion to a secluded beach on an uninhabited castaway island along with a gourmet packed lunch.

Arawak's seven-night 'Island Adventure' package, which also includes a full-day trip via

ferry to Marigot on French St. Martin, is $849 per person. The four-night 'Escape' package is $499 per person and the two-night 'Escape' package is $289 per person. Packages include airport transfers as well as between one- and three-day car rental.
-more-
Award-winning Cap Juluca, a secluded, sophisticated and romantic 179-acre retreat, is offering two special programs from January 5 to April 5. The 'Romantic Rendezvous' includes seven nights' beachfront accommodations for two, four dinners for two at any of the resort's three restaurants or room service, a one-hour couples massage and an all day snorkeling trip to Prickly Pear with a special "Cap Juluca" barbeque lunch. Rates for two start at $5,835 for a superior room, and continue up to $7,850 for a junior suite.

The 'Quick Getaway' offers four nights' beachfront accommodation for two, four dinners provided by the Cap Juluca expert chefs and a half-day snorkeling trip to Little Bay Marine preserve. Rates for two begin at $3,440 for a superior room, and go up to $4,595 for a junior suite. Both packages include daily continental breakfast, accommodation tax and service charges, along with airport and ferry transfers.

CuisinArt Resort & Spa, a stylish and distinctively Mykonos-influenced beachfront resort and spa, is also offering a number of value-added packages for travelers to Anguilla this winter, beginning January 4 and continuing to April 4.

The 'Relaxation' package includes three nights' accommodations, daily continental breakfast, one 50-minute massage, one 40-minute Renewal Facial, a dinner for two at the resort's Santorini restaurant and a lunch for two at CuisinArt's Café Mediterraneo. This package ranges from $2,520 for a luxury room up to $6,520 for a luxury two-bedroom suite, with options in between.

The 'Indulgence' package includes seven nights' accommodations, along with daily continental breakfast, four 50-minute spa treatments, one half-day snorkel excursion, one lunch for two at CuisinArt's Hydroponics Café, a dinner for two at Santorini and one Tuesday-evening Caribbean lobster barbeque for two. This package ranges from $5,910 for a luxury room and culminates with $15,165 for a luxury two-bedroom suite, with options in between. These winter packages also include daily tax and service charges as well as roundtrip airport transfers.
-more-

The Frangipani Beach Club, set amidst a lush tropical garden on Meads Bay, is offering the 'Seven Warm, Winter Nights' package from January 4 to April 15. Along with seven nights' accommodations, the package includes daily continental breakfast, a boat ride to Sandy Island and fresh flowers in each guest room. The rates for this package begin with a one-bedroom suite at $3,500, and continue up through a two-bedroom penthouse for $7,700.

Paradise Cove, a secluded and restful apartment hotel situated at the western end of Anguilla, is a tranquil hideaway offering a seven-night "Escape to Paradise" package from December 19 to March 31. In addition to seven nights' accommodations, the package includes a wine and fruit platter on arrival, daily breakfast for two, two dinners for two at some of the resort's favorite local dining spots, seven-day car rental and all service charges and taxes. A one-bedroom suite package is $3,270 and a one-bedroom penthouse suite package is $4,440.

HOTELS

Hotels		ACC	WIN	SUM	RMS
	Anguilla Great House Rendezvous Bay T: 264-497-6061 • F: 264-497-6019 Toll Free: 800-583-9247 flemingw@anguillanet.com www.anguillagreathouse.com	SG DB	$220+ $250+	$140+ $155+	27
	Arawak Beach Inn Island Harbor T: 264-497-4888 • F: 264-497-4889 Toll Free: 800-4-ARAWAK relax@arawakbeach.com www.arawakbeach.com	STU/STE DB	$225+ $195+	$125+ $95+	17
	Cap Juluca Maundays Bay T: 264-497-6666 • F: 264-497-6617 Toll Free: 888-858-5822 capjuluca@anguillanet.com www.capjuluca.com	LUX.RM JR. STE 3-5 BR	$735+ $905+ $3585+	$395+ $500+ $1720+	98
	Enclave at Cinnamon Reef Little Harbor T: 264-497-2727 • F: 264-497-3727 Toll Free: 800-223-1108 cinnamonreef@boutiqueresortsintl.com www.boutiqueresortsintl.com	VILLA BEACH STE OTHER	$525 $475 $350+	$225+ $200+ $175+	22
	Cocoloba Beach Resort Barnes Bay T: 264-497-8800 • F: 264-497-8126 www.cocolobaresort.com	SG DBL OTHER	$160+ $180+ $320+	$110+ $120+ $160+	100
	Covecastles Shoal Bay West T: 264-497-6801 • F: 264-497-6051 Toll Free: 800-223-1108 covecastles@anguillanet.com www.covecastles.com	1 BR 2 BR 3-4 BR	$795+ $995+ $1295+	$525+ $625+ $825+	14

Hotels	ACC	WIN	SUM	RMS

	Cuisinart Resort & Spa Rendezvous Bay T: 264-498-2002• F: 264-498-2010 Toll Free: 800-937-9956 igiusti@cuisinart.ai www.cuisinartresort.com	LUX JR STE 1,2 BR PH	$495 $595+ $995+	$295 $350+ $595+	93
	Frangipani Beach Club Meads Bay T: 264-497-6442 • F: 264-497-6440 Toll Free: 800-829-4564 frangipani@anguillanet.com www.frangipani.ai	SGL DBL 1-3BR PENT	$300+ $400 $550-1120 $700	$185 $185+ $270-560 $330	16
	La Sirena Meads Bay T: 264-497-6827 • F: 264-497-6829 Toll Free: 800-331-3358 lasirena@anguillanet.com www.la-sirena.com	SGL DBL JR STE 2-3BR	$200+ $260+ $400+ $400-560+	$110+ $145+ $230+ $230-360+	25
	Malliouhana Hotel & Spa Meads Bay T: 264-497-6111 • F: 264-497-6011 Toll Free: 800-835-0796 malliouhana@anguillanet.com www.malliouhana.com	DB JR STE 1 BR 2 BR	$575+ $940+ $860+ $1,705	$275+ $470+ $470+ $815+	55
	Rendezvous Bay Hotel & Villas Rendezvous Bay T: 264-497-6549 • F: 264-497-6026 Toll Free: 800-274-4893 info@rendezvousbay.com www.rendezvousbay.com	2BR DB Deluxe VILLA	$300+ $235+ $700+	$200+ $135+ $375+	45
	Shoal Bay Villas Shoal Bay T: 264-497-2051 • F: 264-497-3631 sbvillas@anguillanet.com www.sbvillas.ai	STUDIO 1BR 2BR SUITE	$270 $295+ $445+ $360+	$165 $195+ $260+ $240+	13

Apartments, Villas & Condos		ACC	WIN	SUM	RMS
	Altamer Villas Shoal Bay West	VILLA	$38,000 Weekly Rates	$24,000	1

	Apartments, Villas & Condos	ACC	WIN	SUM	RMS
	P.O. Box 3001 Toll Free: 888-652-6888 Tel:498-4000 • Fax: 498-4010 www.altamer.com	VILLA	$38,000 Weekly Rates	$24,000	1
	Blue Waters Beach Apartments Shoal Bay West Tel 264-497-6292 Fax: 264-497-6982 www.altamer.com	1 BR 2 BR	$250+ $360+	$125+ $175+	
	Brookland Island View Crocus Hill Tel: 497-5078 crissybrooks978@hotmail.com http://www.brooklandsislandview.com	1 BR 2 BR 3 BR	$650/w $750/w $850/w	$450/w $550/w $650/w	9
	Caribbean Seavi ew Long Path T: 264-497-4662 • F: 264-497-3526 d-3ent@anguillanet.com www.seaview.ai	1 BR	$110+	$95+	10
	Caribella Resort Barnes Bay T: 264-497-6045 • F: 264-497-8929 lambertventures@yahoo.com www.lambertventures.com/caribell.htm	1 BR 2 BR (Wkly Rates)	$1,800 $2,100	$1,050 $1,255	6
	Carimar Beach Club Meads Bay T: 264-497-6881 • F: 264-497-6071 Toll Free: 800-235-8667 carimar@anguillanet.com www.carimar.com	1 BR 2 BR	$320+ $430+	$140+ $210+	24
	Coyaba Manor Lockrum Estate T: 264-497-3400 • F: 264-497-6410 coyaba@anguillanet.com www.coyaba.ai	VILLA (Wkly Rates)	$13,500+	$8,500	6
	Easy Corner Cottages South Hill T: 264-497-6433 • F: 264-497-6410 Toll Free: 800-633-7411 lucy@sintmaarten.com	STUDIO 1 BR 2BR 3 BR	$110+ $160 $195+ $240+	$120+ $125 $155+ $195+	22
		STUDIO 1 BR 2 BR	$150 $130 $205	$120 $110 $180	12

	Harbor Lights Island Harbour T: 264-497-4435 • F: 264-497-4435 Toll Free: 800-759-9870	STUDIO	$80- 130	Closed	4
	Madeariman Beach Club Shoal Bay East T: 264-497-3833 • F: 264-497-5751 info@madeariman.com www.madeariman.com	STUDIO SUITE PVT VILLA	$175+ $225+ $400+	$125+ $175+ $300+	5
		A/C			
	Maria's Beach Apartments The Valley, Anguilla P.O. Box 1144 Tel: 264-497-2427 Email: shermah@anguillanet.com	2 BR	$175+	$125+	2
		A/C			
	Masara Resort Katouche T: 264-497-3200 • F: 264-497-3223 lambertventures@yahoo.com www.lambertventures.com/masara.htm	1 BR 2 BR	$175+ $250+	$100+ $125+	9
		A/C			
	Nathans' Cove Meads Bay T: 264-497-2596	1 BR 2 BR 4 BR	$200 $300 $550	$100 $200 $400	8
		A/C			
	Ocean Breeze Long Path T: 264-497-2466 • F: 264-497-3084 www.mycaribbean.com	1 BR 2 BR	$60 $120	$60 $120	8
	Paradise Cove The Cove T: 264-497-6603 • F: 264-497-6927 para-cove@anguillanet.com www.paradise.ai	1 BR SUITE 2 BR SUITE STUDIO PENTHOUSE	$290+ $420+ $235 $550	$165+ $250+ $150+ $375+	29
		A/C			
	Royal Palms South Hill T: 264-497-6484 • F: 264-497-6448 royalpalms@anguillanet.com www.royalpalms.ai	2 BR	$200+	$135+	12
		A/C			
		1 BR 2 BR VILLA	$125 $170	$65 $85	6
		A/C			

CURRENCY, BANKS, EXCHANGE, TRAVELERS CHEQUES

Anguilla uses US dollars everywhere, but EC dollars are the official currency. Prices are quoted in either currency, so ask if you are unsure. Credit cards are accepted at most hotels, car rental agencies, gift shops and gourmet restaurants, but not at beach bars, supermarkets, local shops.

ATM MACHINES

As of January 2002, the ATM machine at the Scotiabank is still connected to the outside world and allows you to get cash from your home account. There is also an ATM at the NBA that may allow you to make a cash withdrawal against your VISA card.

SERVICE CHARGES?

My wife and I are traveling to your island in September, and our travel agent mentioned that there was a service charge on the exchange of money and the redemption of travelers cheques. Could you tell us if this is, indeed, true, and if so, what the percentage rate of the charge would be?

Not True. There is no charge for cashing US travelers cheques and no charge to change US money. There is a 2% government tax on converting EC dollars into US, but not US into EC. The exchange rate has been unchanged for quite a few years. As a tourist you can function entirely in US$ and never exchange any money to EC at all. (Note: I lived here for 2 years before I learned about the 2% tax and heard rumours of grey market dealers at the ferry dock.)

Exchange Rates for CASH	
EC to US	2.73 EC per US + 2% gov tax
US to EC	2.67 EC per US, no tax
Exchange Rates for CHEQUES	
EC to US cash	2.73 + 2% gov tax
EC to US account	2.7619 + 2% gov tax
US to EC	2.6882, no gov tax

A US$ cheque that is drawn on a US bank can be deposited into an Anguillian bank, but it takes a long time to clear. At the Carribean Commercial Bank, for example, it takes one month to clear if the amount is less than $1000, two weeks if greater. You can wire transfer from anywhere in the world to Anguilla in a day or two and have it credited immediately.

OPENING A BANK ACCOUNT IN ANGUILLA

It is possible to open a personal savings account in US or EC dollars by mail. Banks are reluctant to open a checking account for strangers (you might write a lot of bad checks and then run off). Interest on savings accounts is about 4% at most banks, but interest is not calculated in a very generous way (i.e., it is **not** daily interest on the minimum balance). As at any bank, you complete a signature card giving the names on the account, address, telephone number, how many signatures required, etc. For example, here are the requirements for the Caribbean Commercial Bank:

1. Personal banking reference from a recognized banking institution.
2. Personal identification (copy of passport or Driver's license, etc.)
3. Signatures on signature card must be notarized
4. Minimum deposit for savings account - $25 in the currency of the account.
5. Minimum deposit for checking account - $100 in the currency of the account.

For more information, contact the banks directly. These are not US banks - deposits are primarily protected by the assets of the bank, not by the FDIC.

National Bank of Anguilla 264-497-2101
Caribbean Commercial Bank 264-497-2571 ccbaxa@anguillanet.com
Barclays 264-497-2301
Scotiabank 264-497-3333
Revised: January 24, 19102

SUPPLEMENTS

MARKET PARTICIPANTS

BANKS

Domestic

Caribbean Commercial Bank (Anguilla) Limited

P.O. Box 23
The Valley
Anguilla, B.W.I.
Tel: (264) 497-2571
Fax: (264) 497-3570

FirstCaribbean International Bank (Barbados) Limited

P. O. Box 140
The Valley
Anguilla, B.W.I.
Tel: (264) 497-2301
Fax: (264) 497-2980

National Bank of Anguilla Limited

P. O. Box 44
The Valley
Anguilla, B.W.I.
Tel: (264) 497-2201
Fax: (264) 497-3310

Scotiabank Anguilla Limited

Fairplay Commercial Complex
P.O. Box 250
The Valley
Anguilla, B.W.I.
Tel: (264) 497-3333
Fax: (264) 497-3344

Offshore

Caribbean Commercial Investment Bank Ltd.

2 St. Mary's Street
P.O. Box 23
The Valley
Anguilla, B.W.I.
Tel: (264) 497-2242
Fax: (264) 497-7054

Foreign Commerce Bank Limited

The Anguilla Professional Complex
P.O. Box 1648
The Valley
Anguilla, B.W.I.
Tel: (264) 498-5576
Fax: (264) 498-5578

National Bank of Anguilla (Private Banking and Trust) Limited

Conrad W Fleming Corporate Bldg
St. Mary's Road
P. O. Box 44
The Valley
Anguilla, B.W.I.
Tel: (264) 497-7096
Fax: (264) 497-2296

MONEY SERVICES BUSINESSES

Anguilla Post Office

P O Box 60
The Valley
Anguilla, B.W.I.
Tel: (264) 497-2528
Fax: (264) 497-5455
Email: **angstamp@gov.ai**

GraceKennedy Money Services (Anguilla) Limited

Lake's World
P.O. Box 76
The Valley
Anguilla, B.W.I.
Tel: (264) 497-2240
Fax: (264) 497-2511

COMPANY MANAGERS

Anguilla Insurance Management Inc.

Anguilla Professional Complex
P.O Box 335
The Valley
Anguilla, B.W.I.
Tel: (264) 498-4246
Fax: (264) 498-2228

Astaphan, Thomas

Herbert's Commercial Center
P.O. Box 350
The Valley

Anguilla, B.W.I.
Tel: (264) 497-5555
Fax: (264) 497-5310

AXA Offshore Management Limited

The Law Building
P.O. Box 687
The Valley
Anguilla, B.W.I.
Tel: (264) 497-3142
Fax: (264) 497-5753

Banx Professional Services Ltd.

Caribbean Commercial Centre
P.O. Box 20
The Valley
Anguilla, B.W.I.
Tel: (264) 497-5388
Fax: (264) 497-3286

Benjamine Company Services Limited

Hannah-Waver House
P.O. Box 801
The Valley
Anguilla, B.W.I.
Tel: (264) 497-5270
Fax: (264) 497-5271

Blenheim Trust (Anguilla) Limited

Heywood House
P.O. Box 294
The Valley
Anguilla, B.W.I.
Tel: (264) 461-6468 or (264) 497-6468
Fax: (264) 461-6080 or (264) 497-6800

Capital Corporate Services Anguilla Limited

The Barbrow Building
P.O. Box 371
The Valley
Anguilla, B.W.I.
Tel: (264) 498-4224
Fax: (264) 497-5504

Capstone Insurance Management (Anguilla) Ltd

The Hansa Bank Building
P.O. Box 727
The Valley
Anguilla, B.W.I.
Tel: (264) 498-3800
Fax: (264) 498-3805
www.capstoneassociated.com

Captiva (Anguilla) Ltd

P O Box 941
201 Rogers Office Building
Edwin Wallace Rey Drive
George Hill
Anguilla, B.W.I.
Tel: (264) 498-5858
Fax: (264) 497-5504

C.E.G. Ltd.

Heywood House
P.O. Box 294
The Valley
Anguilla, B.W.I.
Tel: (264) 461-6468 or (264) 497-6468
Fax: (264) 461-6080 or (264) 497-6800

Centurion Financial Services Inc

Spencer House
P.O. Box 821
The Valley
Anguilla, B.W.I.
Tel: (264) 497-8129
Fax: (264) 497-8289
Email: **cfs@anguillanet.com**

CMF International Ltd

Mitchell's House
P.O. Box 174
The Valley
Anguilla, B.W.I.
Tel: (264) 498-8800
Fax: (264) 498-8880

CMS Management Ltd.

Heywood House
P.O. Box 294
The Valley
Anguilla, B.W.I.
Tel: (264) 461-6468 or (264) 497-6468
Fax: (264) 461-6080 or (264) 497-6800

Counsel Limited

The Hansa Bank Building
P.O. Box 727
The Valley
Anguilla, B.W.I.
Tel: (264) 498-3800
Fax: (264) 498-3805

CR Hodge & Associates

The Haskins Bldg
P.O. Box 1486
The Valley
Anguilla, BWI
Tel: (264) 498-8800
Fax: (264) 498-8880

Crystal Anguilla Ltd

P.O. Box 941
201 Rogers Office Building
Edwin Wallace Rey Drive
George Hill
Anguilla, B.W.I.
Tel: (264) 498-5858
Fax: (264) 497-5504

D-3 Enterprises

Caribbean Commercial Complex
P.O Box 350
The Valley
Anguilla, B.W.I.
Tel: (264) 497-3525
Fax: (264) 497-5310

Executive Corporate Services Inc.

The Mason Complex, Suite 19 & 20
P.O. Box I4052
The Valley
Anguilla, B.W.I.
Tel: (264) 497-7416
Fax: (264) 497-7417

Fidelis Company Management Limited

P.O. Box 1330
The Valley
Anguilla, B.W.I.
Tel: (264) 497-7889
Fax: (264) 497-0779

First Management Company Limited

Caribbean Commercial Centre
P.O. Box 68
The Valley
Anguilla, B.W.I.
Tel: (264) 497-5578
Fax: (264) 497-5589

Fleming, Keesha A. N. Attorney & Counselor at Law

Gem Exclusiv Building
P.O Box 1707
The Valley
Anguilla, B.W.I.
Tel: (264) 497-1254/1244
Fax: (264) 497-2209

H & P Corporate Services (Anguilla) Ltd

Maico Building
The Valley
Anguilla BWI
Tel: (264) 497-0361
Fax: (264) 497-8617

HBM (Anguilla) Ltd

Heywood House
P.O. Box 294
The Valley
Anguilla BWI
Tel (264) 497-6468
Fax (264) 497-6800

Hudsun (Anguilla) Limited

P O Box 1341
Babrow's Commercial Complex
The Valley, AI-2640
Anguilla, B.W.I.
Tel: (264) 461-7275
Fax: (264) 462-7275
Email: **admin@hudsun.vg**
Website: **www.hudsuntrust.com**

Icaza, Gonzalez-Ruiz & Aleman (Anguilla) Limited

P O Box 941
201 Rogers Office Building
Edwin Wallace Rey Drive
George Hill
Anguilla, B.W.I.
Tel: (264) 498-5858
Fax: (264) 497-5504

ICS Trust (Anguilla) Limited

The Hallmark Building
P.O. Box 227
The Valley
Anguilla, B.W.I.
Tel: (264) 497-3575
Fax: (264) 497-3577

IMC Management (Anguilla) Ltd.

Heywood House
P.O. Box 294
The Valley
Anguilla, B.W.I.
Tel: (264) 461-6468 or (264) 497-6468
Fax: (264) 461-6080 or (264) 497-6800

International Company Services (Anguilla) Limited

Gilwell Offices
P.O. Box 2
The Valley
Anguilla, B.W.I.
Tel: (264) 497-2744
Fax: (264) 497-3350

Intershore Consult (Anguilla) Ltd

P.O. Box 941
201 Rogers Office Building
Edwin Wallace Rey Drive

George Hill
Anguilla, B.W.I.
Tel: (264) 498-5858
Fax: (264) 497-5504

J.A.G. Company Services Ltd.

The Anguilla Professional Complex
P.O. Box 1398
The Valley
Anguilla, B.W.I.
Tel: (264) 497-1212
Fax: (264) 497-1214

Joyce Kentish & Associates

Auckland House
P.O. Box 259
The Valley
Anguilla, B.W.I.
Tel: (264) 497-2582
Fax: (264) 497-5496

M & R Corporate Services Limited

Hansa Bank Building
P.O. Box 671
The Valley
Anguilla, B.W.I.
Tel: (264) 497-5621
Fax: (264) 497-5220

McCleery, Samuel, Daniela & Louis

Hansa Bank Building
P.O. Box 1027
The Valley
Anguilla, B.W.I.
Tel: (264) 497-2527
Fax: (264) 497-5638

Meridian Corporate Services Ltd

Kamilah House
P.O. Box 637
Rock Farm
Anguilla, B.W.I.
Tel: (264) 476-1621
Fax: (264) 497-7891

OBN Limited

Long Path Rd. Suite 2A
P.O. Box 1015
The Valley
Anguilla, B.W.I.
Tel: (264) 498-2644
Fax: (264) 498- 2640

On-Island (Anguilla) Corporate Services. Ltd.

West Commercial Village
Lower South Hill
P O Box 1010
Anguilla, B.W.I.
Tel: (264) 497-5505
Fax: (264) 497-3975

Overseas Management Company (Anguilla) Limited

Victoria House
P.O. Box 58
The Valley
Anguilla, B.W.I.
Tel: (264) 497-2060
Fax: (264) 497-3096

Offshore Incorporations (Anguilla) Limited

Offshore Incorporations Centre
P.O. Box 1026
The Valley
Anguilla, B.W.I.
Tel: (264) 498-5000
Fax: (264) 498-5001

Paragon Corporate Services Ltd.

The Barbrow Building
P.O. Box 371
The Valley
Anguilla
Tel: (264) 498-4224
Fax: (264) 498-4220

P.M.A Legal & Corporate Services (Anguilla) Ltd.

P.O. Box 941
201 Rogers Office Building
Edwin Wallace Rey Drive
George Hill
Anguilla, B.W.I.
Tel: (264) 498-5858
Fax: (264) 497-5504

PMP Anguilla) Ltd

Mitchell House
P.O. Box 174
The Valley
Anguilla, BWI
Tel: (264) 498-8800
Fax: (264) 498-8880<

Professional Corporate Services (Anguilla) Limited

The Hallmark Building
P.O. Box 227
The Valley
Anguilla, B.W.I.
Tel: (264) 497-3575
Fax: (264) 497-3577

Span-Hansa Group Limited

The Technology Campus – TV1 02P
The Valley
AI-2640, Anguilla, B.W.I.
Tel: (264) 497-3800
Tel: (264) 461-2647
Fax: (702) 447-8567

Stafford Corporate Services Ltd

P.O. Box 941
201 Rogers Office Building
Edwin Wallace Rey Drive
George Hill
Anguilla, B.W.I.
Tel: (264) 498-5858
Fax: (264) 497-5504

Sterling Corporate Services Limited

P O Box 1341
The Valley
Anguilla, B.W.I.
Tel: (264) 498-7275
Fax: (264) 498-7276
Email: **kimberlyfg@anguillanet.com**

Stott & Company Limited

Gilwell Offices
P.O. Box 2
The Valley
Anguilla, B.W.I.
Tel: (264) 497-2744
Fax: (264) 497-3350

Sucre & Sucre (Anguilla) Limited

Victoria House
P.O. Box 58
The Valley
Anguilla, B.W.I.
Tel: (264) 497-2060
Fax: (264) 497-3096

Trufima Management (Anguilla) Ltd

P.O. Box 941
201 Rogers Office Building
Edwin Wallace Rey Drive
George Hill
Anguilla, B.W.I.
Tel: (264) 498-5858
Fax: (264) 497-5504

Wintrust (Anguilla) Limited

The Mason Complex, Suite 19 & 20
P.O. Box I4052
The Valley
Anguilla, B.W.I.
Tel: (264) 497-7416
Fax: (264) 497-7417

RESTRICTED COMPANIES

Bennie's Ltd

P.O. Box 254
Blowing Point
Anguilla
Tel: (264) 497-6221
Fax (264)497-5052

Corporate Management Services Ltd

P.O. Box 1000
The Valley
Anguilla
Tel: 264-497-2500
Fax: 264-498-2500

Fortress Holding Ltd

Maico Building
The Valley
Anguilla BWI
Tel: (264) 497-0361
Fax: (264) 497-8617

H & P (Anguilla) Ltd

Maico Building
The Valley
Anguilla BWI
Tel: (264) 497-0361
Fax: (264) 497-8617

Hudson & Partners Inc

Maico Building
The Valley
Anguilla BWI
Tel: (264) 497-0361
Fax: (264) 497-8617

INSURERS

Lloyds Underwriters

Lloyd's Underwriters

One Lime Street
London
EC3M 7HA
United Kingdom
Tel: (+44) 020 7327 5351
Fax: (+44) 0207 327 5255

Domestic

American Bankers Life Assurance Company Limited

Caribbean Commercial Complex
P.O. Box 1377
The Valley
Anguilla, B.W.I.
Tel: (264) 497-3525
Fax: (264) 497-3526

Atlantic Southern Insurance Company Limited

P.O. Box 1377
The Valley
Anguilla, B.W.I.
Tel: (264) 497-3525
Fax: (264) 497-3526

Best Meridian Insurance Company

Caribbean Commercial Complex
P.O. Box 1377
The Valley
Anguilla, B.W.I.
Tel: (264) 497-3525
Fax: (264) 497-3526

British American Insurance Company Ltd.

P.O. Box 148
The Valley
Anguilla, B.W.I.
Tel: (264) 497-2653
Fax: (264) 497-5933

Bupa Insurance Company

Caribbean Commercial Complex
P.O Box 1377
The Valley
Anguilla, B.W.I.
Tel: 264 497-3525
Fax: 264 497-3526

Caribbean Alliance Insurance Company Limited

P.O. Box 1377
The Valley
Anguilla, B.W.I.
Tel: (264) 497-3525
Fax: (264) 497-3526

CLICO International General Insurance Limited

44 Caribbean Commercial Centre
The Valley
Anguilla, B.W.I.

CLICO International Life Insurance Limited

44 Caribbean Commercial Centre
The Valley
Anguilla, B.W.I.

East Caribbean Reinsurance Company Limited

Hannah Waver House
P.O. Box 801
The Valley
Anguilla, B.W.I.
Tel: (264) 497-3470
Fax: (264) 497-3177

Guardian General Insurance Ltd

Old Factory Plaza
P.O. Box 6
The Valley
Anguilla, B.W.I.
Tel: (264) 497-5757
Fax: (264) 497-2122

Gulf Insurance Limited

P.O. Box 189
Blowing Point
Anguilla, B.W.I.
Tel: (264) 497-6613
Fax: (264) 497-6713

Heritage Insurance Company (Caribbean) Limited

P.O. Box 9109
St Thomas
VI 00801
Tel: (340) 776-8050
Fax: (340) 774-8095

Island Heritage Insurance Company Ltd.

P.O. Box 671
The Valley
Anguilla, B.W.I.
Tel: (264) 497-5621
Fax: (264) 497-5220

Malliouhana-Anico Insurance Company Limited

P.O. Box 492
The Valley
Anguilla, B.W.I.
Tel: (264) 497-3712
Fax: (264) 497-3710

Midland National Life Insurance Limited

P.O. Box 1377
The Valley
Anguilla, B.W.I.
Tel: (264) 497-3525
Fax: (264) 497-3526

Nagico Insurance Company Limited (NAGICO)

P O Box 428
Albert Lake Drive
The Valley
Anguilla, B.W.I.
Tel: 264-497-7318
Fax: 264-497-5839

Nagico Reinsurance Company Limited

P O Box 428
Albert Lake Drive
The Valley
Anguilla, B.W.I.
Tel: (264) 497-5555
Fax: (264) 497-5310

National Caribbean Insurance Company Limited

Caribbean Commercial Complex
P.O. Box 323
The Valley
Anguilla, B.W.I.
Tel: (264) 497-2865
Fax: (264) 497-3783

Occidental Life Insurance Company of North Carolina Limited

P.O. Box 79
The Valley
Anguilla, B.W.I.
Tel: (264) 497-2976
Fax: (264) 497-3303

SAGICOR Life Inc

P.O. Box 492
The Valley
Anguilla, B.W.I.
Tel: (264) 497-3712
Fax: (264) 497-3710

The New India Insurance Company (T&T)

1st Floor
The Hansa Bank Building
The Valley
Anguilla, B.W.I.

OFFSHORE

Citadel Insurance Co Ltd

AXA Offshore Company Limited
PO Box 687,
The Law Building
The Valley
Anguilla, B.W.I.
Tel: (264) 497-3142
Fax: (264) 497-5753

Dean Speciality

Heywood House
P.O. Box 294
The Valley
Anguilla, B.W.I.
Tel: (264) 461-6468 or (264) 497-6468
Fax: (264) 461-6080 or (264) 497-6800

Fidelity Insurance Company

The Law Building
P.O Box 14
The Valley
Anguilla, B.W.I.
Tel: (264) 497-3142
Fax: (264) 497-5753

Kennedy International

Heywood House
P.O. Box 294
The Valley
Anguilla, B.W.I.
Tel: (264) 461-6468 or (264) 497-6468
Fax: (264) 461-6080 or (264) 497-6800

Maven Assurance Limited

Heywood House
P.O. Box 294
The Valley
Anguilla, B.W.I.
Tel: (264) 497-6468
Fax: (264) 497-6800
Email: **info@atlascaptives.com**
Website: **www.atlascaptives.com**

Maven International Life Insurance

Heywood House
P.O. Box 294
The Valley
Anguilla, B.W.I.
Tel: (264) 497-6468
Fax: (264) 497-6800
Email: **info@atlascaptives.com**
Website: **www.atlascaptives.com**

Millenium Re Insurance Company

Spencer House
The Valley
Anguilla, B.W.I.
Tel: (264) 497-8129
Fax: (264) 497-8289

MTD Insurance

Heywood House
P.O. Box 294

The Valley
Anguilla, B.W.I.
Tel: (264) 461-6468 or (264) 497-6468
Fax: (264) 461-6080 or (264) 497-6800

Olympia Insurance Company Limited

P.O. Box 1026
Harlaw Chambers
The Valley
Anguilla, B.W.I.
Tel: (264) 498-5000
Fax: (264) 498-5001

Physicians Excess

P O Box 1338
Caribbean Suite, NBA Corporate Building
St Mary's Road
The Valley
Anguilla, B.W.I.
TV1 11P
Tel: (264) 497 2189
Fax: (264) 497 5007

Security Atlantic Life Insurance Limited

Heywood House
P.O. Box 294
The Valley
Anguilla, B.W.I.
Tel: (264) 461-6468 or (264) 497-6468
Fax: (264) 461-6080 or (264) 497-6800

Trans Global Re Insurance Company Ltd

P.O. Box 941
201 Rogers Office Building
Edwin Wallace Rey Drive
George Hill
Anguilla, B.W.I.
Tel: (264) 498-5858
Fax: (264) 497-5504

Universal Select

First Anguilla Trust Company Limited
Mitchell House
P O BOX 174
The Valley
Anguilla, B.W.I.
Tel: (264) 498-8800
Fax: (264) 498-8880

MANAGERS

Active Insurance Management

Mitchell House
P.O Box 174
The Valley
Anguilla, B.W.I.

Anguilla Insurance Management Inc

Anguilla Professional Complex
P.O. Box 335
The Valley
Anguilla, B.W.I.
Tel: (264) 498-4246
Fax: (264) 497-2228

AON Insurance Managers (Panama), S.A

The Anguilla Professional Complex
P.O. Box 1648
The Valley
Anguilla, B.W.I.
Tel: (264) 498-5576
Fax: (264) 498-5578

Atlas Insurance Management

Heywood House
P.O. Box 294
The Valley
Anguilla, B.W.I.
Tel: (264) 497-6468
Fax: (264) 497-6800
Email: **info@atlascaptives.com**
Website: **www.atlascaptives.com**

ARC Insurance Management

The Anguilla Professional Complex
P.O. Box I4052
The Valley
Anguilla, B.W.I.
Tel: (264) 497-7416
Fax: (264) 497-7417

Atu Insurance Management (Anguilla) Inc

Mitchell House
P .O. Box 174
The Valley
Anguilla, B.W.I.
Tel: 264-498-8800
Fax: 264-498-8880

Azimuth Risk Solutions LLC

The Barbrow Building
P.O. Box 371
The Valley
Anguilla, B.W.I.
Tel: (264) 498-4224
Fax: (264) 498-4220

Belmont Insurance Management (Anguilla) Limited

Heywood House
P.O. Box 294
The Valley
Anguilla, B.W.I.

Tel: 264-497-6468
Fax: 264-497-6080

Blenheim Insurance Management BVI

Heywood House
P.O. Box 294
The Valley
Anguilla, B.W.I.
Tel: (264) 497-6468
Fax: (264) 497-6800

Capstone Insurance Management (Anguilla), Ltd

The Hansa Bank Building
P.O. Box 727
The Valley
Anguilla, B.W.I.
Tel: (264) 498-3800
Fax: (264) 498-3805
www.capstoneassociated.com

Captiva Managers Ltd

P O Box 941
201 Rogers Office Building
Edwin Wallace Rey Drive
George Hill
Anguilla, B.W.I.
Tel: (264) 498-5858
Fax: (264) 497-5504

First Anguilla Insurance Management

Mitchell House
P.O Box 174
The Valley
Anguilla, B.W.I.
Tel: (264) 498-8800
Fax: (264) 498-8880

Folio Insurance Management Limited

Paragon Corporate Services
Barbrow Building
P.O. Box 371
The Valley
Anguilla, B.W.I.
Tel: (264) 498 4224
Fax: (264) 498 4220

ISC Management Services Limited

The Law Building
P.O. Box 687
The Valley
Anguilla, B.W.I.
Tel: (264) 497-3142
Fax: (264) 497-5753

Millennium Insurance Management Company

Wigley & Associates Inc
Spencer House
The Valley
Anguilla, B.W.I.
Tel: (264) 497 8129
Fax: (264) 497 8289

Offshore Trust Services

The Law Building
P.O. Box 687
The Valley
Anguilla, B.W.I.
Tel: (264) 497 3142
Fax: (264) 497-5753

Premier Insurance Management

Mitchell House
P.O Box 174
The Valley
Anguilla, B.W.I.
Tel: (264) 498-8800
Fax: (264) 498-8880

~~RSG Limited~~ (dissolved)

Webster Dyrud Mitchell
P.O. Box 58
Victoria House
The Valley
Anguilla, B.W.I.
Tel: (264) 498-8800
Fax: (264) 498-8880

Stafford Insurance Managers (Anguilla) Ltd

P.O. Box 941
201 Rogers Office Building
Edwin Wallace Rey Drive
George Hill
Anguilla, B.W.I.
Tel: (264) 498-5858
Fax: (264) 497-5504

Symphony Management Ltd

P.O. Box HM 1538
Hamilton HM FX
Bermuda
Tel: (441) 295-2447 ext. 226
Fax: (441) 292-0511

Taino Insurance Managers, Ltd

Mitchell House
P.O Box 174
The Valley
Anguilla, B.W.I.
Tel: (264) 498-8800
Fax: (264) 498-8880

The Tower Management Group (Anguilla) Limited

Babrow's Commercial Complex
P.O. Box 1341
The Valley
Anguilla, B.W.I.
Tel: (264) 461-7275
Fax: (264) 462-7275

Tradewinds Insurance Management

Mitchell House
P.O Box 174
The Valley
Anguilla, B.W.I.

Wealth Management Solutions LLC

120 E. Main Street
Suite 101, Ramsey
NJ, USA
07446-1925
Tel: (201) 995-9085 ext. 5
Fax: (201) 995-9087

INTERMEDIARIES

Agents

A-Affordable Insurance Services Ltd

Mason Complex, Unit 21
P.O. Box 35
The Valley, AI-2640
Anguilla, B.W.I.
Tel: 264 497-5757
Fax 264-497-2122

Caribbean Craft Innovations Limited

NBA Corporate Buildings
St. Mary's Road
The Valley
Anguilla, B.W.I.
TV1 11P
Tel: (268) 779-6388
Fax: (268) 562-6077

Caribbean Insurers (Anguilla) Limited

Hansa Bank Building
P.O. Box 671
The Valley
Anguilla, B.W.I.
Tel: (264) 497-5621
Fax: (264) 497-5220

D-3 Enterprises Limited

Caribbean Commercial Complex
P.O. Box 1377
The Valley
Anguilla, B.W.I.
Tel: (264) 497-3525
Fax: (264) 497-3526

Mallíouhana – ANICO Insurance Company Limited

P.O. Box 492
The Valley
Anguilla, B.W.I.
Tel: (264) 497-3712
Fax: (264) 497-3710

Marjorie McClean

P.O. Box 189
The Valley
Anguilla, B.W.I.
Tel: (264) 497-6613
Fax: (264) 497-6713

North Eastern Insurance Services Ltd.

P.O. Box 350
The Valley
Anguilla, B.W.I.
Tel: (264) 497-5554
Fax: (264) 497-5310

Scotia Anguilla Ltd.

Fairplay Commercial Complex
P.O. Box 250
The Valley
Anguilla, B.W.I.
Tel: (264) 497-3333
Fax: (264) 497-3344

Whitfield Investments Ltd.

Old Factory Plaza
P O Box 6
Wallblake
Anguilla, AI-2640
Tel: (264) 498-2886
Fax: (264) 498-7233

Brokers

Alliance Insurance Services Limited

Kamilah House
P.O. Box 637
Rock Farm
Anguilla, B.W.I.
Tel: (264) 476-1621
Fax: (264) 497-7891

Caribbean Insurance Brokers (Anguilla) Limited

P.O. Box 727
The Valley
Anguilla, B.W.I.
Tel: (264) 497-3420
Fax: (264) 498-3805

CGM Insurance Brokers Limited

Babrow Building
P O Box 371
The Valley, Anguilla, B.W.I.
Tel: (264) 497-4224
Fax (264) 497-4220

CMRT Reinsurance Brokers Limited

Fairplay Commercial Complex
P.O. Box 428
The Valley
Anguilla, B.W.I.
Tel: (264) 497-7073
Fax: (264) 497 5836

Erica Delphine Fleming

P.O. Box 428
The Valley
Anguilla, B.W.I.
Tel: (264) 497-7073
Fax: (264) 497-5836

Fairplay Management Services Limited

Fair Play Commercial Complex
P.O. Box 79
The Valley
Anguilla, B.W.I.
Tel: (264) 497-2976
Fax: (264) 497-3303

Global Reinsurance Brokers Inc.

The Barbrow Building
P.O. Box 371
The Valley
Anguilla
Tel: (264) 498-4224
Fax: (264) 498-4220

Hyperion Risk Solutions Limited

Heywood House
P.O. Box 294
The Valley
Anguilla, B.W.I.
Tel: 264-497-6468
Fax: 264-497-6080

International Insurance Brokers Ltd

Auckland House
P.O. Box 259
The Valley
Anguilla, B.W.I.
Tel: (264) 497-2582
Fax: (264) 497-5496

Quantum Investment Services

Caribbean Commercial Complex
P.O. Box 1377
The Valley
Anguilla, B.W.I.
Tel: (264) 497-3525
Fax: (264) 497-3526

Securus International Limited

Mitchell House
P .O. Box 174
The Valley
Anguilla, B.W.I.
Tel: 264-498-8800
Fax: 264-498-8880

The Special Family Management S.A (SFMS)

Professional Complex
P.O. Box l4052
The Valley
Anguilla, BWI
Tel: (264) 497-7416
Fax: (264) 497-7417

CAPTIVE

A & M Indemnity, Ltd.
A.M.Y. Property & Casualty Insurance Corporation
Abbey Insurance Ltd.
ACE Risk Corp.
Acropolis Insurance Company Ltd.
Adair Insuance PCC
Adam Property & Casualty Insurance Corporation
ADR Insurance PCC
Adrasteak Insurance Corporation
Advantage Business Insurance Company
Aesthetics Concepts Insurance PCC
Alchemy Insurance Resources, Ltd
ALCO Risk Management Corp
All American Reinsurance Company PCC
All Liberty Insurance Ltd.
Alpha Assurance Company Ltd.
Ariel Assurance, Ltd.
Arrowhead Insurance Ltd.
Aspen Insurance Company Ltd.
Assured Solutions Unlimited Inc.
~~Automation Property & Casualty Insurance Corporation~~ (surrendered)
Autoworks Property & Casualty Insurance

Corporation
Bennington Insurance Company Limited
Bessemer Casualty Corp.
Big River Insurance Company, Inc
Blackhawl Indemnity, Ltd.
Blackstar Re Ltd.
Blue Roof Insurance Company Ltd.
Blue Sea Assurance Limited
Blue Sky Reinsurance Company Corp.
Caguas Casualty Corp.
Captiva Insurance Group Limited
Captive Insurance, Ltd.
Carlton Insurance Company Limited
Carnegie Casualty Corp.
Casings Casualty Corp.
Castle Indemnity Limited
Catalina Insurance Company Ltd.
Cedar Insurance, Ltd.
Central Casualty Corp.
Chamsa Insurance Ltd.
Chesapeake Casualty Corp.
Chiller Casualty Corp.
Chiminea Insurance Ltd.
CJA Insurance Company
Colorado River Insurance Ltd.
Columbia Casualty Corp.
Columbia Group Insurance Inc.
Commonwealth Mutual Limited
Concrete Casualty Corp.
Connection Casualty Corp.
Consolidated Casualty Corp.
Consolidated Insuranace Group, Ltd
Construction Casualty Corp.
Corporate National Insurance Ltd.
Cosmos Insurance Company Limited
Cotswold Insurance Limited
CRAC Insurance Company Ltd.
Credit Reassurance Ltd.
CRH Insurance, Ltd.
Crosspointe Casualty Ltd.
Crucible Casualty Corp.
CW Insurance Limited
CWC Insurance Ltd.
DAP Associates Insurance, Ltd.
Dasia Equities & Fidelity Ltd.
Dawg Insurance Ltd.
D&D Insurance, Ltd.
Delta Team Ltd.
~~Desert Trails Insurance Co.~~ (revoked)
Devonshire Property & Casualty Insurance Corporation
Diversified Risk & Assessment, Ltd.
Dublan Insurance Company, Ltd.
Dynagen Insurance, Ltd.
~~Earthworks Property & Casualty Insurance Corporation~~ (dissolved)
Eastrock Property & Casualty Insurance Corporation
Edwards Mutual Limited
Emerald Insurance Company Ltd
Empire Insurance Ltd
Empower Assurance Ltd.
Environ Ltd.
Environmental Casualty Corp.
Euston Property & Casualty Insurance Corporation
Extra Shield Insurance Company
Family Casualty Corp.
FinServ Casualty Corp.
First Trust Property & Casualty, Ltd.
Fluids Casualty Corp.
Florida United Insurance Company
Foreign Commerce Reinsurance Ltd.
Forge Casualty Corp.
Friday Insurance Company PCC
Fundamental Business Insurance Ltd.
Global Casualty Unlimited Inc.
Graces Management Ltd
Grayfin Insurance Co. Ltd.
Great Bay Insurance Company Limited
Great Circle Business Insurance, Ltd.
Green Hill Insurance Limited
Greystone Assurance Company, Ltd.
GRN Insurance Services Ltd.
Guardian Business Insurance, Ltd.
Hammock International Group Limited
Hampstead Casualty Corp.
Harbour International Insurance Company, Inc.
~~Hayden Insurance Ltd.~~ (revoked)
HealthCo Property & Casualty Insurance Corporation
Heart Safe Insurance Company Ltd.
Heath Insurance Company Ltd.
High Ground Insurance Ltd.
HomeCare Casualty Corp.
Hover Aviation Insurance Ltd.
Illini 21 Inc.
Industrial Casualty Corp.
Infinity General Insurance, Ltd.
Insider Insurance Ltd.
~~Insurion Insurance Company Ltd.~~ (surrendered)
Irish Mutual Insurance Company Limited
Island Harbour Insurance Company (PCC) Limited
IT Captive Insurance, Ltd.
JCJ Insurance Company, Ltd.

JEJ Management Ltd.
JLH Reinsurance Co. , Inc.
JSY Insurance Company, Ltd.
Kerpen Re, Lt.d
KOFS Group 1 Assurances Corp.
KOFS Group 2 Assurances Corp.
KOFS Group 3 Assurances Corp.
KOFS Group 4 Assurances Corp.
Lakhani Eye Group, Inc
Lawyers- Exchange Casualty Corp.
LDH Property & Casualty Ltd.
Legacy Business Insurance, Ltd.
Legacy Ventures Insurance, Ltd.
Liberty Assurance, Ltd.
Lockwood Insurance Inc.
LP Casualty Limited
Mainland Insurance Limited
MBM Group Limited
Mechanical Property & Casualty Insurance Corporation
Medical Liability Assurance Ltd.
Mika One Property & Casualty, Ltd.
Millennium Insurance Ltd.
~~MineSight Insurance Group Ltd.~~ (revoked)
Mirae Insurance Group Ltd.
Mirsol Indemnity, Ltd.
Modern Mutual Insurance Company Limited
Morant Insurance Company Limited
Morianai Insurance Ltd.
MoveCo Casualty Corp.
MRP Insurance, Ltd.
MTI Insurances Services, Ltd.
New Providential Insurance Company Ltd
Newport Casualty PCC
~~NLN Insurance Ltd.~~ (revoked)
NoRam Risk Management PCC
North West Providers Insurance PCC
Northstar Insurance Ltd.
~~Northwest Casualty Corp.~~ (surrendered)
Nutraceutical Casualty Corp.
Old Bailey Insurance Company
Old Concord Insurance Company
Omega Risk Management, Inc
Orion Indemnity, Ltd.
Ortus Insurance Ltd.
Oxford Business Insurance PCC
Pacificus Casualty Corp
Pamilo Insurance PCC
Petroguard Property & Casualty Insurance Corporation
Physicians Casualty Insurance Company, Ltd.
Pommes Frites Casualty Company
PoolRe Insurance Corp
Portland Property & Casualty Insurance Corporation
Premier Insurance Company Ltd
Premier Management Ltd.
Premier Physicians Insurance Company, Ltd.
Premier Protective Insurance Company Ltd
Preservation Alliance Ltd
Prestige Insurance Company Limited
Provincial Insurance PCC
~~Prudent Liability Insurance Company Ltd~~ (surrendered)
Quality Medical Insurance Company Ltd.
Rachis Casualty Corp.
Radiological Risk Assurances Corp.
Radix Insurance and Surety Limited (formerly JALKEMP Insurance Limited)
Rainbow Agency Ltd.
Recovery Casualty Corp.
Reinforce Insurance, Ltd
Republic Resources Inc
Reserve Casualty Corp.
Reservior Casualty Corp
Restoration Casualty Corp.
Ridge Casualty Corp.
Rio Salado Indemnity PCC
Risk Kurb Insurance Ltd.
Risk Management Insurance Company Ltd
Risk Retention Ltd.
Rocky Top Insurance
Roundrock Casualty Corp
S & S Risk Management Limited
Safe Shore Insurance Company
Santa Ana Re Ltd.
Scion Indemnity, Ltd
Security Casualty Corp
Security Insurance PCC
Seer Casualty Corp.
Sentry Insurance Company Ltd
Shalimar Business Insurance PCC
Shasta Surety Ltd
Silverado Insurance PCC
SJ Property & Casualty Ltd
Spectrum Property & Casualty Insurance Company PCC
St. Clair Insurance Inc.
St. Mark Inc.
St. Teresa Insurance LLC
Stafford Casualty Corp.
Starfish Insurance Ltd
Steelco Casualty Corp
Stonebridge Insurance Ltd
Strand Indemnity, Ltd
Summit Casualty Corp

Summit Insurance Company, PCC (formerly Summit Insurance Company, Ltd.)
TDS Insurance Company Limited
Texas Risk Assurances Corp.
~~The RHPI Captive Insurance Company, Ltd.~~ (revoked)
Thistle Crown Insurance, Ltd.
Timonium Insurance, Ltd
Tortuga Insurance Ltd
Training Equipment Property & Casualty Insurance Corporation
~~Trans National Insurance Company~~ (dissolved)
Transpro Property & Casualty Insurance Corporation
Travaglini Insurance Company Limited
Treadstone Insurance PCC
Treadwell Casualty Corp
TWG Insurance Company, Ltd
United Family Insurance Ltd.
~~United International Reinsurance Company (formerly First American Re-Insurance Company)~~ (revoked)
Unity Captive Insurance, Ltd.
Universal Business Insurance, Ltd
Universal P & C Corporation
University Insurance Limited
Ursa Insurance, Ltd
USA Doctors Insurance Company PCC
Ventilation Property & Casualty Insurance Corporation
Veterinary Casualty Corp.
Vienna Mutual Limited
Vindex Insurance, Ltd.
VisionRe Limited
Watchman Insurance Ltd.
Western Pacific Insurance PCC
Western Regional Insurance Group Limited
Westminster Mutual Insurance Company Limited
Westmount Insurance, Ltd
Windsor Re Limited
Wolfe Insurance Company, Ltd.
Woodstock Property and Casualty Ltd.
Worldwide Insurance Company, Inc.

MUTUAL FUNDS

Administrators

ATU Fund Administrators (BVI) Limited

Mitchell House
P O Box 1551
The Valley
Anguilla, B.W.I.
Tel: (264) 461-8800
Fax: (264) 461-8880

Folio Administrators Limited

Mitchell House
P.O Box 174
The Valley
Anguilla, B.W.I.
Tel: (264) 498-8800
Fax: (264) 498-8880

~~Global Fund Administrators (Anguilla) Limited~~ (dissolved)

P O Box 941
201 Rogers Office Building
Edwin Wallace Rey Drive
George Hill
Anguilla, B.W.I.
Tel: (264) 497-5858
Fax: (264) 497-5504

Administrators & Managers

Amikod Assets Management Limited.

P O Box 941
201 Rogers Office Building
Edwin Wallace Rey Drive
George Hill
Anguilla, B.W.I.
Tel: (264) 497-5858
Fax: (264) 497-5504

Cavendish Asset Management Ltd

Spencer House
P O Box 821
The Valley
Anguilla, B.W.I.
Tel: (264) 497-8129
Fax: (264) 498-8289

Drake Fund Services Ltd

P O Box 941
201 Rogers Office Building
Edwin Wallace Rey Drive
George Hill
Anguilla, B.W.I.
Tel: (264) 497-5858
Fax: (264) 497-5504

First Anguilla Trust Company Limited

Mitchell House
Mahogany Tree Road
P.O Box 174

The Valley
Anguilla, B.W.I.
Tel: (264) 461-8800
Fax: (264) 461-8880

Geneva Fund Administrators Limited

P O Box 941
201 Rogers Office Building
Edwin Wallace Rey Drive
George Hill
Anguilla, B.W.I.
Tel: (264) 497-5858
Fax: (264) 497-5504

Global Fund Services Inc

S1 South, Auckland House
P O Box 1533
The Valley
Anguilla, B.W.I.
Tel: (264) 498-0340
Fax: (264) 498-0341

Holtrade Capital Company

The Hansa Bank Building 1st Floor
P.O. Box 727 Landsome Road
The Valley, AI-2640
Anguilla, B.W.I.
Tel: (264) 498-3800
Fax: (264) 498-3805
Email: **fcurtis@cousellimited.com**

SN Trust International Corp

Mrs. Fiona Curtis
The Hansa Bank Building, 1st Floor
P.O. Box 727, Landsome Road,
The Valley, AI-2640
Anguilla, B.W.I.
Tel: (264) 498-3800
Fax: (264) 498-3805
Email: **fcurtis@cousellimited.com**
Website: **www.counsellimited.com**

Stafford Fund Managers and Administrators (Anguilla) Ltd.

P.O. Box 941
201 Rogers Office Building
Edwin Wallace Rey Drive
George Hill
Anguilla, B.W.I.
Tel: (264) 498-5858
Fax: (264) 497-5504

MANAGERS

Alpha Horizon Asset Management Ltd

Mitchell House
P O Box 174
The Valley
Anguilla, B.W.I.
Tel: 264-461-8800
Fax: 264-461-8880

ARF Management Ltd

First Anguilla Trust Company Limited
Mitchell House
P.O Box 174
The Valley
Anguilla, B.W.I.
Tel: (264) 461-8800
Fax: (264) 461-8880

City Credit Asset Management Limited

Babrow Building
P O Box 371
The Valley
Anguilla, B.W.I.
Tel: (264) 497-4224
Fax: (264) 497-4220

CKS Capital Management Ltd.

P O Box 941
201 Rogers Office Building
Edwin Wallace Rey Drive
George Hill
Anguilla, B.W.I.
Tel: (264) 497-5858
Fax: (264) 497-5504

Duquesne Holdings LLC

Mitchell House
P O Box 174
The Valley
Anguilla, B.W.I.
Tel: (264)-461-8800
Fax: (264) 461-8880

Geneve Capital Management Limited

P O Box 941
201 Rogers Office Building
Edwin Wallace Rey Drive
George Hill
Anguilla, B.W.I.
Tel: (264) 498-5858
Fax: (264) 497-5504

Headstart Management Inc

Mitchell House
P O Box 174
The Valley
Anguilla, B.W.I.

Tel: (264) 461-8800
Fax: (264) 461-8880

KiKu Management

C.E.G Limited
P.O Box 294
Heywood House
The Valley
Anguilla, B.W.I.
Tel: (264) 497-6468
Fax: (264) 497-6800

Luxinco Investment management Limited

Hudson & Partners
Malliouhana Insurance Building
The Valley
Anguilla B.W.I

Maximum Capital Management Ltd.

CMS Management Ltd
Heywood House
P.O Box 294
The Valley
Anguilla, B.W.I.
Tel: (264) 497 6468

Monument Street Fund Management Limited

Mitchell House
P.O Box 174
The Valley
Anguilla B.W.I
Tel: (264) 461-8800
Fax: (264) 498-8880
Email: **dbillington@firstanguilla.com**

Star Arrow Funds Expertise Ltd

Mitchell House
P O Box 174
The Valley
Anguilla, B.W.I.
Tel: (264) 461-8800
Fax: (264) 461-8880

Tauri Ursa Partners Ltd.

P O Box 941
201 Rogers Office Building
Edwin Wallace Rey Drive
George Hill
Anguilla, B.W.I.
Tel: (264) 498-5858
Fax: (264) 497-5504

Venture Capital Asset Management Limited

Mitchell House
P O Box 1551
The Valley
Anguilla, B.W.I.
Tel: (284) 494 1100
Fax: (284) 494 1199

PROFESSIONAL FUNDS

Amikod Capital Limited

P O Box 941
201 Rogers Office Building
Edwin Wallace Rey Drive
George Hill
Anguilla, B.W.I.
Tel: (264) 497-5858
Fax: (264) 497-5504

Aquarius Opportunity Fund PCC

Alex Richardson & Associates
Babrow Building
P O Box 371
The Valley
Anguilla, B.W.I.
Tel: (264) 498-4224
Fax: (264) 498-4220
Email: **arichardson@anguillanet.com**

Arboria Fund Limited

Harlaw Chambers
P O Box 1026
The Valley
Anguilla, B.W.I.
Tel: (264) 498-5000
Fax: (264 498-5001

Arcos Investment Fund PCC

Mitchell House
P.O. Box 174
The Valley
Anguilla B.W.I
Tel: (264) 461-8800
Fax: (264) 498-8880
Email: **rmcdowall@firstanguilla.com**

Adurion Global Opportunity Fund Limited

Mitchell House
P O Box 174
The Valley
Anguilla, B.W.I.
Tel: (264) 461-8800
Fax: (264) 461-8880

CKS Global Fund PCC

Babrow Building
P O Box 371
The Valley
Anguilla, B.W.I.

Tel: (264) 498-4224
Fax: (264) 498-4220

Drake Incubator PCC

Babrow Building
P O Box 371
The Valley
Anguilla, B.W.I.
Tel: (264) 497-4224
Fax: (264) 497-4220

Geneve Global Fund PCC

P.O. Box 941
201 Rogers Office Building
Edwin Wallace Rey Drive
George Hill
Anguilla, B.W.I.
Tel: (264) 498-5858
Fax: (264) 497-5504

Global Edge Mutual Fund Limited

Mitchell House
P O Box 174
The Valley
Anguilla, B.W.I.
Tel: (264) 461-8800
Fax: (264) 461-8880

Globe Invest PCC

Mitchell House
P O Box 174
The Valley
Anguilla, B.W.I.
Tel: (264) 498-8800
Fax: (264) 498-8880

Infinity Star Fund

Spencer House
P.O. Box 821
The Valley
Anguilla, B.W.I.
Tel: (264) 497-8129
Fax: (264) 497-8289

Maria Desatadora Dos Nos Master Fund SA

Babrow Building
P.O. Box 371
The Valley
Anguilla, B.W.I.
Tel: (264) 498-4224
Fax: (264) 498-4220
Email: **arichardson@anguillanet.com**

Maria Desatadora Umbrella Fund S.A.

Babrow Building
P O Box 371
The Valley
Anguilla, B.W.I.
Tel: 264 498 4224
Fax: 264 498 4220
Email: **arichardson@anguillanet.com**

New Horizon Investment Fund PCC

Mitchell House
Mahogany Tree Road
P.O Box 174
The Valley
Anguilla, B.W.I.
Tel: (264) 461-8800
Fax: (264) 461-8880

~~P & P Protected Cell Company~~ (surrendered)

Mitchell House
Mahogany Tree Road
P.O Box 174
The Valley
Anguilla, B.W.I.
Tel: (264) 461-8800
Fax: (264) 461-8880

Palmares Investment Fund PCC

Mitchell House
P.O. Box 174
The Valley
Anguilla B.W.I
Tel: (264) 461-8800
Fax: (264) 498-8880
Email: **rmcdowall@firstanguilla.com**

~~R+P International Equity Fund~~ (surrendered)

Mitchell House
Mahogany Tree Road
P.O Box 174
The Valley
Anguilla, B.W.I.
Tel: (264) 461-8800
Fax: (264) 461-8880

Silver Oak Fund Limited

Babrow Building
P O Box 371
The Valley
Anguilla, B.W.I.
Tel (264) 498 4224
Fax (264) 498 4220

Venture Capital Growth Fund PCC Limited

Mitchell House
P O Box 1551
The Valley
Anguilla, B.W.I.

Tel: (264) 497-3891
Fax: (264) 497-3891

Venture Capital Opportunity Fund PCC Limited

Mitchell House
P O Box 1551
The Valley
Anguilla, B.W.I.
Tel: (264) 497-3891
Fax: (264) 497-3891

PUBLIC FUNDS

Anchor Fund Limited

Mitchell House
PO Box 174
The Valley
Anguilla, B.W.I.
Tel: (264) 498 8800
Fax: (264) 498 8880

The White November Fund Limited

Mitchell House
P.O Box 174
The Valley
Anguilla, B.W.I.
Tel: (264) 498-8800
Fax: (264) 498-8880

TRUST COMPANIES

Anglo-Overseas Trust Company Limited

The Mason Complex, Suite 19 & 20
P.O. Box I4052
The Valley
Anguilla, B.W.I.
Tel: (264) 497-7416
Fax: (264) 497-7417

ATU General Trust (Anguilla) Inc.

Mitchell House
P .O. Box 174
The Valley
Anguilla, B.W.I.
Tel: (264) 498-8800
Fax: (264) 498-8880

Codan Trust Company (Anguilla) Limited

Mitchell House
P O Box 174
The Valley
Anguilla, B.W.I.
Tel: (264) 461-8800
Fax: (264) 461-8880

First Anguilla Trust Company Ltd.

Mitchell House
P.O Box 174
The Valley
Anguilla, B.W.I.
Tel: (264) 498-8800
Fax: (264) 498-8880

~~Fortis Intertrust (Anguilla) Limited~~ (surrendered)

The Hansa Bank Building
P.O. Box 727
The Valley
Anguilla, B.W.I.
Tel: (264) 498-3800
Fax: (264) 498-3805

Geneva Trust Corporation

P O Box 941
201 Rogers Office Building
Edwin Wallace Rey Drive
George Hill
Anguilla, B.W.I.
Tel: (264) 498-5858
Fax: (264) 497-5504

Lutea (Anguilla) Limited

P.O. Box 1533
S1 South
Auckland House
The Quarter
Anguilla TV1 13P
Tel: (264) 498-0340
Fax: (264) 498-0341

Mossack Fonseca & Co. (British Anguilla) Limited

#25 Mason Complex
P.O. Box 193
The Valley
Anguilla, BWI
Tel: (264) 498-7777
Fax: (264) 497-3727

Noble Management (Anguilla) Limited

P.O. Box 941
201 Rogers Office Building
Edwin Wallace Rey Drive
George Hill
Anguilla, B.W.I.
Tel: (264) 498-5858
Fax: (264) 497-5504

~~Private International Trust Corporation~~ (revoked)

Caribbean Suite
P.O. Box 1338
The Valley
Anguilla, B.W.I.
Tel: (264) 497-2189
Fax: (264) 497-5007

SN International Trust Corp

The Hansa Bank Building
P.O. Box 727
The Valley
Anguilla, B.W.I.
Tel: (264) 498-3800
Fax: (264) 498-3805

United Trust (Anguilla) Limited

Babrow Building
P O Box 371
The Valley
Anguilla, B.W.I.
Tel: (264) 497-4224
Fax (264) 497-4220

RESTRICTED

Boswell Overseas Investment Limited

P.O. Box 941
201 Rogers Office Building
Edwin Wallace Rey Drive
George Hill
Anguilla, B.W.I.
Tel: (264) 498-5858
Fax: (264) 497-5504

Fairfield Trust

Heywood House
P.O. Box 294
The Valley
Anguilla, BWI
Tel: (264) 497-6468
Fax: (264) 497-6800

Guardian Services Limited

201 Office Rogers Building
P. O Box 941
The Valley
Anguilla, BWI
Tel: (264) 498-5858
Fax: (264) 497-5504

Stafford Trust Company Ltd

P.O. Box 941
201 Rogers Office Building
Edwin Wallace Rey Drive
George Hill
Anguilla, B.W.I.
Tel: (264) 498-5858
Fax: (264) 497-5504

Zetland Corporate Services Limited

The Hallmark Building
P.O. Box 227
The Valley
Anguilla, B.W.I.
Tel: (264) 497-3575
Fax: (264) 497-3577

Zombi Limited

Harlaw Chambers
P.O. Box 1026
The Valley
Anguilla, B.W.I.
Tel: (264) 498-5000
Fax: (264) 498-5001

INFORMATION AND INTERNATIONAL OFFICES

The Anguilla Tourist Board

Old Factory Plaza
The Valley, Anguilla, BWI
1-800-553-4939
Tel: 264-497-2759
Fax: 264-497-2710
Email: atbtour@anguillanet.com

USA

Anguilla Tourist Board

United Kingdom

River Communications

Marketing Office
111 Decatur Street
Doylestown, PA 18901
Tel.: 267-880-3511
Fax: 267-880-3507
Email: enterprisefx@aol.com
anguillabwi@aol.com

Unit 8A Oakwood House
414-422 Hackney Road
London E2 7SY
Tel.: 011-44 207 729 8003
Fax: 011-44 207 729 8829
Email: rivercoms@aol.com
anguilla4info@aol.com

Italy, Monaco and France

Ms. Florence Bersans-Zannoli,
Anguilla Tourist Board, Le Coronado, 20
Avenue De Fontvieille
MC 98000, Monaco

Germany

Anguilla Tourist Board
c/o Sergat Deutschland
IM Guldenen Wingert 8-C
D-64342 Seeheim, Germany
Tel.: 011-49-6257-962920
Fax: 011-49-6257-962919
Email: r.morozow@sergat.de

GOVERNMENT OF ANGUILLA TELEPHONE LISTINGS

Name	**Address**	**Telephone #**
Agriculture Department		
Agriculture Department	The Valley	(264) 497-2615
Agriculture Department	The Valley	(264) 497-2783
Attorney General's Chambers		
Attorney General's Chambers	The Valley	(264) 497-3044
Attorney General's Chambers	The Valley	(264) 497-3126 Fax
Airport		

Airport Manager's Office	Wallblake Airport	(264) 497-2384
VIP Lounge	Wallblake Airport	(264) 497-3510
Airport Manager's Office	Wallblake Airport	(264) 497-2928 Fax
Air Traffic Control Tower	Wallblake Airport	(264) 497-2378 Fax
Air Traffic Control Tower	Wallblake Airport	(264) 497-2526
Fire Station	Wallblake Airport	(264) 497-8395
Security	Wallblake Airport	(264) 497-8395
Emergency Operations Center	Wallblake Airport	(264) 497-5666/5667
Tax Collections	Wallblake Airport	(264) 497-2194
Community Development & Welfare	The Valley	(264) 497-2317/5917
Community Development & Welfare	The Valley	(264) 497-2317/5917
Sports Officer	The Valley	(264) 497-5214
Customs & Excise		
Customs Main Office	The Valley	(264) 497-5313
Customs Main Office	The Valley	(264) 497-2513
Customs Main Office	The Valley	(264) 497-5483 Fax
Customs Main Office	The Valley	(264) 497-2058
Customs Main Office (ASYCUDA)	The Valley	(264) 497-5095
Customs Airport	Wallblake	(264) 497-2514
Customs Blowing Point	Blowing Point	(264) 497-6853
Customs Road Bay	Sandy Ground	(264) 497-2213
Customs Marine Base	Road Bay	(264) 497-5461

Education		
Education Department	The Valley	(264) 497-2874
Education Department	The Valley	(264) 497-2875
Education Department	The Valley	(264) 497-2908 Fax
Teacher Resource Center	The Valley	(264) 497-5403
University Center	The Valley	(264) 497-5245
Albena Lake-Hodge Comprehensive School	The Valley	(264) 497-2416
Albena Lake-Hodge Comprehensive School	The Valley	(264) 497-2417
Albena Lake-Hodge Comprehensive School	The Valley	(264) 497-5416
Island Harbour Primary School	Island Harbour	(264) 497-4181
Morris Vanterpool Primary School	East End	(264) 497-4419
Road Primary School	Blowing Point Road	(264) 497-6348
Stoney Ground Primary School	Stoney Ground	(264) 497-2888
Valley Primary School	The Valley	(264) 497-2887
West End Primary School	West End	(264) 497-6721
Finance & Accounts		
Director of Finance & Planning	The Secretariat	(264) 497-2547
Development Unit	The Secretariat	(264) 497-3635
Deputy Director Finance & Planning	The Secretariat	(264) 497-3635
Accountant General	The Secretariat	(264) 497-3235
Treasury Department	The Secretariat	(264) 497-2451
Finance Department	The Secretariat	(264) 497-2451
Statistical Unit	The Secretariat	(264) 497-5693

Information Systems & Technology Unit	The Secretariat	(264) 497-5233
Finance Department	The Secretariat	(264) 497-3761
Financial Services		
Offshore Finance	The Secretariat	(264) 497-5881
Offshore Finance	The Secretariat	(264) 497-5466
Offshore Finance	The Secretariat	(264) 497-5872 Fax
Director of Financial Services	The Secretariat	(264) 497-5072
Companies Registry	The Secretariat	(264) 497-3881
Companies Registry	The Secretariat	(264) 497-5478
Companies Registry	The Secretariat	(264) 497-2601
Companies Registry	The Secretariat	(264) 497-5566
Companies Registry	The Secretariat	(264) 497-8060
Companies Registry	The Secretariat	(264) 497-8053 Fax
Regestrar of Companies	The Secretariat	(264) 497-3539
Deputy Project Manger	The Secretariat	(264) 497-2979
Fisheries And Marine Resources		
Fisheries & Marine Resources	The Valley	(264) 497-2871
Fisheries & Marine Resources	The Valley	(264) 497-5040
General Post Office		
General Post Office	The Valley	(264) 497-2528
General Post Office	The Valley	(264) 497-5451
General Post Office	The Valley	(264) 497-5452
General Post Office	The Valley	(264) 497-5455 Fax

Postmaster General	The Valley	(264) 497-5453
Government House		
Governor's Office	Old Ta	(264) 497-2621
Governor's Office	Old Ta	(264) 497-2622
Governor's Office	Old Ta	(264) 497-3151 Fax
Governor's Residence	Old Ta	(264) 497-2292
Deputy Governor's Office	Old Ta	(264) 497-3313
Deputy Governor's Office	Old Ta	(264) 497-3312
Deputy Governor's Office	Old Ta	(264) 497-3314 Fax
Government Ministries		
Chief Minister & Minister of Home Affairs Tourism and Lands	The Secretariat	(264) 497-2518/5518
Minister of Finance, Planning & Economic Development	The Secretariat	(264) 497- 2545
Minister of Social Services	The Secretariat	(264) 497-5179
Minister of Infrastructure, Communications & Utilities	The Valley	(264) 497-2442
Health & Family Life Education Unit		
Health Education Office	The Valley	(264) 497-2540
Hospital		
Princess Alexandra Hospital	Pope Hill	(264) 497-2551/2552
Human Resource Management Division		
Permanent Scretary	Social Security Complex	(264) 497-3041
Assistant Secretary	Social Security Complex	(264) 497-3045

Assistant Secretary	Social Security Complex	(264) 497-3811
Training Officer	Social Security Complex	(264) 497-3622
Public Sector Development	Social Security Complex	(264) 497-5035/5282
Passport Office	Social Security Complex	(264) 497-2451
Training Division	Social Security Complex	(264) 497-5873 Fax
Immigration		
Deputy Chief Immigration Officer	The Secretariat	(264) 497-3994
Immigration Main Office	The Secretariat	(264) 497-2451
Immigration Blowing Point	Blowing Point	(264) 497-6665
Immigration Road Bay	Sandy Ground	(264) 497-3611
Immigration Wall Blake Airport	Wall Blake	(264) 497-2411
Judicial Department		
Judicial Department	The Valley	(264) 497-2377/3347
Magistrate's Office	The Valley	(264) 497-2377
Registrar of Courts	The Valley	(264) 497-2377
Labour Department		
Labour Commissioner	Social Security Complex	(264) 497-3511
Lands & Surveys Department		
Lands & Surveys Department	The Valley	(264) 497-2424
Lands & Surveys Department	The Valley	(264) 497-2153
Library		
Anguilla Library Services	The Valley	(264) 497-2441/5402
Anguilla Library Service	The Valley	(264) 497-3408
Teacher Resource Center	The Valley	(264) 497-5403/5704

Public Library	The Valley	(264) 497-2434 Fax
Physical Planning Department		
Physical Planning Department	The Valley	(264) 497 5392
Physical Planning Department	The Valley	(264) 497 5424
Medical & Health Services, Primary Health Care & Secondary Health Care		
Director of Medical and Health Services/ Senior Medical Officer	Pope Hill	(264) 497-2745/5274
Health Services Administrator	Pope Hill	(264) 497-2745
Princess Alexandra Hospital	Pope Hill	(264) 497-2551/2552
Princess Alexandra Hospital	Pope Hill	(264) 497-5745 Fax
Princess Alexandra Hospital	Pope Hill	(264) 497-5102/5103
Secretary Director of Health Services	Pope Hill	(264) 497-2207
Laboratory	Pope Hill	(264) 497-2637
Primary Health Care		
Environmental Health	The Valley	(264) 497-2631
Public Health	The Valley	(264) 497-5485
Clinic East End	East End	(264) 497-4420
Clinic Island Harbour	Island Harbour	(264) 497-4020
Clinic South Hill	Road South Hill	(264) 497-6421
Clinic West End	West End	(264) 497-6898
Valley Clinic	The Valley	(264) 497-2702/8492
Dental Unit	The Valley	(264) 497-2343/3342

Health Education Office	The Valley	(264) 497-2540
Water Laboratory	The Valley	(264) 497-5732
Primary Health Care	The Valley	(264) 497-3845/3763
Primary Health Care	The Valley	(264) 497-5486 Fax
Permanent Secretaries & Principal Assistant Secretaries		
Parliamentary Secretary	The Valley	(264) 497-3089
Permanent Secretary Human Resource Management	The Valley	(264) 497-3041
Principal Assistant Secretary Human Resource Mangement	The Valley	(264) 497-3045
Principal Assistant Secretary Human Resource Mangement	The Valley	(264) 497-3811
Permanent Secretary Ministry Of Infrastructure	The Valley	(264) 497-2442
Permanent Secretary Agriculture & Lands	The Valley	(264) 497-3518
Principal Assistant Secretary Home Affairs, Labour & Immigration	The Valley	(264) 497-2443
Principal Assistant Secretary Tourism	The Valley	(264) 497-8475
Permanent Secretary Ministry of Social Services	The Valley	(264) 497-3930
Permanent Secretary Ministry of Social Services	The Valley	(264) 497-5401
Permanent Secretary Ministry of Social Services	The Valley	(264) 497-3042
Principal Assistant	The Valley	(264) 497-5851

Secretary Ministry of Social Services		
Police Departments		
Valley Police Station	The Valley	(264) 497-2333/5333
Valley Police Station	The Valley	(264) 497-3746 Fax
Sandy Ground Police Station	Sandy Ground	(264) 497-2354
Fort Hill Police Station	Sandy Hill	(264) 497-4332
Blowing Point Police Station	Blowing Point	(264) 497-6533
Commissioner of Police	The Valley	(264) 497-2533
Mitchell Harrigan	Shoal Bay	(264) 497-5349
Deputy Commissioner of Police Operations	The Valley	(264) 497-3752
Superintendent of Police	The Valley	(264) 497-2633
Police Administration	The Valley	(264) 497-3752
Drugs Hotline Valley Police Station	The Valley	(264) 497-4000
Emergency, Ambulance & Fire Services	The Valley	911
Ports Manager Marine Base	Sandy Ground	(264) 497-3467
Ports Manager Blowing Point	Blowing Point	(264) 497-6070
HM Prison	The Valley	(264) 497-3046
Public Works & Water Department		
General Offices	The Valley	(264) 497-2651/2652
General Offices	The Valley	(264) 497-2752/2753
Radio Anguilla	The Valley	(264) 497-2218/3620

Permanent Secretary Public Works	The Valley	(264) 497-2442
Minister Of Infrastructure, Communications & Utilities	The Valley	(264) 497-2796
Secretariat The PBX		
All Departments	The Valley	(264) 497-2451/2452/2453/2454/2455
Tourism Department		
Tourism Main Office	Wall Blake	(264) 497-2759
Tourism Main Office	Wall Blake	(264) 497-3779
Tourism Main Office	Wall Blake	(264) 497-8456
Tourism Main Office	Wall Blake	(264) 497-8457
Tourism Main Office	Wall Blake	(264) 497-3579
Tourism Main Office	Wall Blake	(264) 497-2710 Fax

FINANCIAL SERVICES DIRECTORY

ACCOUNTING FIRMS

Audain & Associates
Fairplay Commercial Complex
P.O. Box 671
The Valley
Anguilla, B.W.I.
Tel: +1 264 497 5621
Fax: +1 264 497 5220
E-mail: mraudain@anguillanet.com
Website: N/A
Contact: Marva Audain-Thompson

Counsel Limited
Physical Address:
The Hansa Bank Building - 1st Floor
Landsome Road
The Valley
Anguilla, B.W.I.

Mailing Address:
P.O. Box 727
The Valley
TV1 02P
Anguilla, B.W.I.

Tel: +1 264 498 3800
Fax: +1 264 498 3805
E-Mail: counsel@counsel.ai
Website: www.counsellimited.com
Contact: Donald R Curtis

KPMG Peat Marwick
P.O. Box 136
The Valley
Anguilla, B.W.I.
Tel: +1 264 497 5500
Fax: +1 264 497 3755
E-Mail: kpmg@anguillanet.com
Website: www.kpmg.com.ai
Contact: Claudel Romney

BANKS

Firstcaribbean International Bank (Barbados) Limited
P.O. Box 140
The Valley
Anguilla, B.W.I.
Tel: +1 264 497 2301
Fax: +1 264 497 2980
E-mail: N/A
Website: N/A
Contact: Mr Bernard Leonce

National Bank of Anguilla
P.O. Box 44
The Valley
Anguilla, B.W.I.
Tel: +1 264 497 2101
Fax: +1 264 497 3310
E-mail: nbabankl@anguillanet.com
Website: N/A
Contact: Icilma Vanterpool

Caribbean Commercial Bank (Anguilla) Ltd.
P.O. Box 23
The Valley
Anguilla, B.W.I.
Tel: +1 264 497 2571
Fax: +1 264 497 3570
E-mail: ccbaxa@anguillanet.com
Website: N/A
Contact: Landia Richardson

Scotiabank Anguilla Ltd.
Fairplay commercial Complex
P.O. Box 250
The Valley
Anguilla, B.W.I.
Tel: +1 264 497 3333
Fax: +1 264 497 3344
E-mail: scotia@anguillanet.com
Website: N/A
Contact: Walter MacCalman

LAW FIRMS

Caribbean Juris Chambers
P.O. Box 328
The Valley
Anguilla, B.W.I.
Tel: +1 264 497 3470
Fax: +1 264 497 3177
E-mail: caribjur@anguillanet.com
Website: www.benjamine.ai
Contact: John Benjamin / Bernadine Romney / Carol Nelson

Caribbean Associated Attorneys
P.O. Box 1010
The Valley
Anguilla, B.W.I.
Tel: +1 264 497 5405
Fax: +1 264 497 3975
E-mail: caa@caribbean-attorneys.com
Website: www.caribbean-attorneys.com
Contact: Courtney Abel

J.A.G. Gumbs & Co
The Anguilla Professional Complex
P.O. Box 1398
The Valley
Anguilla, B.W.I.
Tel: +1 264 497 1212
Fax: +1 264 497 1214
E-Mail:
jaggumbs_co@anguillanet.com
Website: N/A
Contact: Mrs Josephine A G Gumbs-Connor

Harney Westwood & Riegels
Harlaw Chambers
P.O. Box 1026
The Valley
Anguilla, B.W.I.
Tel: +1 264 498 5000
Fax: +1 264 498 5001
E-Mail: hwr@anguillanet.com
Website: www.harneys.com
Contact: Alex Richardson

Hodge's Chambers
Hodge's Chambers
PO Box 840
The Valley
Anguilla, B.W.I.
Tel: +1 264 497 3793
Fax: +1 264 497 2863
E-mail: N/A
Website: N/A
Contact: V. R. Hodge

Keithley Lake & Associates
The Law Building
P.O. Box 14
The Valley
Anguilla, B.W.I.
Tel: +1 264 497 2069
Fax: +1 264 497 3012
E-mail: information@anguilla-attorney.com
Website: www.anguilla-attorney.com
Contact: Keithley Lake, Kenneth Porter or Yvette Wallace

Lake & Kentish
PO Box 259
The Valley
Anguilla, B.W.I.
Tel: +1 264 497 2582
Fax: +1 264 497 5496
E-mail: laken@anguillanet.com
Website: N/A
Contact: Bernice V Lake QC / Joyce Kentish / Lorna Rogers

Myrna R. Walwyn & Associates
The Valley
Anguilla, B.W.I.
Tel: +1 264 497 2484
Fax: +1 264 497 3706
E-mail: N/A
Website: N/A
Contact: Myrna R. Walwyn

Samuel McCleery
Hansa Bank Building
P.O. Box 1027
The Valley
Anguilla, B.W.I.
Tel: +1 264 497 2527
Fax: +1 264 497 5638
E-Mail: ultra@anguillanet.com
Website: www.smccleery.com
Contact: Samuel McCleery

T W R Astaphan
P.O. Box 350
The Valley
Anguilla, B.W.I.
Tel: +1 264 497 5555
Fax: +1 264 497 5310
E-mail: N/A
Website: N/A
Contact: Thomas WR Astaphan

Webster Dyrud Mitchell

Wigley's Chambers

P.O. Box 58
The Valley
Anguilla, B.W.I.
Tel: +1 264 497 2060
Fax: +1 264 497 3096
E-mail:
information@websterdyrud.com
Website: www.websterdyrud.com
Contact: Palmavon J Webster

P.O. Box 821
The Valley
Anguilla, B.W.I.
Tel: +1 264 497 8129
Fax: +1 264 497 8289
E-Mail: information@offshore-lawyer.com
Website: www.offshore-lawyer.com
Contact: John Wigley

COMPANY MANAGERS

Anglo-Overseas Trust Company Limited
Intertrust Office
The Valley
Anguilla
British West Indies
E-mail: intertrust@anguillanet.com
Website: N/A
Contact: Anthony Shiffers

Angwal Corporate Services Limited
Myrna R. Walwyn & Associates
Chambers
P.O. Box 397
The Valley
Anguilla
Tel: (264) 497-2484/3868
Fax: (264) 497-3706
E-mail: angwal@anguillanet.com
Website: N/A

Antilles International Management Services Limited
The Valley
Anguilla
E-mail: ault@kensingtontrust.com
Website: N/A
Contact: Douglas Calder

Astaphan & Kelsick
Herbert's Commercial Center
The Valley
Anguilla
British West Indies
E-mail:
astaphankelsick@anguillanet.com
Website: N/A
Contact: Thomas Astaphan

AXA Offshore Management Limited
The Law Building
P.O. Box 687
The Valley
Anguilla, B.W.I.
Tel: +1 264 497 3142
Fax: +1 264 497 5753
E-mail: axa-offshore@anguillanet.com
Website: www.axaoffshore.com
Contact: Esther Fleming

Banx Professional Services Ltd.
Caribbean Commercial Centre
P.O. Box 20
The Valley
Anguilla, B.W.I.
Tel: +1 264 497 5388
Fax: +1 264 497 3286
E-mail: banksv@anguillanet.com
Website: N/A
Contact: Olivia Gumbs Hodge

Benjamine Company Svcs. Ltd.
Hannah-Waver House
P.O. Box 801

C.E.G. Limited
Heywood House
P.O. Box 294

The Valley
Anguilla, B.W.I.
Tel: +1 264 497 5270
Fax: +1 264 497 5271
E-mail: caribjur@anguillanet.com
Website: www.benjamine.ai
Contact: Bernadine Romney / John Benjamin / Carol Nelson

Codan Trust Company (Anguilla) Limited
Principal Office
Clarendon House
2 Church Street
P.O. Box HM 666
Hamilton HM CX
Bermuda
Tel: +1 441 295 1422
Fax: +1 441 292 4720

Anguilla Office
c/o Intertrust Offices
P.O. Box 147
The Valley
Anguilla, BWI
Tel: 264 497 2189
Fax: 264 497 5007

E-Mail: see Contacts
Website: www.cdp.bm
Contact: David Astwood or John C.R. Collis

Euro-American Trust and Management Services Limited
Principal Office
R.G. Hodge Plaza, 3rd Floor
P.O. Box 3483
Wickhams Cay 1
Road Town
Tortola
British Virgin Islands

Anguilla Office
P.O. Box 1388
The Valley
Anguilla, B.W.I.
Tel: +507 269 2272

The Valley
Anguilla, B.W.I.
Tel: +1 264 497 6468
Fax: +1 264 497 6080
E-mail: info@ceg.ai
Website: www.ceg.ai
Contact: Graham Crabtree

Counsel Limited
Physical Address:
The Hansa Bank Building - 1st Floor
Landsome Road
The Valley
Anguilla, B.W.I.

Mailing Address:
P.O. Box 727
The Valley
TV1 02P
Anguilla, B.W.I.

Tel: +1 264 498 3800
Fax: +1 264 498 3805
E-Mail: counsel@counsel.ai
Website: www.counsellimited.com
Contact: Donald R Curtis

First Anguilla Trust Company Ltd
Mitchell House
P.O. Box 174
The Valley
Anguilla, B.W.I.
Tel: +1 264 498 8800
Fax: +1 264 498 8880
E-mail: information@firstanguilla.com
Website: www.firstanguilla.com
Contact: John O. Dyrud

Fax: +507 269 2714

E-Mail: eamsbvi@surfbvi.com
Website: N/A
Contact: Pauline Robinson

First Management Company Ltd.
#40 Caribbean Commercial Centre
P.O. Box 68
The Valley
Anguilla, B.W.I.
Tel: +1 264 497 5578
Fax: +1 264 497 5589
E-mail:
firstmanagement@anguillanet.com
Website: N/A
Contact: Icilma Woodley

Hansa Bank & Trust Company Limited
NBA Corporate Building
First Floor
St. Mary's Road
The Valley
Anguilla, B.W.I.
TV1 02P
Tel: +1 264 497 3800
J.Fax: +1 702 447 8567
E-Mail: hansa@attglobal.net
Website: www.hansa.net
Contact: Lynwood S. Bell

HWR Services (Anguilla) Limited
Harlaw Chambers
P.O. Box 1026
The Valley
Anguilla, B.W.I.
Tel: +1 264 498 5000
Fax: +1 264 498 5001
E-Mail: hwr@anguillanet.com
Website: www.harneys.com
Contact: Alex Richardson / Heather Wallace

Icaza, Gonzalez-Ruiz & Aleman
Principal Office
Aquilino de la Guardia Street, No. 8
IGRA Building
5th Floor
PO Box 87-1371 - 7
Panama
Republic of Panama

Anguilla Office
P.O. Box 1388
The Valley
Anguilla, B.W.I.

Tel: +507 263 5555
Fax: +507 259 4891
E-Mail: igranet@icazalaw.com
Website: www.icazalaw.com
Contact: Dr. Roberto R. Alemán H. and/or Dr. Domingo A. Díaz S.

ICS Trust (Anguilla) Limited
The Hallmark Building, Old Airport Road
PO Box 227
The Valley
Anguilla, B.W.I.
Tel: +852 2854 4544

Intertrust (Anguilla) Limited
P.O. Box 1388
The Valley
Anguilla, B.W.I.
Tel: +1 264 497 2189
Fax: +1 264 497 5007
E-mail: Anguilla@intertrustgroup.com

Fax: +852 2543 5555
E-Mail: ew@icstrust.com
Website: www.icstrust.com
Contact: Eliza S. Y. Wu

J.A.G. Gumbs & Co
The Anguilla Professional Complex
P.O. Box 1398
The Valley
Anguilla, B.W.I.
Tel: +1 264 497 1212
Fax: +1 264 497 1214
E-Mail:
jaggumbs_co@anguillanet.com
Website: N/A
Contact: Mrs Josephine A G Gumbs-Connor

KPMG Corporate Services LLC
P.O. Box 136
The Valley
Anguilla, B.W.I.
Tel: +1 264 497 5500
Fax: +1 264 497 3755
E-mail: kpmg@anguillanet.com
Website: www.kpmg.com.ai
Contact: Claudel Romney

Lutea (Anguilla) Limited
c/o Intertrust Offices
The Valley
Anguilla
E-mail: jfleetwood@lutea.com
Website: N/A
Contact: John Fleetwood

Offshore Incorporations (Anguilla) Limited
Principal Office
9/F Ruttonjee House
11 Duddell Street
Central
Hong Kong
Anguilla Office
Harlaw Chambers
The Valley

Website: www.intertrust-group.com
Contact: Joseph Brice

Samuel McCleery
Hansa Bank Building
P.O. Box 1027
The Valley
Anguilla, B.W.I.
Tel: +1 264 497 2527
Fax: +1 264 497 5638
E-Mail: ultra@anguillanet.com
Website: www.smccleery.com
Contact: Samuel McCleery

Lake & Kentish
P.O. Box 259
The Valley
Anguilla, B.W.I.
Tel: +1 264 497 2582
Fax: +1 264 497 5496
E-mail: laken@anguillanet.com
Website: N/A
Contact: Bernice V Lake QC / Joyce Kentish / Lorna Rogers

M & R Corporate Services
P.O. Box 671
The Valley
Anguilla, B.W.I.
Tel: +1 264 497 5620
Fax: +1 264 497 5220
E-mail: mraudain@anguillanet.com
Website: N/A
Contact: Marva Audain-Thompson

On-Island (Anguilla) Corporate Svcs. Ltd.
P.O. Box 1010
The Valley
Anguilla, B.W.I.
Tel: +1 264 497 5405
Fax: +1 264 497 3975
E-mail: abelc@anguillanet.com
Website: www.on-island.com
Contact: Courtney Abel

Anguilla, B.W.I.

Tel: +852 2521 2517
Fax: +852 2810 4525
E-Mail: administration@offshore-inc.com
Contact: Wendy O'Donnell

Overseas Management Company (Anguilla) Limited
Victoria House
The Valley
Anguilla
E-mail: eileen@omcpty.com
Contact: Eileen Marquez

Professional Corporate Services (Anguilla) Ltd.
The Hallmark Building, Old Airport Road
PO Box 227
The Valley
Anguilla, B.W.I.
Tel: +1 264 497 3573
Fax: +1 264 497 3577
E-mail: procorp@profgroup.com
Website: www.profgroup.com
Contact: Scott Hauser

ProServices (Anguilla) Limited
Victoria House
The Valley
Anguilla
E-mail: haleue@amicorp.vg
Website: N/A
Contact: Humphry Leue

Rathbone (Anguilla) Ltd.
P.O. Box 136
#7 Herberts Commercial Centre
The Valley
Anguilla, B.W.I.
Tel: +1 264 497 5500
Fax: +1 264 497 3755
E-mail: rathbone@surfbvi.com
Website: N/A
Contact: Mr. Peter W Poole or Ms. Annetta Williams

Renaissance International Trust Ltd
The Law Building
The Valley
E-mail: tmaynard@renaissancetrust.ai
Website: N/A
Contact: Joan Johnson

Sinel Trust Anguilla Limited
Sinel Chambers
PO Box 1269
The Valley
Anguilla, BWI
Tel: +1 264 497 3311
Fax: +1 264 497 5659
E-mail: jbrice@sineltrust.com
Website: www.sineltrust-anguilla.com
Contact: Joseph Brice

Sterling Trust (Anguilla) Ltd
Principal Office
Sterling ACS, Ltd.
British American Building
Ground Floor

Stott & Company Limited
P.O. Box 2
The Valley
Anguilla, B.W.I.
Tel: +1 264 497 2744

Malborough & Navy Lyon Road
Nassau
Bahamas
Anguilla Office
National Bank Corporate Building
Airport Road
The Valley
Anguilla, B.W.I.

Tel: +1 264 497 5578
Fax: +1 264 497 5589
E-Mail: hwoltz@sterlinggroup.bs
Contact: Howell Woltz

Sucre & Sucre Anguilla Limited
Principal Office
48th East Street, Bella Vista
Sucre Building
P.O. Box 6277, Zone 5
Panama
Republic of Panama

Anguilla Office
P.O. Box 58
Victoria House
The Valley
Anguilla, B.W.I.

Tel: +507 264 1355
Fax: +507 264 1168
E-mail: sucre@sucre.net
Website: N/A
Contact: Mr. Carlos Sucre, Mr. RamÓn Anzola, Ms. Yavel Francis or Ms. Thays de Salas

Fax: +1 264 497 3350
E-mail: information@stottco.com
Website: www.stottco.com
Contact: Denise Stott-Brown

INVESTMENT BANKERS & STOCK BROKERS

Hansa Bank & Trust Company Limited
Hansa Bank Building
P.O. Box 213
The Valley
Anguilla, B.W.I.
TV1 02P
Tel: +1 264 497 3800
Fax: +1 264 497 3801

Talisman Securities Limited.
Fairplay Commercial Complex
P.O. Box 726
The Valley
Anguilla, B.W.I.
Tel: +1 264 497 5840
Fax: +1 264 497 5834
E-mail: talisman@anguillanet.com
Website: www.talisman.ai

E-Mail: hansa@attglobal.net
Website: www.hansa.net
Contact: Lynwood S. Bell

Contact: Robert McNair

OVERSEAS AGENTS

ALCO Trust B.V.
Sophialaan 33
1075 BL-Amsterdam
The Netherlands
Email: manager@alcotrust.nl
Contact: Albert Verstijnen
Local Agent: C.E.G. Limited

ARPAD Corporate Services, Inc
Karikas
42 Rue
Raoul Servant
69007
Lyon
France
Email: arpad-corporate-services@attglobal.net
Contact: Michel Rakoczi
Local Agent: Wigley & Associates Inc.

ATU General Trust (BVI) Limited
076 Sir Francis Drake Highway
P.O.Box 3463
Road Town
Tortola
British Virgin Islands
Email: atu@atubvi.com
Contact: Michael Parton
Local Agent: Euro-American Trust and Management Services Limited

Thomas Azzara
54 Sandyport Drive
Nassau
Bahamas
Email: taxman@mail.batelnet.bs
Contact: Thomas Azzara
Local Agent: Wigley & Associates Inc.

Colombo Fiduciaria SA
Via San Salvatore 10
6902 Paradiso
The Swiss Confederation
Email: Raffaella@colombo-group.com
Contact: Diego Colombo
Local Agent: Professional Corporate Services (Anguilla) Ltd.

Corporate Agents Group
Werfstraat 6
P.O. Box 3914
Willemstad
Curacao
Netherlands Antilles
Tel: +1 305 358 7872
Fax: +1 305 358 7873
E-Mail: wal001@aol.com
Website: www.corporate-agents.com
Contact: James Walfenzao
Local Agent: HWR Services (Anguilla) Limited

Morris K Ebeling
44 W. Broadway, Suite 601
Salt Lake City
Utah 84101
Tel. No: +1 801 983 5000

Equinox Trustees Limited
Thorp House
Rouge Bouillon
St Helier
Jersey

Fax No.: +1 801 983 5005
Email: morty@goluxul.com
Contact: Morris Ebeling
Local Agent: Professional Corporate Services (Anguilla) Ltd.

Email: clive.tomes@clivetomes.com
Contact: Clive Tomes
Local Agent: Sinel Trust Anguilla Limited

Euro-American Trust and Management Services Limited (BVI)
Euro American Building
Box 3161
Road Town, Tortola
British Virgin Island
Email: eamsbvi@surfbvi.com
Contact: Kay Reddy
Local Agent: Euro-American Trust and Management Services Limited (Anguilla)

Euro-American Trust and Management Services Limited (Guernsey)
St. Peter Port
The Grange
Guernsey
Channel Islands, 971 2QJ
Email: howep@ffg.co.gg
Contact: Kay Reddy
Local Agent: Euro-American Trust and Management Services Limited (Anguilla)

Euro-American Trust and Management Services Limited (Panama)
PO Box 4281
Panama City
Republic of Panama
Email: eamspty@sinfo.netv
Contact: Martha Salazar
Local Agent: Euro-American Trust and Management Services Limited (Anguilla)

Fiduvalor Services Limited
13 Orchard Way
Lapford Crediton
Devon
EX17 6PR
United Kingdom
Tel: +44 709 216 4250
Fax: +44 709 216 4253
E-Mail: fiduvalor@valorgroup.net
Website: www.valorgroup.biz
Contact: René Wetzel, TEP
Local Agent: Professional Corporate Services (Anguilla) Ltd.

FINAB International Corporate Management Services, Ltd
Genesis Building 3/F
Georgetown
Grand Cayman
Cayman Islands
BVI
Email: finab@candw.ky
Contact: Valdemar B Lopes
Local Agent: Professional Corporate Services (Anguilla) Ltd.

First Class Company Services Limited
72 New Bond Street
London W1S 1RR
UK
Email: jdixon@4business.com
Contact: John Dixon
Local Agent: Professional Corporate Services (Anguilla) Ltd.

Goodman & Richter, LLP
501 West Broadway
Suite 1335
San Diego

Gordon Down and Partners
23 Allenbank Road
Heath
Cardiff

California, 92101
Email: srichter@goodman-richter.com
Contact: Steven Richter
Local Agent: Benjamine Company Services Limited

Hebert Schenk, P.C.
1440 E Missouri
Suite 125
Phoenix
AZ 85014
Email: prr@hs-law.com
Contact: Philip Rupprecht
Local Agent: Anguilla Offshore Management Limited

Interface Management International (UK) Ltd
Green Dragon House, 64-70 High Street
Croydon, United Kingdom
CRO 9XN
Email: dolores@interface-management.com
Contact: Dolores McCarthy
Local Agent: HWR Services (Anguilla) Limited

Intertrust (Isle of Man) Limited
Clinch's House
Lord Street
Douglas
Isle of Man, IM99 IRZ
Email: richardorton@intertrustlimited.com
Contact: Melanie Sarapuk
Local Agent: Intertrust (Anguilla) Ltd.

Intrust Ltd.
66 Wigmore Street
London
WIH OHQ
England
Tel: +44 20 7467 4000 Fax: +44 20

Wales
UK
CF14 3PN
Email: l.cohen1@ntlworld.com
Contact: Laurence Cohen
Local Agent: Benjamine Company Services Limited

HWR Services Limited (BVI)
Craigmuir Chambers
Road Town
Tortola
British Virgin Islands
Email: acorn@hwr.org
Contact: Richard Peters
Local Agent: HWR Services (Anguilla) Limited

Intertrust (Hong Kong) Limited
2001 Central Plaza
18 Harbour Road
Wanchai
Hong Kong
Email: HongKong@intertrustgroup.com
Contact: Katherine Chiu
Local Agent: Intertrust (Anguilla) Ltd.

Intertrust Management S.A. - Geneva Branch
Rue de la Pélisserie 16
P.O. Box 3292
CH - 1211 Geneva 3
Switzerland
Tel: +41 22 317 8000
Fax: +41 22 317 8011
E-mail: Geneva@intertrustgroup.com
Website: www.intertrustgroup.com
Contact: Walter Stressemann
Local Agent: Intertrust (Anguilla) Ltd.

Jordans Limited
21 St Thomas Street
Bristol BS1 6JS
England
Tel: +44 117 923 0600
Fax: +44 117 923 0063

7467 4081 E-mail: info@intrust.com
Contact: Peter Stone
Local Agent: Professional Corporate Services (Anguilla) Ltd.

Everett, Krebs
256 Bronte Road
Oakville
Ontario, L6L 3C6
Canada
Tel: +1 905 825 8535
Fax: +1 905 469 9967
E-mail: lawgod@offshore-tax.com
Website: www.offshore-tax.com
Contact: Randall J. Krebs
Local Agent: Wigley & Associates Inc

Newport Pacific Financial Group SA/Le Groupe Financiér Newport Pacific SA
Suite 1860, Manulife Place
10180 - 101 Street
Edmonton
Alberta
Canada T5J 3S4
Tel: +1 780 424 5700
Fax: +1 780 428 5100
E-mail: mritter@newpac.com
Website: www.newpac.com
Contact: Michael P. Ritter
Local Agent: HWR Services (Anguilla) Limited

Offshore Incorporations Limited
9/F Ruttonjee House
11 Duddell Street
Central, Hong Kong
Email: administration@offshore-inc.co
Contact: Wendy O'Donnell
Local Agent: HWR Services (Anguilla) Limited

Overseas Management Company (Jersey) Limited

Email: international@jordans.co.uk
Website: www.jordans-international.com
Contact: Anna Goddard
Local Agent: Finsco Limited

Mr. Duncan MacDonald
C.P.024
AC Betim D/R
Betim
MG 32501-970
Brazil
Tel: +55 31 3531 5681
Fax: N/A
E-mail: epopeia@netscape.net
Website: N/A
Contact: Duncan MacDonald
Local Agent: Finsco Limited

OCRA World Wide
Grosvenor Court
Tower Street
Ramsey
Isle of Man, IM8 1JA
British Isles
Tel: +44 1624 825544
Fax: +44 1624 815548
E-mail: ocra@ocra.com
Website: www.ocra-worldwide.com
Contact: Christopher Oldfield
Local Agent: Professional Corporate Services (Anguilla) Ltd.

Overseas Management Company (Asia) Limited
2706 NatWest Tower
Times Square
1 Matheson Street
Causeway Bay
Hong Kong
Email: omcasia@omchk.com.hk
Contact: Irma Herrera
Local Agent: Overseas Management Company Anguilla Limited

Overseas Management Company Inc (Panama)

P.O. Box 740
31 Broad Street
St Helier
Jersey
JE4 8ZP
Tel: +44 1534 737776
Fax: +44 1534 759909
E-mail: omcj@omcjersey.com
Website: www.omcgroup.com
Contact: Mrs Brigette Homer or Miss Carol Beaugie
Local Agent: N/A

Via Espana # 122
Bank of Boston Building
Panama
Republic of Panama
Email: corp.ops@omcpty.com
Contact: Eileen Marquez
Local Agent: Overseas Management Company Anguilla Limited

Overseas Services International Corp (Miami)
Suite 850
1401 Brickell Avenue
Miami
Florida
33131
Email: andromaji@omcpty.com
Contact: Andromaji Tzanetatos
Local Agent: Overseas Management Company Anguilla Limited

Jason Ellis Perry
918 Town Colony Drive
Middletown
Connecticut
06547
USA
Email: jadmperry@aol.com
Contact: Jason Perry
Local Agent: C.E.G Limited

ProServices Limited
Ellen L. Skelton Building, 4th Floor
Fisher's Estate
Road Town
Tortola
B.V.I
Email: haleue@amicorp.vg
Contact: Humphry Leue
Local Agent: ProServices (Anguilla) Limited

Sovereign Trust International
1601-1603 Kinwick Centre
32 Hollywood Road
Central
Hong Kong
Tel: +852 2542 1177
Fax: +852 2545 0550
E-mail: hk@sovereigngroup.com
Website: www.sovereigngroup.com
Contact: Michael Foggo, Stuart Stobie or Michael Tsang
Local Agent: Professional Corporate Services (Anguilla) Ltd.

SUCRE, ARIAS, CASTRO & REYES
48th East Street
Bella Vista
Sucre Building
Panama
Republic of Panama
Email: sucre@sucre.net
Website: www.sucre.net Contact: Mr Carlos Sucre, Mr Ramon Anzola, and Ms Thays De Salas

Sterling ACS, Ltd.
British American Building
Ground Floor
Malborough & Navy Lyon Road
Nassau, Bahamas
Email: hwoltz@sterlinggroup.bs
Contact: Howell Woltz
Local Agent: Sterling Trust (Anguilla), Ltd

Local Agent: Sucre & Sucre Anguilla Ltd

St Peters Trust Company Limited
Quay House, South Esplanade
St Peter Port
Guernsey GY 4EJ
Email: quay@quayport.demon.co.uk
Contact: Andy Stoaling
Local Agent: HWR Services (Anguilla) Limited

Angela Wang & Co
24/F, Entertainment Building
30 Queen's Road
Central
Hong Kong
Tel: +852 2869 7772
Fax: +852 2868 0708
E-mail: lawyers@angelawangco.com
Website: N/A
Contact: Kevin L Jones, Angela Wang
Local Agent: Professional Corporate Services (Anguilla) Ltd.

Scott Wilson
701 Rossland Road, Suite 258
Whitby
Canada L1N 9K3
Tel: +1 905 430 5359
Email: offshore2001@rogers.com
Contact: Scott Wilson
Local Agent: Professional Corporate Services (Anguilla) Ltd.

G. Wiseman & Associates
Rossland, BC
Canada VOG 1YO
Email: gideon@invest-wise.com
Contact: Gideon Wiseman
Local Agent: HWR Services (Anguilla) Limited

Zetland Corporate Services Limited
13/F. Silver Fortune Plaza
1 Wellington Street, Central
Hong Kong
Tel: +852 2525 7800
Fax: +852 2140 6833
E-Mail: intray@offshore.com.hk
Website: www.offshore.com.hk
Contact: Michael H. Horne or Ms Hanna Cheung
Local Agent: On-Island (Anguilla) Corporate Svcs. Ltd.

TRUST COMPANIES

Codan Trust Company (Anguilla) Limited
c/o Intertrust Offices
P.O. Box 147
The Valley
Anguilla, BWI

First Anguilla Trust Company Ltd
Mitchell House
P.O. Box 174
The Valley
Anguilla, B.W.I.
Tel: +1 264 498 8800

Fax: 264 497 5007
E-Mail: see Contact
Website: www.cdp.bm
Contact: David Astwood or John C.R. Collis

E-mail: information@firstanguilla.com
Website: www.firstanguilla.com
Contact: John O. Dyrud

HWR Services (Anguilla) Ltd.
Harlaw Chambers
P.O. Box 1026
The Valley
Anguilla, B.W.I.
Tel: +1 264 498 5000
Fax: +1 264 498 5001
E-mail: hwr@anguillanet.com
Website: www.harneys.com
Contact: Alex Richardson / Heather Wallace

Intertrust (Anguilla) Limited
P.O. Box 1388
The Valley
Anguilla, B.W.I.
Tel: +1 264 497 2189
Fax: +1 264 497 5007
E-mail: Anguilla@intertrustgroup.com
Website: www.intertrust-group.com
Contact: Joseph Brice

Renaissance International Trust
P.O. Box 687
The Valley
Anguilla, B.W.I.
Tel: +1 264 498 7878
Fax: +1 264 498 7872
E-mail: renaissance@anguillanet.com
Contact: Guy Defresne or Keithley Lake

Sinel Trust Anguilla Limited
Sinel Chambers
PO Box 1269
The Valley
Anguilla, BWI
Tel: +1 264 497 3311
Fax: +1 264 497 5659
E-mail: jbrice@sineltrust.com
Website: www.sineltrust-anguilla.com
Contact: Joseph Brice

PUBLICATIONS

Anguilla Life Magazine
PO Box 1622 Anguilla, B.W.I. Tel: 264.497.3080 ~ Fax: 264.497.4196 E-mail: anguillalife@anguillanet.com or kedivar@aol.com "The Magazine That Covers Anguilla in Depth ~ From A to Z" Subscription: One Year (3 issues — April, August and December) EC$54; US$20; UK£14. Checks or money orders should be made payable to Anguilla Life Magazine.
The Anguillian
Weekly Newspaper PO Box 98 The Valley Anguilla, B.W.I. Tel: 264.497.3823 ~ Fax: 264.497.8706

E-mail: theanguillian@anguillanet.com Subscription Rates: One Year US$120; EC$352 www.anguillian.com
The Light
Weekly Newspaper PO Box 1373 The Valley Anguilla, B.W.I. Tel: 264.497.5641 ~ Fax: 264.497.5795 E-mail: thelight@anguillanet.com Subscription Rates: One Year US$39; EC$104 www.thelight-anguilla.com
What We Do In Anguilla
Annual Magazine Monthly Edition (Update) PO Box 1373 The Valley Anguilla, B.W.I. Tel: 264.497.5641 ~ Fax: 264.497.5795 Subscription Rates: US$50 www.anguillatourguide.com

PACE OF ECONOMIC DEVELOPMENT.

Fellow Anguillians, success has its own problems and challenges. Over the past three years, Anguilla has enjoyed quite significant success in stimulating foreign as well as domestic investment, especially in luxury tourism. This has returned our country to robust economic growth, full employment and increasing disposable income. The Government's financial situation is the best it has ever been. The prospects are good for the growth we are now experiencing to be sustained well into the future. This is critical for us, as a people, in achieving economic self-reliance, self-determination and ultimately economic independence.

The economic success achieved in the past three years, now threatens to overwhelm us. The enthusiasm of foreign investors is extremely high. Many are scrambling to grasp the investment opportunities they perceive to be available in Anguilla.

The light at the end of the tunnel of which I spoke repeatedly during the dark economic days of 2000 to 2002 has now become so bright, that it threatens to blind us. It threatens to throw us off-course from the path of controlled, modest and steady economic growth. Indeed, as your Government, we are in serious danger of being distracted from our commitment to place the highest priority on social development over the next five years.

We find ourselves today facing the very real prospect of overdeveloping. We are in danger of creating unprecedented shortages in the labour force, of having to rely heavily on imported labour. We are experiencing the early symptoms associated with a rapidly deteriorating social environment. We are under tremendous pressure to deviate from the low volume high value investment strategy, which has sustained us over the years.

Fellow Anguillians, in the past week, September 19th to 25th, two events have powerfully demonstrated to the Government the immediacy and urgency of this reality. Firstly, the ongoing deterioration in behaviour among some elements of our youth again reared its ugly head. Fighting with dangerous weapons erupted resulting in serious injury to one male student of the Albena Lake-Hodge Comprehensive School. Government will ensure that this trend of youth violence and deviant behaviour is arrested.

The second event, which is the focus of my address, concerns the developments in the latest round of the on-going negotiations held during September 20 - 22 for a Memorandum of Agreement for the tourism project proposed for the Junks Hole Estate and adjoining lands. This past week, the Government was faced with extremely tough choices and placed under tremendous pressure by competing interests as we sought to finalize the terms for a Memorandum of Agreement for the Junks Hole Project. The Government was exposed to the harsh reality of the inherent danger in approving large projects in very small countries such as Anguilla.

Fellow Anguillians, in our 2000 Manifesto, a commitment re-pledged in the 2005 Manifesto, the Anguilla United Front Government, as part of our programme priorities, pledged and I quote "to review the tourism plant and supply and develop a phased investment strategy consistent with projected demand, carrying capacities, labour market supply as well as accessibility to the island", unquote. This from a tourism perspective is consistent with the island's positioning as an upscale tourism destination, offering an unrivalled and unique experience to its visitors.

In the recent past, when commenting on the surge in investor interest in Anguilla that has taken place since 2002, I have said that "whilst we are pleased with the interest in Anguilla, we must be careful that the increased demand for a bit of the peace and tranquility of Anguilla, does not lead to over-development, a huge mass of visitors, congestion, overcrowding, collapse of our social and physical infrastructure and eventual economic decline".

One of the proposals to come before Government in recent times has been for a major tourism project in the eastern end of Anguilla. As we indicated in the 2005 Budget Address, Government in November 2004 received a formal proposal from Urban Nicklaus Holdings in conjunction with the Property Markets Group, which I will refer to as the UNH-PMG Group, to establish a major project on over 500 acres of land encompassing Junks Hole, Captains Bay and Windward Point. We indicated to the developers in November, that Government was in the midst of finalizing the 2005 Budget, and given our small administration, could not immediately devote resources to appraising the project. However, in the new year Government would turn priority attention to the project.

This we did and beginning in January 2005, Government through the Ministry of FEDICT and the Tourism Investment Review Committee began the painstaking task of conducting the due diligence and appraisal of the project proposal. This task was completed at the end of March and in April, following the decision of the Executive Council to this effect, Government communicated to the developers that it had approved the grant of "Investment Approval in Principle" for the project. This meant that the project concept and UNH-PMG, as the proposed developers, along with their strategic partners, which they had identified, were acceptable to the Government. Government was at pains though, to stress that the granting of "investment approval in principle" should not be taken as implying that Government committed itself to the details of the project as proposed by the developers. The design, scope, and scale of the project, as well as any concessions to be granted had to be determined during negotiations between the GoA and UNH-PMG, which if successful, would lead to a Memorandum of Agreement representing "Investment Approval in Full". It was furthermore communicated that investment approval in full could only be granted by the Executive Council.

Negotiations on a Memorandum of Agreement (MOA) commenced on May 2, 2005 and have continued on a start-stop basis, as both parties tried to come to grips with the issues that a project of this magnitude (over 500 acres of land and 2083 bedrooms) would have on Anguilla. Government was mindful of its responsibility to take into consideration the overall investment situation in the economy, the rate of growth, employment, income generation and the social impacts and implications arising as a result of other investment projects and other economic developments as a whole, which have been taking place in Anguilla since 2002. The negotiations have therefore been conducted at all times by the Government against the backdrop of the total economic and social picture. This framework was painstakingly laid out to the UNH-PMG Negotiating Team by the Government's Negotiating Team from the first day of formal negotiations in May.

Two key concerns of Government with the Junks Hole Project were the start date and phasing of the project. Government was mindful that major construction of buildings (hotel, estate homes, villas, condos, etc) should not coincide with peak construction activity of the Flag Temenos-St. Regis and Viceroy Projects at Merrywing-Rendezvous and Barnes Bay, respectively. Government has consistently underscored its grave concern over the growing labour shortage situation and wished at all times to avoid the need to undertake the massive importation of labour.

We are extremely concerned about the significant attendant stress this would place on social and physical infrastructure and services (including housing, education and health). These and other issues were debated between both sides over the course of May and June and were informed by the public consultations, which Government held concerning the project. Of course the large scale of the project was an underlying cause for concern and was a most significant factor in Government's concerns about the timing and phasing of the project.

In late July, an impasse developed between the two negotiating teams. Government by way of an Executive Council decision, took a firm position on the issues on which the negotiations had become deadlocked and communicated its position to UNH-PMG. UNH-PMG responded to the Government, that it accepted the GOA's position. As a result the Government and the UNH-PMG came to agreement in principle on all of the major issues raised during the negotiations, including a project building construction start date and a project phasing, which would balance the needs of both parties. Further consideration of the project proposal however, would be subject to the developers submitting certain documentary evidence as it related to, inter alia, business plan, financing plans and contracts entered into and under consideration before the investment approval in full process could be further advanced. Negotiations towards the finalisation of the MOA were recessed, due to the start of the Annual Summer Festival activities.

When negotiations resumed on September 6, UNH-PMG represented to Government that they wished to reopen the issues surrounding the project building construction start date and indicated that their project was not viable if they could not start construction within nine months of the approval of the Memorandum of Agreement, owing to commitments which they had to make to their bankers. Negotiations with UNH-PMG at this stage reached an impasse after Government indicated that it could not agree to such a request.

Fellow Anguillians, from time to time, any and all Governments face pressure from stakeholders and parties seeking to promote their particular interests.

The owners of the Junks Hole Estate after learning that there was impasse in the negotiations between the GoA and UNH-PMG during the three weeks from September 4, 2005 exerted relentless pressure and lobbied extensively with Ministers of Government to accommodate the demands of the developers and thereby enable the project to proceed speedily.

In the face of this pressure and mindful of its commitment to having a significant project in the East, Ministers reluctantly yielded to the pressure to make further concessions to the developers. As a result Ministers indicated to the developers that they would be prepared to concede that the building construction could start some twelve months after the signing of the Memorandum of Agreement. The developers indicated that this was acceptable to them.

Both sides resumed face to face negotiations on Tuesday September 20 with a view to ironing out remaining issues standing in the way of investment approval in full. At the close of these negotiations on Wed Sept. 21 the significant issues remaining to be resolved was language as it related to:

(i) the Environmental Impact Assessment process;
(ii) the Economic-Social Impact Assessment process;

(iii) the Government of Anguilla's processes and procedures governing the grant of permits and approvals particularly in regard to labour, immigration, physical planning, building and other required approvals;
(iv) provisions as they related to the project lenders;
(v) intra-company transfers; and,
(vi) performance provisions.
Legal counsel for UNH-PMG was then expected to revise the draft MOA to take into account all negotiations and discussions to date and forward the revised draft MOA to the Attorney General's Chambers for consideration.

Government took great pains to point out that the AG's Chambers would take at least 2-3 weeks to fully vet and revise the latest draft of the proposed MOA. Subject to the language in the revised draft MOA being satisfactory to both the GoA and the developers, the Minister of FEDICT would then submit the draft Memorandum of Agreement to Executive Council for consideration.

Upon hearing that the GoA was close to resolving the outstanding issues that could serve to prevent another golf tourism and resort residential real estate project for the island to be located in the east, the principals of Flag Luxury Properties strongly represented to Government that approval of such a project to proceed at this time would jeopardize the viability of their project which had commenced since early 2003. The Flag principals further indicated that if approval was granted to the project proposed by UNH-PMG, at this time, the lending institutions with whom they had been in contact would not lend the funds necessary to continue with the project. If no loans funds were forthcoming the project would have to be discontinued with immediate effect.

The apparent fears in some segments of the banking community is that if two such large projects were to come on stream at the same time, there was the strong possibility of product oversupply and that the market, in terms of the sales of vacation homes which are critical to the success of the financial model of both projects, could in fact only bear one such project at the current time.

Fellow Anguillians, my Ministerial colleagues and I came face to face in the past week with the possibility of suddenly losing the economic growth we are now enjoying and slipping back to where we were just a few short years ago. We were faced with representation from the owners of Flag Luxury Properties of the possibility of the immediate cessation of work on the Temenos-St. Regis golf tourism project, if the Government signed a Memorandum of Agreement with Urban Nicklaus Holdings and the Property Markets Group for the development of the Junks Hole Project with a commencement date sooner than 30 months into the future from the signing of an MOA.

My Ministerial Colleagues and I carefully considered the situation and did much soul searching. We seriously contemplated dis-regarding the representation made by Flag Luxury Properties. However, out of an abundance of concern firstly for the approximately 500 construction workers currently employed on the Temenos-St. Regis Project and their dependents, which could well amount to another 1000 or more persons, we decided against this. The decision was not easy and it was and is quite painful. We also considered the negative ripple effects likely to spread throughout the entire economy in the immediate future. We came to the stark conclusion that our responsibilities to and on behalf of all of us, the people of the Anguillian community, required that we should not risk the robust, yet fragile growth, which we have been enjoying for less than two years in a head on confrontation. This growth fellow Anguillians has been stimulated and made possible to a significant degree, as a result of the implementation of the Temenos-St. Regis project over the past two years.

In the circumstances, we felt that it was our primary duty in the short term, and in the interest of Anguilla to err on the side of protecting the economic gains already being realized by all of us and to seek an accommodation in terms of the timing of the development of the Junks Hole project that could be a win-win situation for all concerned over the medium to long term.

Fellow Anguillians, what would be the implications you may ask of the Flag project closing down due to lack of funding to continue. 500 construction workers would be out of work, heavy equipment and other suppliers would have their contracts terminated, their loan commitments to the local banking community would be in serious jeopardy. The ripple effect on Anguilla's economy would be disastrous. The Government was faced therefore with a potentially very painful option, even if the pain could have begun to ease significantly within a year or two.

It is being said on the street that Government has relinquished its power as Government to the principals of Flag. We argue to the contrary. We argue that Government has been decisive in the face of an exceedingly difficult position. Protecting jobs on the ground has always been something that Governments in small countries like ours and big countries like the UK have faced.

The possibility of cessation of work on the Temenos-St. Regis project coupled with the Government's strong reservations about allowing an early build out of the proposed UNH-PMG project, convinced Ministers that Government ought to maintain its original position about judiciously phasing major construction on Anguilla and to re-open the issue with UNH –PMG about a start date for their proposed project. This decision was communicated to the members of the UNH-PMG team on the island on Thursday September 22, 2005.

While it is entirely fortuitous, it is instructive that the violent incident at the Comprehensive School, to which I referred earlier, should have taken place on the very day when my colleague Ministers and I had to grapple with the fundamental challenge of how to respond in the face of competing interests of large projects on the island.

Ministers informed UNH-PMG's representatives at the meeting on September 22, that the project building construction would have to be timed to commence 30 months after the signing of the Memorandum of Agreement. The members of the UNH-PMG indicated that that this was not acceptable to them and that Government should be prepared to face the consequences of its decision.

In my speech amidst economic recession in 2002, I assured you the people of Anguilla that there was light at the end of the tunnel. Today however, we cannot allow ourselves to be blinded by this light but rather allow our eyes to gradually adjust as we transition from the darkness of the tunnel to the light on the outside. We must make our assessments and then take action. Our decision of the past week must be viewed within this context.

Let me elaborate. We must take into consideration the labour realities on Anguilla, the physical, environmental and social infrastructure of the island, the human and financial resource capacity of the Government, the supply of accommodation facilities in the tourism sector, and the stages of implementation of already approved local and foreign projects when considering applications for further investment projects. We must also be aware of the history of failed projects on Anguilla and the need to avoid such recurrences. These are the sorts of considerations that the Government has taken into account concerning its present position with regards the proposed UNH-PMG project for Junks Hole-Captains Bay-Windward Point.

Indeed in that meeting last Thursday 22, I indicated to the UNH-PMG team that Anguilla seemed to be a "convict of its own success". Anguilla is currently at a state of full employment, particularly within the construction sector, as a result of the development at Flag Luxury Properties project, other tourism, commercial and residential projects as well as public sector projects such as the on-going road development programme. Economic growth last year was 13.7%, the highest among Caribbean Development Bank borrowing member countries. One side effect of rapid economic growth is usually rising inflation. We are beginning to see this, with inflation for the year so far running at around 5% compared to 3% in 2004. As Government, we have to guard against this and other effects of over expansion, such as the need to import massive amounts of labour, which I mentioned earlier in this address.

On Thursday 22 we met with some of those family members (who were available to attend) whose lands would be sold to the UNH-PMG Group in order for them to undertake the project. We indicated to them that in keeping with its manifesto pledge for a major project in the East, the Government of Anguilla is keeping the door open for the UNH-PMG Group.

Fellow Anguillians, most people who know me, would agree that I am always optimistic. As I have indicated, Government's desire to re-open the issue of the project building construction start date has been communicated to UNH-PMG and I am hopeful that some way can be found to continue with the negotiations. At this time, when emotions are running high, I implore all stakeholders involved – the principals of UNH-PMG, members of the Junks Hole and Webster Estates, residents of the East – to let us all keep a sense of perspective. Anguilla is a beautiful jewel, which none of us wishes to see despoiled or destroyed.

The self-reliant, self-determined, orderly and sustained development of Anguilla is the underlying motivation of your Government. The struggle for the sustained economic and social development and security of all of us is not won nor lost on a single turn of events. The progress we have made in two short years is too fragile to suffer any major shocks at this time.

Thank you for listening. And may God bless you all and continue to bless Anguilla.

MORATORIUM ON MAJOR NEW FOREIGN INVESTMENT TOURISM RELATED PROJECTS

The Valley, Anguilla, Monday, October 31st , 2005 –The Government of Anguilla in keeping with its commitment to carefully manage the development of the economy to achieve long term sustainability and mindful of the current labour and social challenges facing the Anguillian community and the high risk of over-development has decided to place a general moratorium on major new foreign investment tourism related projects with effect from November 1st, 2005 as follows:

i) An embargo will be placed on the announcement of any approved major new foreign tourism project for a period of 20 months after November 1st, 2005;
ii) No presales of real estate products by major new foreign investment projects will be approved to be undertaken for 20 months from November 1st, 2005;
iii) No site preparation nor construction of infrastructure will be approved to commence until 24 months after November 1st, 2005; and
iv) No construction work on the accommodations/real estate products and amenities will be approved to commence until 30 months after November 1st, 2005.

This policy decision shall be generally applicable to approved major new foreign investment tourism related projects. The Honourable Chief Minister early this month in a radio-address to the nation regarding projects of this nature said" Fellow Anguillians, success has its own problems and challenges. Over the past three years, Anguilla has enjoyed quite significant success in stimulating foreign as well as domestic investment, especially in luxury tourism. This has returned our country to robust economic growth, full employment and increasing disposable income. The Government's financial situation is the best it has ever been. The prospects are good for the growth we are now experiencing to be sustained well into the future. This is critical for us, as a people, in achieving economic self-reliance, self-determination and ultimately economic independence.

The honourable Osbourne Fleming said "the economic success achieved in the past three years, now threatens to overwhelm us. The enthusiasm of foreign investors is extremely high. Many are scrambling to grasp the investment opportunities they perceive to be available in Anguilla.

The light at the end of the tunnel of which I spoke repeatedly during the dark economic days of 2000 to 2002 has now become so bright, that it threatens to blind us. It threatens to throw us off-course from the path of controlled, modest and steady economic growth. Indeed, as your Government, we are in serious danger of being distracted from our commitment to place the highest priority on social development over the next five years. We find ourselves today facing the very real prospect of overdeveloping. We are in danger of creating unprecedented shortages in the labour force, of having to rely heavily on imported labour. We are experiencing the early symptoms associated with a rapidly deteriorating social environment. We are under tremendous pressure to deviate from the low volume high value investment strategy, which has sustained us over the years."

The chief minister in this same speech went on to further stated"fellow Anguillians, in our 2000 Manifesto, a commitment re-pledged in the 2005 Manifesto, the Anguilla United Front Government, as part of our programme priorities, pledged and I quote "to review the tourism plant and supply and develop a phased investment strategy consistent with projected demand, carrying capacities, labour market supply as well as accessibility to the island", unquote. This from a tourism perspective is consistent with the island's positioning as an upscale tourism destination, offering an unrivalled and unique experience to its visitors.

In the recent past, when commenting on the surge in investor interest in Anguilla that has taken place since 2002, I have said that "whilst we are pleased with the interest in Anguilla, we must be careful that the increased demand for a bit of the peace and tranquility of Anguilla, does not lead to over-development, a huge mass of visitors, congestion, overcrowding, collapse of our social and physical infrastructure and eventual economic decline".

In the same speech the Chief Minister went on to further declare "Anguilla is a beautiful jewel, which none of us wishes to see despoiled or destroyed. The self-reliant, self-determined, orderly and sustained development of Anguilla is the underlying motivation of your Government. The struggle for the sustained economic and social development and security of all of us is not won nor lost on a single turn of events. The progress we have made in two short years is too fragile to suffer any major shocks at this time.

NEW! WORLD OFFSHORE TAX GUIDES

Price: $149.95 each

1.	Andorra Offshore Tax Guide
2.	Anguilla Offshore Tax Guide
3.	Bahamas Offshore Tax Guide
4.	Barbados Offshore Tax Guide
5.	Belize Offshore Tax Guide
6.	Bermuda Offshore Tax Guide
7.	British Virgin Islands Offshore Tax Guide
8.	Cayman Islands Offshore Tax Guide
9.	Cook Islands Offshore Tax Guide
10.	Costa Rica Offshore Tax Guide
11.	Cyprus Offshore Tax Guide
12.	Dubai Offshore Tax Guide
13.	Gibraltar Offshore Tax Guide
14.	Grenada Offshore Tax Guide
15.	Guernsey Offshore Tax Guide
16.	Hong Kong Offshore Tax Guide
17.	Ireland Offshore Tax Guide
18.	Isle of Man Offshore Tax Guide
19.	Jersey Offshore Tax Guide
20.	Labuan Offshore Tax Guide
21.	Liechtenstein Offshore Tax Guide
22.	Luxembourg Offshore Tax Guide
23.	Madeira Offshore Tax Guide
24.	Malta Offshore Tax Guide
25.	Mauritius Offshore Business and Investment Opportunities Handbook
26.	Mauritius Offshore Tax Guide
27.	Monaco Offshore Tax Guide
28.	Nauru Offshore Tax Guide
29.	Netherlands Antilles Offshore Tax Guide
30.	Panama Offshore Tax Guide
31.	Seychelles Offshore Tax Guide
32.	Switzerland Offshore Tax Guide
33.	Turks & Caicos Islands Offshore Tax Guide
34.	Vanuatu Offshore Tax Guide

To order and for additional analytical and marketing information, please contacrt
International Business Publications, USA at:
P.O. Box 15343, Washington, DC 20003, USA. Phone: (202) 546-2103. Fax: (202) 546-3275.
World Business Info Catalog: http://www.ibous.com. E-mail: ibpusa@comcast.net

NEW! WORLD OFFSHORE, LAW, INVESTMENT & BUSINESS LIBRARY

Detailed Information on conducting business and investment activity in the countries with special offshore status
Price: $149.95 each

Andorra Offshore Investment and Business Guide
Anguilla Offshore Investment and Business Guide
Bahamas Offshore Investment and Business Guide
Barbados Offshore Investment and Business Guide
Belize Offshore Investment and Business Guide
Bermuda Offshore Investment and Business Guide
British Virgin Islands Offshore Investment and Business Guide
Cayman Islands Offshore Investment and Business Guide
Cook Islands Offshore Investment and Business Guide
Costa Rica Offshore Investment and Business Guide
Cyprus Offshore Investment and Business Guide
Dubai Offshore Investment and Business Guide
Gibraltar Offshore Investment and Business Guide
Grenada Offshore Investment and Business Guide
Guernsey Offshore Investment and Business Guide
Hong Kong Offshore Investment and Business Guide
Ireland Offshore Investment and Business Guide
Isle of Man Offshore Investment and Business Guide
Jersey Offshore Investment and Business Guide
Labuan Offshore Investment and Business Guide
Liechtenstein Offshore Investment and Business Guide
Luxembourg Offshore Investment and Business Guide
Madeira Offshore Investment and Business Guide
Malta Offshore Investment and Business Guide
Mauritius Offshore Business and Investment Opportunities Handbook
Mauritius Offshore Investment and Business Guide
Monaco Offshore Investment and Business Guide
Nauru Offshore Investment and Business Guide
Netherlands Antilles Offshore Investment and Business Guide
Panama Offshore Investment and Business Guide
Seychelles Offshore Investment and Business Guide
Switzerland Offshore Investment and Business Guide
Turks & Caicos Islands Offshore Investment and Business Guide
Vanuatu Offshore Investment and Business Guide

To order and for additional analytical and marketing information, please contacrt
International Business Publications, USA at:
P.O. Box 15343, Washington, DC 20003, USA. Phone: (202) 546-2103. Fax: (202) 546-3275.
E-mail: rusric@erols.com

Basic Laws and Regulations for conducting business and investment activity in the countries with special offshore status

Andorra Offshore Business Law Handbook
Anguilla Offshore Business Law Handbook
Bahamas Offshore Business Law Handbook
Barbados Offshore Business Law Handbook
Belize Offshore Business Law Handbook
Bermuda Offshore Business Law Handbook
British Virgin Islands Offshore Business Law Handbook
Cayman Islands Offshore Business Law Handbook
Cook Islands Offshore Business Law Handbook
Costa Rica Offshore Business Law Handbook
Cyprus Offshore Business Law Handbook
Dubai Offshore Business Law Handbook
Gibraltar Offshore Business Law Handbook
Grenada Offshore Business Law Handbook
Guernsey Offshore Business Law Handbook
Hong Kong Offshore Business Law Handbook
Ireland Offshore Business Law Handbook
Isle of Man Offshore Business Law Handbook
Jersey Offshore Business Law Handbook
Labuan Offshore Business Law Handbook
Liechtenstein Offshore Business Law Handbook
Luxembourg Offshore Business Law Handbook
Madeira Offshore Business Law Handbook
Malta Offshore Business Law Handbook
Mauritius Offshore Business and Investment Opportunities Handbook
Mauritius Offshore Business Law Handbook
Monaco Offshore Business Law Handbook
Nauru Offshore Business Law Handbook
Netherlands Antilles Offshore Business Law Handbook
Panama Offshore Business Law Handbook
Seychelles Offshore Business Law Handbook
Switzerland Offshore Business Law Handbook
Turks & Caicos Islands Offshore Business Law Handbook
Vanuatu Offshore Business Law Handbook

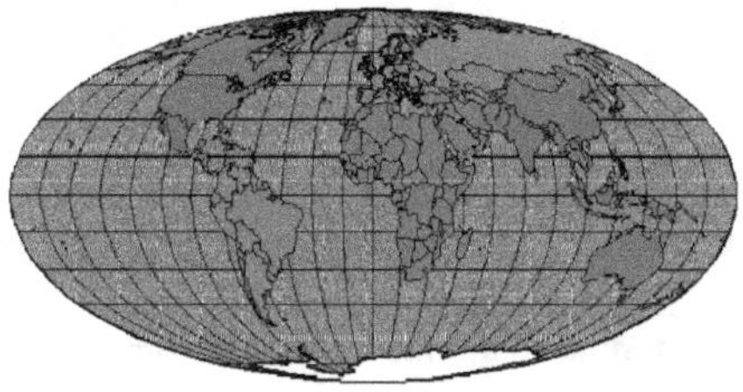

WORLD BUSINESS AND INVESTMENT OPPORTUNITIES YEARBOOK LIBRARY

World Business Information Catalog, USA: http://www.ibpus.com
Email: ibpusa3@gmail.com

Price: $99.95 Each

TITLE
Abkhazia (Republic of Abkhazia) Business and Investment Opportunities Yearbook Volume 1 Strategic, Practical Information and Opportunities
Afghanistan Business and Investment Opportunities Yearbook Volume 1 Strategic, Practical Information and Opportunities
Aland Business and Investment Opportunities Yearbook Volume 1 Strategic, Practical Information and Opportunities
Albania Business and Investment Opportunities Yearbook Volume 1 Strategic, Practical Information and Opportunities
Algeria Business and Investment Opportunities Yearbook Volume 1 Strategic, Practical Information and Opportunities
Andorra Business and Investment Opportunities Yearbook Volume 1 Strategic, Practical Information and Opportunities
Angola Business and Investment Opportunities Yearbook Volume 1 Strategic, Practical Information and Opportunities
Anguilla Business and Investment Opportunities Yearbook Volume 1 Strategic, Practical Information and Opportunities
Antigua and Barbuda Business and Investment Opportunities Yearbook Volume 1 Strategic, Practical Information and Opportunities
Antilles (Netherlands) Business and Investment Opportunities Yearbook Volume 1 Strategic, Practical Information and Opportunities
Argentina Business and Investment Opportunities Yearbook Volume 1 Strategic, Practical Information and Opportunities
Armenia Business and Investment Opportunities Yearbook Volume 1 Strategic, Practical Information and Opportunities
Aruba Business and Investment Opportunities Yearbook Volume 1 Strategic, Practical Information and Opportunities
Australia Business and Investment Opportunities Yearbook Volume 1 Strategic, Practical Information and Opportunities
Austria Business and Investment Opportunities Yearbook Volume 1 Strategic, Practical Information and Opportunities
Azerbaijan Business and Investment Opportunities Yearbook Volume 1 Strategic, Practical Information and Opportunities
Bahamas Business and Investment Opportunities Yearbook Volume 1 Strategic, Practical Information and Opportunities
Bahrain Business and Investment Opportunities Yearbook Volume 1 Strategic, Practical Information and Opportunities
Bangladesh Business and Investment Opportunities Yearbook Volume 1 Strategic, Practical Information and Opportunities
Barbados Business and Investment Opportunities Yearbook Volume 1 Strategic, Practical Information and Opportunities
Belarus Business and Investment Opportunities Yearbook Volume 1 Strategic, Practical Information and Opportunities

For additional analytical, business and investment opportunities information,
Please contact Global Investment & Business Center, USA
at (202) 546-2103. Fax: (202) 546-3275. E-mail: ibpusa3@gmail.com

TITLE
Belgium Business and Investment Opportunities Yearbook Volume 1 Strategic, Practical Information and Opportunities
Belize Business and Investment Opportunities Yearbook Volume 1 Strategic, Practical Information and Opportunities
Benin Business and Investment Opportunities Yearbook Volume 1 Strategic, Practical Information and Opportunities
Bermuda Business and Investment Opportunities Yearbook Volume 1 Strategic, Practical Information and Opportunities
Bhutan Business and Investment Opportunities Yearbook Volume 1 Strategic, Practical Information and Opportunities
Bolivia Business and Investment Opportunities Yearbook Volume 1 Strategic, Practical Information and Opportunities
Bosnia and Herzegovina Business and Investment Opportunities Yearbook Volume 1 Strategic, Practical Information and Opportunities
Botswana Business and Investment Opportunities Yearbook Volume 1 Strategic, Practical Information and Opportunities
Brazil Business and Investment Opportunities Yearbook Volume 1 Strategic, Practical Information and Opportunities
Brunei Business and Investment Opportunities Yearbook Volume 1 Strategic, Practical Information and Opportunities
Bulgaria Business and Investment Opportunities Yearbook Volume 1 Strategic, Practical Information and Opportunities
Burkina Faso Business and Investment Opportunities Yearbook Volume 1 Strategic, Practical Information and Opportunities
Burundi Business and Investment Opportunities Yearbook Volume 1 Strategic, Practical Information and Opportunities
Cambodia Business and Investment Opportunities Yearbook Volume 1 Strategic, Practical Information and Opportunities
Cameroon Business and Investment Opportunities Yearbook Volume 1 Strategic, Practical Information and Opportunities
Canada Business and Investment Opportunities Yearbook Volume 1 Strategic, Practical Information and Opportunities
Cape Verde Business and Investment Opportunities Yearbook Volume 1 Strategic, Practical Information and Opportunities
Cayman Islands Business and Investment Opportunities Yearbook Volume 1 Strategic, Practical Information and Opportunities
Central African Republic Business and Investment Opportunities Yearbook Volume 1 Strategic, Practical Information and Opportunities
Chad Business and Investment Opportunities Yearbook Volume 1 Strategic, Practical Information and Opportunities
Chile Business and Investment Opportunities Yearbook Volume 1 Strategic, Practical Information and Opportunities
China Business and Investment Opportunities Yearbook Volume 1 Strategic, Practical Information and Opportunities
Colombia Business and Investment Opportunities Yearbook Volume 1 Strategic, Practical Information and Opportunities
Comoros Business and Investment Opportunities Yearbook Volume 1 Strategic, Practical Information and Opportunities
Congo Business and Investment Opportunities Yearbook Volume 1 Strategic, Practical Information and Opportunities
Congo, Democratic Republic Business and Investment Opportunities Yearbook Volume 1 Strategic, Practical Information and Opportunities
Cook Islands Business and Investment Opportunities Yearbook Volume 1 Strategic, Practical Information and Opportunities
Costa Rica Business and Investment Opportunities Yearbook Volume 1 Strategic, Practical Information and Opportunities

TITLE
Cote d'Ivoire Business and Investment Opportunities Yearbook Volume 1 Strategic, Practical Information and Opportunities
Croatia Business and Investment Opportunities Yearbook Volume 1 Strategic, Practical Information and Opportunities
Cuba Business and Investment Opportunities Yearbook Volume 1 Strategic, Practical Information and Opportunities
Cyprus Business and Investment Opportunities Yearbook Volume 1 Strategic, Practical Information and Opportunities
Czech Republic Business and Investment Opportunities Yearbook Volume 1 Strategic, Practical Information and Opportunities
Denmark Business and Investment Opportunities Yearbook Volume 1 Strategic, Practical Information and Opportunities
Djibouti Business and Investment Opportunities Yearbook Volume 1 Strategic, Practical Information and Opportunities
Dominica Business and Investment Opportunities Yearbook Volume 1 Strategic, Practical Information and Opportunities
Dominican Republic Business and Investment Opportunities Yearbook Volume 1 Strategic, Practical Information and Opportunities
Ecuador Business and Investment Opportunities Yearbook Volume 1 Strategic, Practical Information and Opportunities
Egypt Business and Investment Opportunities Yearbook Volume 1 Strategic, Practical Information and Opportunities
El Salvador Business and Investment Opportunities Yearbook Volume 1 Strategic, Practical Information and Opportunities
Equatorial Guinea Business and Investment Opportunities Yearbook Volume 1 Strategic, Practical Information and Opportunities
Eritrea Business and Investment Opportunities Yearbook Volume 1 Strategic, Practical Information and Opportunities
Estonia Business and Investment Opportunities Yearbook Volume 1 Strategic, Practical Information and Opportunities
Ethiopia Business and Investment Opportunities Yearbook Volume 1 Strategic, Practical Information and Opportunities
Falkland Islands Business and Investment Opportunities Yearbook Volume 1 Strategic, Practical Information and Opportunities
Faroes Islands Business and Investment Opportunities Yearbook Volume 1 Strategic, Practical Information and Opportunities
Fiji Business and Investment Opportunities Yearbook Volume 1 Strategic, Practical Information and Opportunities
Finland Business and Investment Opportunities Yearbook Volume 1 Strategic, Practical Information and Opportunities
France Business and Investment Opportunities Yearbook Volume 1 Strategic, Practical Information and Opportunities
Gabon Business and Investment Opportunities Yearbook Volume 1 Strategic, Practical Information and Opportunities
Gambia Business and Investment Opportunities Yearbook Volume 1 Strategic, Practical Information and Opportunities
Georgia Business and Investment Opportunities Yearbook Volume 1 Strategic, Practical Information and Opportunities
Germany Business and Investment Opportunities Yearbook Volume 1 Strategic, Practical Information and Opportunities
Ghana Business and Investment Opportunities Yearbook Volume 1 Strategic, Practical Information and Opportunities
Gibraltar Business and Investment Opportunities Yearbook Volume 1 Strategic, Practical Information and Opportunities
Greece Business and Investment Opportunities Yearbook Volume 1 Strategic, Practical Information and Opportunities

TITLE
Greenland Business and Investment Opportunities Yearbook Volume 1 Strategic, Practical Information and Opportunities
Grenada Business and Investment Opportunities Yearbook Volume 1 Strategic, Practical Information and Opportunities
Guam Business and Investment Opportunities Yearbook Volume 1 Strategic, Practical Information and Opportunities
Guatemala Business and Investment Opportunities Yearbook Volume 1 Strategic, Practical Information and Opportunities
Guernsey Business and Investment Opportunities Yearbook Volume 1 Strategic, Practical Information and Opportunities
Guinea Business and Investment Opportunities Yearbook Volume 1 Strategic, Practical Information and Opportunities
Guinea-Bissau Business and Investment Opportunities Yearbook Volume 1 Strategic, Practical Information and Opportunities
Guyana Business and Investment Opportunities Yearbook Volume 1 Strategic, Practical Information and Opportunities
Haiti Business and Investment Opportunities Yearbook Volume 1 Strategic, Practical Information and Opportunities
Honduras Business and Investment Opportunities Yearbook Volume 1 Strategic, Practical Information and Opportunities
Hungary Business and Investment Opportunities Yearbook Volume 1 Strategic, Practical Information and Opportunities
Iceland Business and Investment Opportunities Yearbook Volume 1 Strategic, Practical Information and Opportunities
India Business and Investment Opportunities Yearbook Volume 1 Strategic, Practical Information and Opportunities
Indonesia Business and Investment Opportunities Yearbook Volume 1 Strategic, Practical Information and Opportunities
Iran Business and Investment Opportunities Yearbook Volume 1 Strategic, Practical Information and Opportunities
Iraq Business and Investment Opportunities Yearbook Volume 1 Strategic, Practical Information and Opportunities
Ireland Business and Investment Opportunities Yearbook Volume 1 Strategic, Practical Information and Opportunities
Israel Business and Investment Opportunities Yearbook Volume 1 Strategic, Practical Information and Opportunities
Italy Business and Investment Opportunities Yearbook Volume 1 Strategic, Practical Information and Opportunities
Jamaica Business and Investment Opportunities Yearbook Volume 1 Strategic, Practical Information and Opportunities
Japan Business and Investment Opportunities Yearbook Volume 1 Strategic, Practical Information and Opportunities
Jersey Business and Investment Opportunities Yearbook Volume 1 Strategic, Practical Information and Opportunities
Jordan Business and Investment Opportunities Yearbook Volume 1 Strategic, Practical Information and Opportunities
Kazakhstan Business and Investment Opportunities Yearbook Volume 1 Strategic, Practical Information and Opportunities
Kenya Business and Investment Opportunities Yearbook Volume 1 Strategic, Practical Information and Opportunities
Kiribati Business and Investment Opportunities Yearbook Volume 1 Strategic, Practical Information and Opportunities
Korea, North Business and Investment Opportunities Yearbook Volume 1 Strategic, Practical Information and Opportunities
Korea, South Business and Investment Opportunities Yearbook Volume 1 Strategic, Practical Information and Opportunities

TITLE
Kosovo Business and Investment Opportunities Yearbook Volume 1 Strategic, Practical Information and Opportunities
Kurdistan Business and Investment Opportunities Yearbook Volume 1 Strategic, Practical Information and Opportunities
Kuwait Business and Investment Opportunities Yearbook Volume 1 Strategic, Practical Information and Opportunities
Kyrgyzstan Business and Investment Opportunities Yearbook Volume 1 Strategic, Practical Information and Opportunities
Laos Business and Investment Opportunities Yearbook Volume 1 Strategic, Practical Information and Opportunities
Latvia Business and Investment Opportunities Yearbook Volume 1 Strategic, Practical Information and Opportunities
Lebanon Business and Investment Opportunities Yearbook Volume 1 Strategic, Practical Information and Opportunities
Lesotho Business and Investment Opportunities Yearbook Volume 1 Strategic, Practical Information and Opportunities
Liberia Business and Investment Opportunities Yearbook Volume 1 Strategic, Practical Information and Opportunities
Libya Business and Investment Opportunities Yearbook Volume 1 Strategic, Practical Information and Opportunities
Liechtenstein Business and Investment Opportunities Yearbook Volume 1 Strategic, Practical Information and Opportunities
Lithuania Business and Investment Opportunities Yearbook Volume 1 Strategic, Practical Information and Opportunities
Luxembourg Business and Investment Opportunities Yearbook Volume 1 Strategic, Practical Information and Opportunities
Macao Business and Investment Opportunities Yearbook Volume 1 Strategic, Practical Information and Opportunities
Macedonia Business and Investment Opportunities Yearbook Volume 1 Strategic, Practical Information and Opportunities
Madagascar Business and Investment Opportunities Yearbook Volume 1 Strategic, Practical Information and Opportunities
Madeira Business and Investment Opportunities Yearbook Volume 1 Strategic, Practical Information and Opportunities
Malawi Business and Investment Opportunities Yearbook Volume 1 Strategic, Practical Information and Opportunities
Malaysia Business and Investment Opportunities Yearbook Volume 1 Strategic, Practical Information and Opportunities
Maldives Business and Investment Opportunities Yearbook Volume 1 Strategic, Practical Information and Opportunities
Mali Business and Investment Opportunities Yearbook Volume 1 Strategic, Practical Information and Opportunities
Malta Business and Investment Opportunities Yearbook Volume 1 Strategic, Practical Information and Opportunities
Man Business and Investment Opportunities Yearbook Volume 1 Strategic, Practical Information and Opportunities
Marshall Islands Business and Investment Opportunities Yearbook Volume 1 Strategic, Practical Information and Opportunities
Mauritania Business and Investment Opportunities Yearbook Volume 1 Strategic, Practical Information and Opportunities
Mauritius Business and Investment Opportunities Yearbook Volume 1 Strategic, Practical Information and Opportunities
Mayotte Business and Investment Opportunities Yearbook Volume 1 Strategic, Practical Information and Opportunities
Mexico Business and Investment Opportunities Yearbook Volume 1 Strategic, Practical Information and Opportunities

TITLE
Micronesia Business and Investment Opportunities Yearbook Volume 1 Strategic, Practical Information and Opportunities
Moldova Business and Investment Opportunities Yearbook Volume 1 Strategic, Practical Information and Opportunities
Monaco Business and Investment Opportunities Yearbook Volume 1 Strategic, Practical Information and Opportunities
Mongolia Business and Investment Opportunities Yearbook Volume 1 Strategic, Practical Information and Opportunities
Montserrat Business and Investment Opportunities Yearbook Volume 1 Strategic, Practical Information and Opportunities
Montenegro Business and Investment Opportunities Yearbook Volume 1 Strategic, Practical Information and Opportunities
Morocco Business and Investment Opportunities Yearbook Volume 1 Strategic, Practical Information and Opportunities
Mozambique Business and Investment Opportunities Yearbook Volume 1 Strategic, Practical Information and Opportunities
Myanmar Business and Investment Opportunities Yearbook Volume 1 Strategic, Practical Information and Opportunities
Nagorno-Karabakh Republic Business and Investment Opportunities Yearbook Volume 1 Strategic, Practical Information and Opportunities
Namibia Business and Investment Opportunities Yearbook Volume 1 Strategic, Practical Information and Opportunities
Nauru Business and Investment Opportunities Yearbook Volume 1 Strategic, Practical Information and Opportunities
Nepal Business and Investment Opportunities Yearbook Volume 1 Strategic, Practical Information and Opportunities
Netherlands Business and Investment Opportunities Yearbook Volume 1 Strategic, Practical Information and Opportunities
New Caledonia Business and Investment Opportunities Yearbook Volume 1 Strategic, Practical Information and Opportunities
New Zealand Business and Investment Opportunities Yearbook Volume 1 Strategic, Practical Information and Opportunities
Nicaragua Business and Investment Opportunities Yearbook Volume 1 Strategic, Practical Information and Opportunities
Niger Business and Investment Opportunities Yearbook Volume 1 Strategic, Practical Information and Opportunities
Nigeria Business and Investment Opportunities Yearbook Volume 1 Strategic, Practical Information and Opportunities
Niue Business and Investment Opportunities Yearbook Volume 1 Strategic, Practical Information and Opportunities
Northern Cyprus (Turkish Republic of Northern Cyprus) Business and Investment Opportunities Yearbook Volume 1 Strategic, Practical Information and Opportunities
Northern Mariana Islands Business and Investment Opportunities Yearbook Volume 1 Strategic, Practical Information and Opportunities
Norway Business and Investment Opportunities Yearbook Volume 1 Strategic, Practical Information and Opportunities
Oman Business and Investment Opportunities Yearbook Volume 1 Strategic, Practical Information and Opportunities
Pakistan Business and Investment Opportunities Yearbook Volume 1 Strategic, Practical Information and Opportunities
Palau Business and Investment Opportunities Yearbook Volume 1 Strategic, Practical Information and Opportunities
Palestine (West Bank & Gaza) Business and Investment Opportunities Yearbook Volume 1 Strategic, Practical Information and Opportunities
Panama Business and Investment Opportunities Yearbook Volume 1 Strategic, Practical Information and Opportunities

TITLE
Papua New Guinea Business and Investment Opportunities Yearbook Volume 1 Strategic, Practical Information and Opportunities
Paraguay Business and Investment Opportunities Yearbook Volume 1 Strategic, Practical Information and Opportunities
Peru Business and Investment Opportunities Yearbook Volume 1 Strategic, Practical Information and Opportunities
Philippines Business and Investment Opportunities Yearbook Volume 1 Strategic, Practical Information and Opportunities
Pitcairn Islands Business and Investment Opportunities Yearbook Volume 1 Strategic, Practical Information and Opportunities
Poland Business and Investment Opportunities Yearbook Volume 1 Strategic, Practical Information and Opportunities
Polynesia French Business and Investment Opportunities Yearbook Volume 1 Strategic, Practical Information and Opportunities
Portugal Business and Investment Opportunities Yearbook Volume 1 Strategic, Practical Information and Opportunities
Qatar Business and Investment Opportunities Yearbook Volume 1 Strategic, Practical Information and Opportunities
Romania Business and Investment Opportunities Yearbook Volume 1 Strategic, Practical Information and Opportunities
Russia Business and Investment Opportunities Yearbook Volume 1 Strategic, Practical Information and Opportunities
Rwanda Business and Investment Opportunities Yearbook Volume 1 Strategic, Practical Information and Opportunities
Sahrawi Arab Democratic Republic Volume 1 Strategic Information and Developments
Saint Kitts and Nevis Business and Investment Opportunities Yearbook Volume 1 Strategic, Practical Information and Opportunities
Saint Lucia Business and Investment Opportunities Yearbook Volume 1 Strategic, Practical Information and Opportunities
Saint Vincent and The Grenadines Business and Investment Opportunities Yearbook Volume 1 Strategic, Practical Information and Opportunities
Samoa (American) A Business and Investment Opportunities Yearbook Volume 1 Strategic, Practical Information and Opportunities
Samoa (Western) Business and Investment Opportunities Yearbook Volume 1 Strategic, Practical Information and Opportunities
San Marino Business and Investment Opportunities Yearbook Volume 1 Strategic, Practical Information and Opportunities
Sao Tome and Principe Business and Investment Opportunities Yearbook Volume 1 Strategic, Practical Information and Opportunities
Saudi Arabia Business and Investment Opportunities Yearbook Volume 1 Strategic, Practical Information and Opportunities
Scotland Business and Investment Opportunities Yearbook Volume 1 Strategic, Practical Information and Opportunities
Senegal Business and Investment Opportunities Yearbook Volume 1 Strategic, Practical Information and Opportunities
Serbia Business and Investment Opportunities Yearbook Volume 1 Strategic, Practical Information and Opportunities
Seychelles Business and Investment Opportunities Yearbook Volume 1 Strategic, Practical Information and Opportunities
Sierra Leone Business and Investment Opportunities Yearbook Volume 1 Strategic, Practical Information and Opportunities
Singapore Business and Investment Opportunities Yearbook Volume 1 Strategic, Practical Information and Opportunities
Slovakia Business and Investment Opportunities Yearbook Volume 1 Strategic, Practical Information and Opportunities

TITLE
Slovenia Business and Investment Opportunities Yearbook Volume 1 Strategic, Practical Information and Opportunities
Solomon Islands Business and Investment Opportunities Yearbook Volume 1 Strategic, Practical Information and Opportunities
Somalia Business and Investment Opportunities Yearbook Volume 1 Strategic, Practical Information and Opportunities
South Africa Business and Investment Opportunities Yearbook Volume 1 Strategic, Practical Information and Opportunities
Spain Business and Investment Opportunities Yearbook Volume 1 Strategic, Practical Information and Opportunities
Sri Lanka Business and Investment Opportunities Yearbook Volume 1 Strategic, Practical Information and Opportunities
St. Helena Business and Investment Opportunities Yearbook Volume 1 Strategic, Practical Information and Opportunities
St. Pierre & Miquelon Business and Investment Opportunities Yearbook Volume 1 Strategic, Practical Information and Opportunities
Sudan (Republic of the Sudan) Business and Investment Opportunities Yearbook Volume 1 Strategic, Practical Information and Opportunities
Sudan South Business and Investment Opportunities Yearbook Volume 1 Strategic, Practical Information and Opportunities
Suriname Business and Investment Opportunities Yearbook Volume 1 Strategic, Practical Information and Opportunities
Swaziland Business and Investment Opportunities Yearbook Volume 1 Strategic, Practical Information and Opportunities
Sweden Business and Investment Opportunities Yearbook Volume 1 Strategic, Practical Information and Opportunities
Switzerland Business and Investment Opportunities Yearbook Volume 1 Strategic, Practical Information and Opportunities
Syria Business and Investment Opportunities Yearbook Volume 1 Strategic, Practical Information and Opportunities
Taiwan Business and Investment Opportunities Yearbook Volume 1 Strategic, Practical Information and Opportunities
Tajikistan Business and Investment Opportunities Yearbook Volume 1 Strategic, Practical Information and Opportunities
Tanzania Business and Investment Opportunities Yearbook Volume 1 Strategic, Practical Information and Opportunities
Thailand Business and Investment Opportunities Yearbook Volume 1 Strategic, Practical Information and Opportunities
Timor Leste (Democratic Republic of Timor-Leste) Business and Investment Opportunities Yearbook Volume 1 Strategic, Practical Information and Opportunities
Togo Business and Investment Opportunities Yearbook Volume 1 Strategic, Practical Information and Opportunities
Tonga Business and Investment Opportunities Yearbook Volume 1 Strategic, Practical Information and Opportunities
Trinidad and Tobago Business and Investment Opportunities Yearbook Volume 1 Strategic, Practical Information and Opportunities
Tunisia Business and Investment Opportunities Yearbook Volume 1 Strategic, Practical Information and Opportunities
Turkey Business and Investment Opportunities Yearbook Volume 1 Strategic, Practical Information and Opportunities
Turkmenistan Business and Investment Opportunities Yearbook Volume 1 Strategic, Practical Information and Opportunities
Turks & Caicos Business and Investment Opportunities Yearbook Volume 1 Strategic, Practical Information and Opportunities
Tuvalu Business and Investment Opportunities Yearbook Volume 1 Strategic, Practical Information and Opportunities

TITLE
Uganda Business and Investment Opportunities Yearbook Volume 1 Strategic, Practical Information and Opportunities
Ukraine Business and Investment Opportunities Yearbook Volume 1 Strategic, Practical Information and Opportunities
United Arab Emirates Business and Investment Opportunities Yearbook Volume 1 Strategic, Practical Information and Opportunities
United Kingdom Business and Investment Opportunities Yearbook Volume 1 Strategic, Practical Information and Opportunities
United States Business and Investment Opportunities Yearbook Volume 1 Strategic, Practical Information and Opportunities
Uruguay Business and Investment Opportunities Yearbook Volume 1 Strategic, Practical Information and Opportunities
Uzbekistan Business and Investment Opportunities Yearbook Volume 1 Strategic, Practical Information and Opportunities
Vanuatu Business and Investment Opportunities Yearbook Volume 1 Strategic, Practical Information and Opportunities
Vatican City (Holy See) Business and Investment Opportunities Yearbook Volume 1 Strategic, Practical Information and Opportunities
Venezuela Business and Investment Opportunities Yearbook Volume 1 Strategic, Practical Information and Opportunities
Vietnam Business and Investment Opportunities Yearbook Volume 1 Strategic, Practical Information and Opportunities
Virgin Islands, British Business and Investment Opportunities Yearbook Volume 1 Strategic, Practical Information and Opportunities
Wake Atoll Business and Investment Opportunities Yearbook Volume 1 Strategic, Practical Information and Opportunities
Wallis & Futuna Business and Investment Opportunities Yearbook Volume 1 Strategic, Practical Information and Opportunities
Western Sahara Business and Investment Opportunities Yearbook Volume 1 Strategic, Practical Information and Opportunities
Yemen Business and Investment Opportunities Yearbook Volume 1 Strategic, Practical Information and Opportunities
Zambia Business and Investment Opportunities Yearbook Volume 1 Strategic, Practical Information and Opportunities
Zimbabwe Business and Investment Opportunities Yearbook Volume 1 Strategic, Practical Information and Opportunities

WORLD INSOLVENCY (BANKRUPTCY) LAWS AND REGULATIONS HANDBOOK LIBRARY

STRATEGIC INFORMATION AND BASIC LAWS

UPDATED ANNUALLY: PLEASE CONTACT IBP, INC FOR ISBN NUMBERS

978 ISBN	COMPLETE FULL TITLE
9781433084997	Afghanistan Insolvency (Bankruptcy) Laws and Regulations Handbook - Strategic Information and Basic Laws
9781433085000	Albania Insolvency (Bankruptcy) Laws and Regulations Handbook - Strategic Information and Basic Laws
9781433086793	Algeria Insolvency (Bankruptcy) Laws and Regulations Handbook - Strategic Information and Basic Laws
9781433085017	Angola Insolvency (Bankruptcy) Laws and Regulations Handbook - Strategic Information and Basic Laws
9781433086250	Antigua and Barduba Insolvency (Bankruptcy) Laws and Regulations Handbook - Strategic Information and Basic Laws
9781433085024	Argentina Insolvency (Bankruptcy) Laws and Regulations Handbook - Strategic Information and Basic Laws
9781433086786	Armenia Insolvency (Bankruptcy) Laws and Regulations Handbook - Strategic Information and Basic Laws
9781433085031	Australia Insolvency (Bankruptcy) Laws and Regulations Handbook - Strategic Information and Basic Laws
9781433086779	Austria Insolvency (Bankruptcy) Laws and Regulations Handbook - Strategic Information and Basic Laws
9781433085048	Azerbaijan Insolvency (Bankruptcy) Laws and Regulations Handbook - Strategic Information and Basic Laws
9781433086762	Bahamas Insolvency (Bankruptcy) Laws and Regulations Handbook - Strategic Information and Basic Laws
9781433085055	Bahrain Insolvency (Bankruptcy) Laws and Regulations Handbook - Strategic Information and Basic Laws
9781433086243	Bangladesh Insolvency (Bankruptcy) Laws and Regulations Handbook - Strategic Information and Basic Laws
9781433085062	Barbados Insolvency (Bankruptcy) Laws and Regulations Handbook - Strategic Information and Basic Laws
9781433086755	Belarus Insolvency (Bankruptcy) Laws and Regulations Handbook - Strategic Information and Basic Laws
9781433085079	Belgium Insolvency (Bankruptcy) Laws and Regulations Handbook - Strategic Information and Basic Laws
9781433086748	Belize Insolvency (Bankruptcy) Laws and Regulations Handbook - Strategic Information and Basic Laws
9781433085086	Benin Insolvency (Bankruptcy) Laws and Regulations Handbook - Strategic Information and Basic Laws
9781433086731	Bermuda Insolvency (Bankruptcy) Laws and Regulations Handbook - Strategic

978 ISBN	COMPLETE FULL TITLE
	Information and Basic Laws
9781433085093	Bhutan Insolvency (Bankruptcy) Laws and Regulations Handbook - Strategic Information and Basic Laws
9781433086595	Bolivia Insolvency (Bankruptcy) Laws and Regulations Handbook - Strategic Information and Basic Laws
9781433085109	Bosnia and Herzegovina Insolvency (Bankruptcy) Laws and Regulations Handbook - Strategic Information and Basic Laws
9781433086236	Brazil Insolvency (Bankruptcy) Laws and Regulations Handbook - Strategic Information and Basic Laws
9781433086236	Bulgaria Insolvency (Bankruptcy) Laws and Regulations Handbook - Strategic Information and Basic Laws
9781433085123	Burkina Faso Insolvency (Bankruptcy) Laws and Regulations Handbook - Strategic Information and Basic Laws
9781433086717	Cabo Verde Insolvency (Bankruptcy) Laws and Regulations Handbook - Strategic Information and Basic Laws
9781433085130	Cambodia Insolvency (Bankruptcy) Laws and Regulations Handbook - Strategic Information and Basic Laws
9781433086847	Cameroon Insolvency (Bankruptcy) Laws and Regulations Handbook - Strategic Information and Basic Laws
9781433085147	Canada Insolvency (Bankruptcy) Laws and Regulations Handbook - Strategic Information and Basic Laws
9781433086694	Cayman Insolvency (Bankruptcy) Laws and Regulations Handbook - Strategic Information and Basic Laws
9781433085154	Central African Republic Insolvency (Bankruptcy) Laws and Regulations Handbook - Strategic Information and Basic Laws
9781433086687	Chad Insolvency (Bankruptcy) Laws and Regulations Handbook - Strategic Information and Basic Laws
9781433085161	Chile Insolvency (Bankruptcy) Laws and Regulations Handbook - Strategic Information and Basic Laws
9781433086670	China Insolvency (Bankruptcy) Laws and Regulations Handbook - Strategic Information and Basic Laws
9781433085178	Colombia Insolvency (Bankruptcy) Laws and Regulations Handbook - Strategic Information and Basic Laws
9781433086663	Comoros Insolvency (Bankruptcy) Laws and Regulations Handbook - Strategic Information and Basic Laws
9781433085208	Congo Democratic Republic Insolvency (Bankruptcy) Laws and Regulations Handbook - Strategic Information and Basic Laws
9781433085185	Costa Rica Insolvency (Bankruptcy) Laws and Regulations Handbook - Strategic Information and Basic Laws
9781433086229	Croatia Insolvency (Bankruptcy) Laws and Regulations Handbook - Strategic Information and Basic Laws
9781433085192	Cyprus Insolvency (Bankruptcy) Laws and Regulations Handbook - Strategic Information and Basic Laws
9781433086212	Czech Insolvency (Bankruptcy) Laws and Regulations Handbook - Strategic Information and Basic Laws
9781433086656	Denmark Insolvency (Bankruptcy) Laws and Regulations Handbook - Strategic Information and Basic Laws
9781433085215	Dominican Republic Insolvency (Bankruptcy) Laws and Regulations Handbook - Strategic Information and Basic Laws
9781433086649	Ecuador Insolvency (Bankruptcy) Laws and Regulations Handbook - Strategic Information and Basic Laws
9781433085222	Egypt Insolvency (Bankruptcy) Laws and Regulations Handbook - Strategic Information and Basic Laws

To order and for additional analytical and marketing information, please contacts
International Business Publications, USA at:
P.O. Box 15343, Washington, DC 20003, USA. Phone: (202) 546-210 Fax: (202) 546-32
E-mail: ibpusa@comcast.net

978 ISBN	COMPLETE FULL TITLE
9781433086632	El Salvador Insolvency (Bankruptcy) Laws and Regulations Handbook - Strategic Information and Basic Laws
9781433085239	Estonia Insolvency (Bankruptcy) Laws and Regulations Handbook - Strategic Information and Basic Laws
9781433086625	Ethiopia Insolvency (Bankruptcy) Laws and Regulations Handbook - Strategic Information and Basic Laws
9781433085246	European Union Insolvency (Bankruptcy) Laws and Regulations Handbook - Strategic Information and Basic Laws
9781433086076	Fiji Insolvency (Bankruptcy) Laws and Regulations Handbook - Strategic Information and Basic Laws
9781433085253	Finland Insolvency (Bankruptcy) Laws and Regulations Handbook - Strategic Information and Basic Laws
9781433086199	France Insolvency (Bankruptcy) Laws and Regulations Handbook - Strategic Information and Basic Laws
9781433085260	Gabon Insolvency (Bankruptcy) Laws and Regulations Handbook - Strategic Information and Basic Laws
9781433086311	Gambia Insolvency (Bankruptcy) Laws and Regulations Handbook - Strategic Information and Basic Laws
9781433085277	Georgia Republic Insolvency (Bankruptcy) Laws and Regulations Handbook - Strategic Information and Basic Laws
9781433086175	Germany Insolvency (Bankruptcy) Laws and Regulations Handbook - Strategic Information and Basic Laws
9781433085284	Ghana Insolvency (Bankruptcy) Laws and Regulations Handbook - Strategic Information and Basic Laws
9781433086618	Gibraltar Insolvency (Bankruptcy) Laws and Regulations Handbook - Strategic Information and Basic Laws
9781433085291	Greece Insolvency (Bankruptcy) Laws and Regulations Handbook - Strategic Information and Basic Laws
9781433086168	Grenada Insolvency (Bankruptcy) Laws and Regulations Handbook - Strategic Information and Basic Laws
9781433085307	Guatemala Insolvency (Bankruptcy) Laws and Regulations Handbook - Strategic Information and Basic Laws
9781433086601	Guyana Insolvency (Bankruptcy) Laws and Regulations Handbook - Strategic Information and Basic Laws
9781433085314	Haiti Insolvency (Bankruptcy) Laws and Regulations Handbook - Strategic Information and Basic Laws
9781433086977	Honduras Insolvency (Bankruptcy) Laws and Regulations Handbook - Strategic Information and Basic Laws
9781433085321	Hong Kong Insolvency (Bankruptcy) Laws and Regulations Handbook - Strategic Information and Basic Laws
9781433086151	Hungary Insolvency (Bankruptcy) Laws and Regulations Handbook - Strategic Information and Basic Laws
9781433085338	Iceland Insolvency (Bankruptcy) Laws and Regulations Handbook - Strategic Information and Basic Laws
9781433086144	India Insolvency (Bankruptcy) Laws and Regulations Handbook - Strategic Information and Basic Laws
9781433085345	Indonesia Insolvency (Bankruptcy) Laws and Regulations Handbook - Strategic Information and Basic Laws
9781433086991	Iran Insolvency (Bankruptcy) Laws and Regulations Handbook - Strategic Information and Basic Laws
9781433085352	Iraq Insolvency (Bankruptcy) Laws and Regulations Handbook - Strategic Information and Basic Laws
9781433086137	Ireland Insolvency (Bankruptcy) Laws and Regulations Handbook - Strategic Information

978 ISBN	COMPLETE FULL TITLE
	and Basic Laws
9781433085369	Island of Jersey Insolvency (Bankruptcy) Laws and Regulations Handbook - Strategic Information and Basic Laws
9781433086724	Israel Insolvency (Bankruptcy) Laws and Regulations Handbook - Strategic Information and Basic Laws
9781433085376	Italy Insolvency (Bankruptcy) Laws and Regulations Handbook - Strategic Information and Basic Laws
9781433087080	Ivory Coast Insolvency (Bankruptcy) Laws and Regulations Handbook - Strategic Information and Basic Laws
9781433085383	Jamaica Insolvency (Bankruptcy) Laws and Regulations Handbook - Strategic Information and Basic Laws
9781433087073	Japan Insolvency (Bankruptcy) Laws and Regulations Handbook - Strategic Information and Basic Laws
9781433085390	Jersey Insolvency (Bankruptcy) Laws and Regulations Handbook - Strategic Information and Basic Laws
9781433087066	Jordan Insolvency (Bankruptcy) Laws and Regulations Handbook - Strategic Information and Basic Laws
9781433085406	Kazakhstan Insolvency (Bankruptcy) Laws and Regulations Handbook - Strategic Information and Basic Laws
9781433086120	Kenya Insolvency (Bankruptcy) Laws and Regulations Handbook - Strategic Information and Basic Laws
9781433085413	Kiribati Insolvency (Bankruptcy) Laws and Regulations Handbook - Strategic Information and Basic Laws
9781433086113	Korea Insolvency (Bankruptcy) Laws and Regulations Handbook - Strategic Information and Basic Laws
9781433085420	Kuwait Insolvency (Bankruptcy) Laws and Regulations Handbook - Strategic Information and Basic Laws
9781433086106	Kyrgyz Republic Insolvency (Bankruptcy) Laws and Regulations Handbook - Strategic Information and Basic Laws
9781433085437	Latvia Insolvency (Bankruptcy) Laws and Regulations Handbook - Strategic Information and Basic Laws
9781433087059	Lebanon Insolvency (Bankruptcy) Laws and Regulations Handbook - Strategic Information and Basic Laws
9781433085444	Lesotho Insolvency (Bankruptcy) Laws and Regulations Handbook - Strategic Information and Basic Laws
9781433087042	Liechtenstein Insolvency (Bankruptcy) Laws and Regulations Handbook - Strategic Information and Basic Laws
9781433085451	Lithuania Insolvency (Bankruptcy) Laws and Regulations Handbook - Strategic Information and Basic Laws
9781433086090	Luxembourg Insolvency (Bankruptcy) Laws and Regulations Handbook - Strategic Information and Basic Laws
9781433085468	Macedonia Insolvency (Bankruptcy) Laws and Regulations Handbook - Strategic Information and Basic Laws
9781433086083	Madagascar Insolvency (Bankruptcy) Laws and Regulations Handbook - Strategic Information and Basic Laws
9781433085475	Malaysia Insolvency (Bankruptcy) Laws and Regulations Handbook - Strategic Information and Basic Laws
9781433087110	Malta Insolvency (Bankruptcy) Laws and Regulations Handbook - Strategic Information and Basic Laws
9781433085482	Marshall Islands Insolvency (Bankruptcy) Laws and Regulations Handbook - Strategic Information and Basic Laws
9781433087035	Mexico Insolvency (Bankruptcy) Laws and Regulations Handbook - Strategic Information and Basic Laws

978 ISBN	COMPLETE FULL TITLE
9781433085499	Micronesia Insolvency (Bankruptcy) Laws and Regulations Handbook - Strategic Information and Basic Laws
9781433087097	Moldova Insolvency (Bankruptcy) Laws and Regulations Handbook - Strategic Information and Basic Laws
9781433085505	Monaco Insolvency (Bankruptcy) Laws and Regulations Handbook - Strategic Information and Basic Laws
9781433087028	Mongolia Insolvency (Bankruptcy) Laws and Regulations Handbook - Strategic Information and Basic Laws
9781433085512	Montenegro Insolvency (Bankruptcy) Laws and Regulations Handbook - Strategic Information and Basic Laws
9781433087011	Mozambique Insolvency (Bankruptcy) Laws and Regulations Handbook - Strategic Information and Basic Laws
9781433085529	Nepal Insolvency (Bankruptcy) Laws and Regulations Handbook - Strategic Information and Basic Laws
9781433086441	Netherlands Insolvency (Bankruptcy) Laws and Regulations Handbook - Strategic Information and Basic Laws
9781433085536	New Zealand Insolvency (Bankruptcy) Laws and Regulations Handbook - Strategic Information and Basic Laws
9781433086465	Nicaragua Insolvency (Bankruptcy) Laws and Regulations Handbook - Strategic Information and Basic Laws
9781433085543	Niger Insolvency (Bankruptcy) Laws and Regulations Handbook - Strategic Information and Basic Laws
9781433087004	Nigeria Insolvency (Bankruptcy) Laws and Regulations Handbook - Strategic Information and Basic Laws
9781433085550	Norway Insolvency (Bankruptcy) Laws and Regulations Handbook - Strategic Information and Basic Laws
9781433086205	Pakistan Insolvency (Bankruptcy) Laws and Regulations Handbook - Strategic Information and Basic Laws
9781433085567	Palau Insolvency (Bankruptcy) Laws and Regulations Handbook - Strategic Information and Basic Laws
9781433086564	Panama Insolvency (Bankruptcy) Laws and Regulations Handbook - Strategic Information and Basic Laws
9781433085574	Papau New Guinea Insolvency (Bankruptcy) Laws and Regulations Handbook - Strategic Information and Basic Laws
9781433086557	Paraguay Insolvency (Bankruptcy) Laws and Regulations Handbook - Strategic Information and Basic Laws
9781433085581	Peru Insolvency (Bankruptcy) Laws and Regulations Handbook - Strategic Information and Basic Laws
9781433087127	Philippines Insolvency (Bankruptcy) Laws and Regulations Handbook - Strategic Information and Basic Laws
9781433085598	Poland Insolvency (Bankruptcy) Laws and Regulations Handbook - Strategic Information and Basic Laws
9781433086540	Portugal Insolvency (Bankruptcy) Laws and Regulations Handbook - Strategic Information and Basic Laws
9781433085604	Romania Insolvency (Bankruptcy) Laws and Regulations Handbook - Strategic Information and Basic Laws
9781433086854	Russia Insolvency (Bankruptcy) Laws and Regulations Handbook - Strategic Information and Basic Laws
9781433085611	Saudi Arabia Insolvency (Bankruptcy) Laws and Regulations Handbook - Strategic Information and Basic Laws
9781433086533	Senegal Insolvency (Bankruptcy) Laws and Regulations Handbook - Strategic Information and Basic Laws
9781433085628	Serbia Insolvency (Bankruptcy) Laws and Regulations Handbook - Strategic Information

To order and for additional analytical and marketing information, please contacts
International Business Publications, USA at:
P.O. Box 15343, Washington, DC 20003, USA. Phone: (202) 546-210 Fax: (202) 546-32
E-mail: ibpusa@comcast.net

978 ISBN	COMPLETE FULL TITLE
	and Basic Laws
9781433086526	Sierra Leone Insolvency (Bankruptcy) Laws and Regulations Handbook - Strategic Information and Basic Laws
9781433085635	Singapore Insolvency (Bankruptcy) Laws and Regulations Handbook - Strategic Information and Basic Laws
9781433087103	Slovak Republic Insolvency (Bankruptcy) Laws and Regulations Handbook - Strategic Information and Basic Laws
9781433086519	Slovenia Insolvency (Bankruptcy) Laws and Regulations Handbook - Strategic Information and Basic Laws
9781433085642	Solomon Islands Insolvency (Bankruptcy) Laws and Regulations Handbook - Strategic Information and Basic Laws
9781433086502	South Africa Insolvency (Bankruptcy) Laws and Regulations Handbook - Strategic Information and Basic Laws
9781433085659	Spain Insolvency (Bankruptcy) Laws and Regulations Handbook - Strategic Information and Basic Laws
9781433086984	Sri Lanka Insolvency (Bankruptcy) Laws and Regulations Handbook - Strategic Information and Basic Laws
9781433085666	St. Kitts & Nevis Insolvency (Bankruptcy) Laws and Regulations Handbook - Strategic Information and Basic Laws
9781433086496	Sweden Insolvency (Bankruptcy) Laws and Regulations Handbook - Strategic Information and Basic Laws
9781433085673	Switzerland Insolvency (Bankruptcy) Laws and Regulations Handbook - Strategic Information and Basic Laws
9781433086489	Taiwan Insolvency (Bankruptcy) Laws and Regulations Handbook - Strategic Information and Basic Laws
9781433085680	Tajikistan Insolvency (Bankruptcy) Laws and Regulations Handbook - Strategic Information and Basic Laws
9781433086472	Tanzania Insolvency (Bankruptcy) Laws and Regulations Handbook - Strategic Information and Basic Laws
9781433085697	Thailand Insolvency (Bankruptcy) Laws and Regulations Handbook - Strategic Information and Basic Laws
9781433085703	Togo Insolvency (Bankruptcy) Laws and Regulations Handbook - Strategic Information and Basic Laws
9781433086960	Trinidad and Tobago Insolvency (Bankruptcy) Laws and Regulations Handbook - Strategic Information and Basic Laws
9781433085710	Tunisia Insolvency (Bankruptcy) Laws and Regulations Handbook - Strategic Information and Basic Laws
9781433086953	Turkey Insolvency (Bankruptcy) Laws and Regulations Handbook - Strategic Information and Basic Laws
9781433085727	Tuvalu Insolvency (Bankruptcy) Laws and Regulations Handbook - Strategic Information and Basic Laws
9781433086946	Uganda Insolvency (Bankruptcy) Laws and Regulations Handbook - Strategic Information and Basic Laws
9781433085734	Ukraine Insolvency (Bankruptcy) Laws and Regulations Handbook - Strategic Information and Basic Laws
9781433086939	United Arab Emirates Insolvency (Bankruptcy) Laws and Regulations Handbook - Strategic Information and Basic Laws
9781433085741	United Kingdom Insolvency (Bankruptcy) Laws and Regulations Handbook - Strategic Information and Basic Laws
9781433086328	Uruguay Insolvency (Bankruptcy) Laws and Regulations Handbook - Strategic Information and Basic Laws
9781433085758	USA Insolvency (Bankruptcy) Laws and Regulations Handbook - Strategic Information and Basic Laws

To order and for additional analytical and marketing information, please contacts International Business Publications, USA at:
P.O. Box 15343, Washington, DC 20003, USA. Phone: (202) 546-210 Fax: (202) 546-32
E-mail: ibpusa@comcast.net

978 ISBN	COMPLETE FULL TITLE
9781433086922	Uzbekistan Insolvency (Bankruptcy) Laws and Regulations Handbook - Strategic Information and Basic Laws
9781433085765	Venezuela Insolvency (Bankruptcy) Laws and Regulations Handbook - Strategic Information and Basic Laws
9781433086915	Vietnam Insolvency (Bankruptcy) Laws and Regulations Handbook - Strategic Information and Basic Laws
9781433085116	Virgin Islands, British Insolvency (Bankruptcy) Laws and Regulations Handbook - Strategic Information and Basic Laws
9781433085772	Zambia Insolvency (Bankruptcy) Laws and Regulations Handbook - Strategic Information and Basic Laws
9781433086458	Zimbabwe Insolvency (Bankruptcy) Laws and Regulations Handbook - Strategic Information and Basic Laws